Beyond
Resilience
to **Rootsilience**

*A Revolutionary Women's
Leadership Framework
for Balance, Well-being
and Success*

Rimi Chakraborty & Samantha Anderson

Paperback: ISBN 978-1-916529-07-6

Ebook: ISBN 978-1-916529-08-3

Library of Congress Control Number: 2023921109

Edited By: Jesse Smart

Cover Art and Layout By: Lynda Mangoro

llustrations by: Maeve Mangine and Copyright (c) 2024, Rimi Chakraborty, Drew Samantha Anderson

Photographs By: Rimi Chakraborty

Printed By IngramSpark in the USA/ UK

DISCLAIMER

Hey unbound one!

Welcome to this magical book brought to you by The Unbound Press.

At The Unbound Press we believe that when women write freely from the fullest expression of who they are, it can't help but activate a feeling of deep connection and transformation in others. When we come together, we become more and we're changing the world, one book at a time!

This book has been carefully crafted by both the author and publisher with the intention of inspiring you to move ever more deeply into who you truly are.

We hope that this book helps you to connect with your Unbound Self and that you feel called to pass it on to others who want to live a more fully expressed life.

With much love,

Nicola Humber

Founder of The Unbound Press

www.theunboundpress.com

DEDICATION

To You, dear Reader, may this book illuminate your path toward a more balanced journey to leadership and success.

Praise for
BEYOND RESILIENCE TO ROOTSILIENCE

Samantha and Rimi have done women a tremendous service in mapping out an approach to a fulfilling, sustainable approach to leadership – and life! The demands on women can be overwhelming, and Rootsilience will help ground and support women leaders as they grow and flourish. I wish I had their insights as I was coming up through the ranks and raising my daughters.

~ Lucinda Duncalfe, EVP, True Technologies and 6-time startup CEO

Beyond Resilience to Rootsilience is an extraordinary guide for leaders who desire a healthier, more balanced integration between themselves, their work, and their lives in general. Rimi Chakraborty and Samantha Anderson offer a navigation framework, mapped via the seven traditional Sanskrit chakras, to help you bridge the connections between your behavior, physical symptoms, and emotions. By completing exercises throughout the book, you will develop increased awareness and a fine-tuned focus on your leadership practices. The authors generously offer stories from their own experiences, which bring their foundations to life.

~ Tammy Gooler Loeb, award-winning author, Work from the Inside Out

As someone who has flirted with chakras I have been overwhelmed and skeptical as they never fit in with my western educated brain. Until now. From the personal assessment, to the individualized mapping, the hand holding through each section and overall integration leading back to the whole - with recipes! What could be better? Beyond Resilience to Rootsilience is the cool drink of water we need as individuals to help nourish our collective parched roots.

~ Wendy Swart Grossman, Co-Founder, Creative Re/Frame; Faculty, Boston University; Author, Behind the Wheel: A Mothers Journal of a Year on the Road

I invite you to embark on a transformative journey of self-discovery and leadership with Beyond Resilience to Rootsilience. This empowering guide takes you on a profound exploration of the Chakras, offering a holistic approach to leadership, personal growth and living each day with reverence. Each chapter delves into a Chakra's unique energy, providing balanced leadership insights, character strengths, and practical exercises.

~ Rochelle Schieck, founder of Qoya Inspired Movement; Author, Qoya: A Compass for Navigating an Embodied Life that is Wise, Wild and Free

Beyond Resilience to Rootsilience is a vibrant book offering each of us a map of wholeness. It offers information, inspiration, and an invitation to connect all the parts of our inner and outer lives, something we need to survive the challenges we individually and collectively face. Rather than another model for self-improvement requiring we change ourselves it guides us to discover more deeply who we are and what matters to us to live and lead more effectively. Beyond Resilience to Rootsilience offers an inclusive and holistic approach, richly grounded in the wisdom of the Feminine, with application to all aspects of our lives. It has the potential to benefit any woman, anytime, anywhere to have a more nourished and nourishing life.

~ Kate Levinson, Ph.D, Author, Emotional Currency: A Woman's Guide to Building a Healthy Relationship with Money

Samantha and Rimi have imagined into being an inspiring and empowered framework to guide our thinking around the important topic of women's leadership. Introducing a new set of metrics for success – metrics that focus on holistic health and well-being – is more than just creative – it's revolutionary. The many tools, exercises and reflections in this beautifully illustrated book provide a roadmap for any woman looking to lead, not solely in the work arena (although the book will help her there too), but in every facet of her being. As someone deeply committed to linking resources to women recovering from trauma, mental health and addiction, I am beyond excited to know that this book exists.

~ Dawn Nickel, PhD, Founder, SHE RECOVERS Foundation; Author, She Recovers Every Day

Every once in a while a book comes out that has information that you didn't know you needed; this is that book. This book offers practical, spiritual, real-life tools to empower our modern-day leaders to reach their fullest potential. The approach taken in Beyond Resilience to Rootsilience resonates deeply with me. I enthusiastically recommend this book to everyone, not just women! I genuinely value that women are at the core of this book; it's high time we embrace a more feminine approach to leadership.

~ Gail Grossman, @yogamom; Author, Restorative Yoga for Life

Beyond Resilience to Rootsilience is about grounding myself in a holistic way. I can tap into my own Character Strengths and utilize what I know about the mind and body and how I can work with them to stay resilient, rooted and continue growing, despite some inevitable setbacks."

~ Rebecca Johnston, NBC-HWC Functional Medicine Health Coach

I have been teaching and attempting to practice resilience and sustainable, grounded leadership for over a decade, and I think this is the medicine of our times, especially for women and people of color. Thank you for sharing your experiences and wisdom and bringing this book to life!

~ Katherine Elmer, M.S., NB-HWC and Lecturer at the University of Vermont in Clinical Herbalism and Whole Foods Nutrition

In their book Beyond Resilience to Rootsilience, Rimi and Samantha have created a ground-breaking approach to modern leadership. Rootsilience provides the perfect blend of grounded leadership strategies with a mix of spiritual guidance and reflective exercises that reinforce the key learnings of how to be a balanced leader in today's chaotic world. This book has become my go-to roadmap for the times when I feel like I have lost my way. It is my compass to assure that I do not lose myself while still giving my all to those who count on me to show up for them.

~ Heidi Solomon-Orlick – Founder & CEO of GirlzWhoSell

Beyond Resilience to Rootsilience promises to alter the consciousness that women bring to leadership. It is a brilliant fabric woven from strengths-based and exquisitely actionable maps, frameworks, and exercises. The book's architecture is designed around the magnificent power of working with chakra energies. It's one thing to talk about women transforming and healing the global character of leadership, and another to outline how this will be possible. This gift does this beautifully.

~ Jack Ricchiuto, 33-time author

Beyond Resilience to Rootsilience is like a best friend you can talk to when you feel you're spinning out of control reminding you who you are and what you need. This book gives you the tools to get back on track, and these are the tools women leaders need to rise beyond resilience, to Rootsilience!

~ Juliet Hahn, Chief Communications Officer at FetTech, Host of Your Next Stop, YNS Live with NFL Thread, and Word Blindness podcasts

The Rootsilience Leadership Map feels like a map to my soul.

~ Ravit Greenberg, Philanthropic Advisor and Inclusive Development Professional

Samantha and Rimi have integrated so much physical, mental, and spiritual wellness wisdom through the guidance and framework of the chakras. I love how they made all of the information and practices accessible and relatable.

~ Chelsea Shea, Certified Nurse Midwife

Beyond Resilience to Rootsilience is a deeply thoughtful guide to reconnecting with and cultivating your inner leadership, wisdom, and resilience. I was fortunate to join one of Rimi's and Samantha's workshops just as I was beginning the search for my own more grounded and authentic path in my life. This is a unique and important book!

~ Patricia Atkinson, Founder, Impetus Global

Contents

Introduction

It was January 2020, and Samantha and her husband Scott set foot upon the Azores, an archipelago of nine beautiful islands in the middle of the Atlantic Ocean, for the third time in just as many years. Scott had been diving into exploring his ancestral roots and connection to São Miguel, the "green island" as it's known. Samantha and Scott returned to stay at the beautiful Minuvida Lodge and Learning Center, owned by Rimi and her Azorean husband, João. Rimi and Samantha spent time planning a retreat to bring women together to learn about conscious leadership and the connections between mind, body, and spirit and were gearing up to announce their April 2020 retreat.

Just two months later, the COVID-19 pandemic threw a major wrench in their plans, and Rimi and Samantha found solace in bridging their worlds, from a small island in the middle of the Atlantic, to New York City. With the majority of the world in lockdown, their weekly check-in calls were soothing balm to their souls. Under the guise of "retreat planning," Samantha and Rimi found support in deeply sharing and reflecting, leaning into being honest with themselves and with each other about what they were experiencing. As business owners, leaders, and coaches, Rimi and Samantha were often holding space for many others, and with the pressure to hold it all together, they could unravel in these calls, share what was raw and real, and what was working and what was not. It was on May 19, 2020, that they had an "Aha" moment.

In the early days of the COVID-19 pandemic, the word "Resilience" was used over and over again. Words like "overcome," "determined," "strength," "effort," "defense," "endurance," and "persistence" were emphasized as we dealt with the stresses of the situation. Samantha suddenly exclaimed, "I'm tired of being told to be resilient! Resilience is simply not enough! We need something more now! We need to be Rootsilient!" And so began our journey to empower women to rise Beyond Resilience to Rootsilience.

Introductory Reflection Exercise

Take a moment to soften your gaze. You can either place your hands on your lap or gently place one hand on your heart and one over your belly. Take a couple of deep breaths. As you inhale, sit a little taller, and as you exhale, allow your shoulders to soften, letting your weight sink downward. Deep breath in, sitting up tall. And exhale, feeling your feet on the ground.

Let's take three more breaths together.

Inhale, exhale. Notice where you feel your breath.

Inhale, exhale. Notice any sensations that are present.

Inhale, exhale. Notice, *how's the weather inside* today?

As you embark on reading this book and your journey to being a Rootsilient leader, consider yourself supported and held by the incredible container of people from all over the world who are taking these breaths with you now. Take a moment to breathe and feel just how far this container reaches.

Bring your attention to what made you show up to open this book. What called you? What are you hoping to learn or share or heal or grow, not only today and during the course of reading this book, but also in your journey to being a Rootsilient leader? Notice if you feel that intention somewhere in your body. Take a few moments to write down your intention.

The Importance of Roots

 The root is certainly a more decisive factor than what is growing above ground. After all, it is the root that looks after the survival of an organism. It is the root that has withstood severe changes in climatic conditions. And it is the root that has regrown trunks time and time again. It is in the roots that centuries of experience are stored, and it is this experience that has allowed the tree's survival.

– Peter Wohlleben, *The Hidden Life of Trees*

The "Biosphere 2" project created the world's largest controlled environment dedicated to understanding the impacts of climate change in the 1990s. During their clinical experiments, scientists observed trees growing quickly, at a much faster pace than their counterparts outside the biosphere. But there was a catch. Despite these trees' rapid growth, they became thin and weak with underdeveloped root systems, many of them falling over before reaching maturity.[1] The scientists discovered there was one element in Biosphere 2 they had *not* accounted for – wind in the environment. The trees needed some level of adversity in order to grow stronger and for their roots to grow deeper. The trees needed a challenge to be more resilient, for their roots to support them during their lifetime.

In 2023, as of the writing of this book, three years into the COVID-19 pandemic and with the threat of world wars and climate catastrophe, we've had our share of challenges and "wind." These events could have made us stronger. But instead of growing deeper and stronger roots, many of us, and especially women leaders, are simply toppling over and being swept away. We are exhausted. We have depleted our "surge capacity" to survive short-term crises by continuous engagement of our "fight/flight/freeze/fawn" responses. Instead of growing roots and realizing that imbalance in our body, behavior or mind is a sign of imbalance within the whole system, many women leaders are numbing out with alcohol, drugs and food, disconnecting from ourselves, disconnecting from our roots, and disconnecting from being the leaders our world needs us to be.

Resilience, "the ability of something to return to its original shape after it's been pulled, stretched, pressed, and bent,"[2] remains an elusive pursuit during traumatic times. If you pull, stress, press, and bend something that is not rooted, it will either break or get pulled along with the force that it's being subjected to. Resilience assumes we are rooted to begin with. However, many women have lost a connection to our roots. We have lost a connection to that which brings us back into balance, into a state of interconnected physical, emotional, mental, and behavioral well-being.

We lack a system to decode the language of our body, behavior, and mind to understand when we are off balance and need to grow or nurture our roots. As of the writing of this book, we are mired in yet another emerging pandemic of mental health crisis. Women leaders are leaving the workforce at record rates,[3] with 43% of women leaders feeling burned out, compared to only 31% of men at their level.[4] Women are now closing the gender gap in alcohol consumption with women now exceeding men in binge drinking for the first time in a century[5] and alcohol-related deaths rising faster in the United States among women than men.[6]

With increasing challenges and severity of events such as global health crises, climate change impacts and economic instability, mounting evidence points out that today's leaders need a way to lead with impact and purpose while not burning out and destroying our health in the process.

We need something more to withstand the winds and challenges of the world today. How can we bounce back to our status quo after a difficult or traumatic experience without strong roots to ground us? How can we bounce back if we're not connected to our whole selves in the first place? Without tending to our physical, emotional, mental, and behavioral health as a whole, the winds and challenges we face sweep us away and we drift further from ourselves.

Beyond Resilience to Rootsilience empowers women to rise in leadership through a revolutionary framework for balance and well-being. Our framework teaches you to recognize your unique signs of ease and dis-ease at the behavioral, physical and emotional level *before* you get thrown off balance, *before* you get stretched beyond your limits, and *before* you end up battling a life-threatening disease or giving up on your hopes and dreams.

Rootsilience (*"root - zeel - ience"*) is a new word and rhymes with resilience. Try saying it a few times. Root - zeel - ience. We invented the word because in order to affect real, transformational change, we need to create new consciousness with new language.[7] Resilience is not enough to deal with the stressors and challenges of the day. Our new word, Rootsilience, takes the notion of resilience a step deeper, and teaches us to be grounded, rooted and able to respond to stressors from a place of stability rather than being stretched beyond our limits. We need to rise beyond resilience to Rootsilience.

The Beyond Resilience to Rootsilience framework is organized around the ancient chakra system, combining three key branches: conscious leadership, healing foods, and mind-body integration. With our revolutionary Rootsilience Leadership Map, you will learn to recognize your unique signs of balance and imbalance, and become literate in the language of your body, behavior and mind. You don't need to be an expert on or believe in the chakras to benefit from this ancient organizational system for making sense of our physical, mental and emotional signs of ease and dis-ease.

The Rootsilience Leadership Map shows you which of the seven chakras' tools, practices, and foods you can focus on first to bring yourself into harmony and balance. Rather than a "one size fits all" solution to your life and leadership challenges, Beyond Resilience to Rootsilience becomes a companion guide, a dear friend that calls you back to your center helping you to make sense of your behavior, body and mind. You will be able to come back to this book time and time again, learning to be a Rootsilient leader, able to stay grounded and rooted, avoiding getting stretched beyond your limits.

This book includes leadership exercises based on key themes in each of the chakras as well as mind-body integration practices to embody those lessons and enable you to thrive as a more effective leader. You will learn how food and movement can be healing medicine for your body, and you'll come away with practices you can prioritize based on your unique Rootsilience Leadership Map. (We'll discuss the Rootsilience Leadership Map further and you'll have the chance to explore your own in Chapter One).

Beyond Resilience to Rootsilience offers a path for women leaders to nurture our roots, finding harmony at the physical, emotional, mental and behavioral levels. It's time we embrace a path to leadership that enables us to embody what we understand intellectually but may find difficult to implement. Beyond Resilience to Rootsilience provides us the path to continually strengthen our roots, to find and stay balanced as our whole selves.

Empowering Disclaimers

Beyond Resilience to Rootsilience amplifies the voices of those who identify as women. We are activating women to embody our roles as guardians of the earth by nurturing and tending to the roots of our whole selves. We've chosen to focus on women for many of the reasons stated thus far and in the themes we expand upon further in the book. We use the word "women" to mean those assigned as women at birth, as we write extensively about aspects of the female anatomy and point to studies and statistics that highlight many of the unique differences in women's and men's mental, physical, and behavioral health. That said, the Rootsilience Leadership Path is available for anyone, regardless of gender or social expression, and we hope that anyone who is drawn to a more inclusive and holistic approach to leadership will gain valuable insights from this book.

Being a woman (or whatever your assigned gender is at birth) is not a medical condition, and you are not damaged.[8] As you read this book, you are empowered to take control of your body and live fully and wholly in it. Each of our bodies contains innate wisdom, and each of us can tell our stories in the way that we feel and sense. A Rootsilient leader is someone who lives in alignment with this innate wisdom. In this book, we'll share many practices, ideas and foods that can support your health and well-being. But you are the owner of your body and only you can tune in and know what's right for you. If you have questions about the work that we share or the practices that we offer, and whether they are appropriate for you, you can always check in with your doctor or trusted medical professional.

This book is not intended to provide medical or clinical advice nor take the place of such advice or treatment from a physician or qualified health professional. All readers/viewers of this content are advised to consult their doctors or qualified health professionals regarding specific health questions. This content is for informational and educational purposes only. All readers/viewers of this content, especially those taking prescription or over-the-counter medications, should consult their physicians or health professionals before beginning any nutrition, supplement, or lifestyle program.

In the guided practices, remember it's not "Simon Says." If we tell you to do something and it doesn't feel right or you know it's contraindicated for you, just don't do it. This book will inspire you to connect and lead with authenticity and will provide practical tools, reflection exercises and real-world opportunities for application of these learnings so you can embrace your whole self.

We are asking you to:

- Have an open heart and mind

- Be aware that if something "strikes a chord" with you, either in agreement or in discord, we encourage you to sit with what you feel and sense, and make space for that to be present while taking this in as a new perspective

- Commit to yourself.

Together we rise Beyond Resilience to Rootsilience.

21

Chapter One

Beyond Resilience to Rootsilience

The Missing Rung
on the Ladder for Women

Despite evidence that having more women in leadership increases overall company health, women are underrepresented at the senior level and lack a path to leadership that enables them to thrive. There's a missing rung on the leadership ladder for women.

Research has shown that firms with more women in senior positions are more profitable, more socially responsible, and provide safer, higher-quality customer experiences – among many other benefits.[1] Female-founded companies outperform the market in key metrics of success for early-stage businesses,[2] and in the banking industry, banks with more women on boards commit less fraud and faced fewer fines for misconduct.[3]

Yet women are grossly underrepresented in leadership. As of the writing of this book, while women represent nearly half of the S&P 500 workforce in the United States, they hold just 8% of the top leadership position as CEOs.[4] While women make up 32% of senior management positions globally,[5] the highest percentage of women on record, we have a long way to go.

The traditional path to leadership is often based on the myopic lens of profit and the exponential desire for more. The never attainable but always dangling carrot pushes us to work harder and aim for more, but deep down, the nagging feeling that "nothing is ever enough" is so ingrained in our path to leadership that it's no wonder we seek external validation for our sense of self-worth and internalize the belief that "I am not enough."

The endless networking events and dinners left little time to spend with my partner or be alone. The intense high-paced rhythm pushed me to be constantly on. I was having recurring urinary tract infections, but I never made the connection that my body was screaming at me to slow down. I just kept popping antibiotics. There was always more to do, more outreach I should be doing, more potential clients I could be reaching, more opportunities to increase revenue. I was haunted by the insatiable desire for more. I sought out new shiny toys and even bought a new car, but there was always more to achieve, more to have, more ways to "be better." I received lavish praise and compensation after bringing in a huge client, but after a brief time, it no longer gave me gratification, that high sensation, that feeling of pride and satisfaction. My successes were short-lived, so I needed more. I needed to find the next great sale, the next praise to feel satisfied again. Meanwhile, the climb never ended.

– Rimi, reflecting on life as an SVP in her management consulting firm

The pressure to "always be on" has led women to work themselves to the bone, taking on even greater responsibilities, often unrecognized, unpaid or underpaid. In the US, women still earn an average of about 82 cents for each dollar earned by a man,[6] full-time employed Black women earn only 67 cents to every dollar a white man earns,[7] and the gap across many countries in Europe is similar.[8] The "caregiver burden," a term given to women who bear household, family, and elderly care responsibilities, has increased exponentially with global catastrophes such as the COVID-19 pandemic adding to the overwork and overwhelm that has pushed many women out of the workforce.[9]

Instead of being resilient, overcoming adversity, and staying determined, many women leaders are opting out of the workforce altogether. The lack of a holistic path to leadership has led more women leaders to leave their companies at the highest rate in nearly a decade, with 43% of women leaders feeling burned out, compared to only 31% of men at their level.[10] Women leaders are now asking:

- How do I lead during difficult times while also practicing self-care?

- How do I create soft but solid boundaries with gentle reminders on how to hold them?

- How do I regain work/life balance and find my "happy place"?

- How do I shed my "fictitious superpower" persona and find time for myself, slow down, and regain my life?

- How do I commit to my own health?

New Metrics of Success Aligned with Health and Well-being

 In early 2001, my long-standing business partnership with my father in a consultancy focused on workplace culture came to a screeching halt when he suffered a fatal heart attack during a family vacation. It was a shock to us all, as a photo of him taken just a few hours earlier shows a healthy, fit, muscular man full of life and gleaming as he held his grandchild in the pool. That sudden tragedy was coupled with a busy, stressful life with three young children and a marriage that was hanging on by its shoestrings. I tried to keep it all together and to be a "superhero" to meet all the expectations I had for myself, and those of others. But, in short, I was a mess. To cope, I turned to unhealthy habits to numb my brain from

all the noise around me and escape the demands. I drank too much, ate processed foods and a lot of sugar, and slept too little, if at all.

As I turned 50, approaching the age my father died, my unhealthy habits started to take a toll. I started noticing a host of health issues such as hair loss, bloating, brain fog, and nagging anxiety which led me to seek medical attention. With each symptom, I was sent to a different doctor focusing on a different specialty, and yet none were able to address the root cause of my health concerns. Finally, a dear friend introduced me to a functional medicine practitioner trained to examine how the body functions as an interconnected, whole system, identifying and addressing the root cause of disease, not just individual symptoms siloed into organ systems. We discovered the root cause of my inflammation, and I removed the triggers that had caused the brain fog, anxiety, and weight gain.

I stopped drinking alcohol. I eliminated gluten from my diet. I added more plant-based rainbow foods to my diet as well as healthy fats. I started to move more frequently and found restorative practices that felt good in my body. Slowly, I worked my way back to wellness, and my health improved.

– Samantha, reflecting on the challenges that led her to learn about functional medicine and pivot her career to become a health coach

We know we should be meditating more often, eating better, making good choices that help us sleep soundly at night. But we don't. We spend that extra hour of free time scrolling social media or surfing the web. We cave into our cravings, eat too much of what we know we shouldn't and too little of what we know we should. We say "yes" when we really mean "no." We slip into making decisions that somewhere deep down we know aren't good for us, and we aren't sleeping well.

Women's health is disproportionately affected by stress and anxiety: 51% of women versus 34% of men said that worry or stress related to global catastrophes, such as the pandemic, has affected their mental health.[11] Women have 30% more neurons firing at any given time than men,[12] which supports their having stronger skills such as empathy, intuition, collaboration, and self-control, but it also makes women vulnerable to anxiety, depression, pain, and insomnia.[13] Women are more likely than men to be diagnosed with Alzheimer's Disease,[14] depression[15] and anxiety disorders[16] and are more severely affected than men by alcohol abuse and heart disease.[17]

We need new metrics of success that incorporate our overall health and well-being, downtime, sleep, and the importance of joy and happiness. However, life is fraught with constant stressors and there are so many distractions that interfere with our ability to deeply connect with ourselves and listen to our bodies. We often ignore the chronic headaches, the all-too-frequent indigestion and stomach upsets. We dismiss the subtle and more obvious signs of falling out of our natural state of balance and "ease." And then we suddenly find ourselves out of balance, in a state of dis-ease and if left unchecked, disease.

The Three Branches of Rootsilience

Mind-Body Integration

Conscious Leadership

Healing Foods

Arianna Huffington wrote, "*2021 was the year we watched the pandemic go from something we thought and hoped would have a defined end to, at best, an endemic virus that will always be part of our lives. And our thinking about resilience is evolving in the same way. Resilience is not, as so many of us thought in the early days of the pandemic, an end state we can reach. It's a constant process of becoming.*"[18]

It's time we tend our roots. Beyond Resilience to Rootsilience is that path. Rootsilience empowers women leaders to reclaim balance and well-being by decoding the language of our body, behavior and mind. Rootsilience provides a path to be grounded, rooted, and able to respond to stressors from a place of security and balance. Rather than being stretched to our limits and toppling over, Rootsilience shows us how to lead and live as our whole selves.

Beyond Resilience to Rootsilience is organized around the ancient Sanskrit chakra system, combining three main "branches" as they relate to each chakra, starting from the top down, clearing a path to our roots.

1. *Conscious Leadership*: Empowering women in our personal and professional lives to lead with meaning and purpose, rooted in self-awareness to rise beyond our individual selves and live and learn in community. We "embody" conscious leadership, instilling the core teachings at the cellular level through deep reflections, journaling and enhanced self-inquiry.

2. *Healing Foods*: With every bite we take, we have the power to influence our health and balance our body. We use a systems approach to exploring the root cause of disease and explore "food as medicine," learning about foods and herbs that can bring us healing and balance, as well as simple recipes and techniques to incorporate healing foods into our day-to-day life.

3. *Mind-Body Integration*: We cultivate literacy in the language of our mind and body to bring balance to our whole system. In this section, we explore yoga, meditation and movement practices that balance the nervous system and embrace the interconnectedness of our thoughts, emotions and physical sensations. Becoming literate in the language of our mind-body enables us to recognize the subtle signals of imbalance before they become screeching alarms.

Conscious Leadership

Even after all this time
The Sun never says to the Earth,
"You owe me."
Look what happens
With a love like that,
It lights the whole sky.

– Hafiz

We didn't *earn* fresh air, we didn't *earn* our breath, or life itself. These were all present for us, "given to us as gifts," so naturally, we have a desire to give back.[19] The desire to give back is what so many of us are searching for. It's what motivates us to take on challenges for causes we care about, and it's also what keeps us up at night. It's likely a big reason you purchased this book. Some call it purpose, some call it living authentically. When you are leading from a connection with this inner guidance, it's like a puzzle piece clicking into place.

Conscious leadership is leading from this connection. Your motivation becomes less and less about winning awards, titles, gaining fame and notoriety (although these things will naturally flow when you lead consciously), and more about leading as a natural outpouring of your unique talents and gifts, and doing what you love. You shine because it's your natural state of being. You shine because you know how to set boundaries and effectively delegate when necessary. You even help other people shine because you feel completely validated and know your self-worth and no longer find yourself feeling slighted or comparing yourself to others. You trust your decision-making, even if sometimes you make a mistake. You take lessons learned in stride and move forward. You lead because you care and you lead without expectation or attachment to results.

Throughout this book, in the exercises and practices, we invite you to embody these lessons not just by thinking about them and wishing yourself to lead from this idyllic image or ideal. We invite you to reflect on your life and leadership experiences, be the observer, detach from ego, and then transform and act in alignment with your values. In each of the chapters of Section II, there are leadership exercises for you to reflect on to embody the lessons of leadership that each of the chapters provides.

Getting to the Root with Healing Foods

 When diet is wrong, medicine is of no use.
When diet is correct, medicine is of no need.

– Ayurvedic Proverb

For thousands of years, healing foods and herbs have been used to prevent imbalance and disease. Food is a key branch in the Rootsilience framework as we explore foods that support and bring us into balance. Nourishing food, and a healthy relationship to it, is foundational to being Rootsilient.

Functional medicine teaches us to look beyond the individual symptoms and explore core clinical imbalances, reaching all the way down to the root level. When we look at a tree, we assess its health based on its leaves, the vigor of its branches, and the integrity of its trunk. However, these are only signs of what is going on at the surface, above the Earth. When a tree shows signs of illness in its leaves, instead of trying to fix the damage in each individual leaf, we investigate what is going on in the soil and roots beneath the surface.

Using this metaphor, if our body is the tree, functional medicine teaches us to look at "the whole tree," i.e., our roots, branches, and leaves. When we look holistically at our health, systemic causes of disease are often uncovered and the healing process can begin. As a tree relies on a strong root structure to absorb nutrients from the soil and water below to support its leaves, branches and trunk, we rely on healthy, nourishing and healing foods to support our overall health. In each chapter of Section II, we provide an overview of the body as it relates to each chakra and the associated body parts and key body processes. With this understanding, along with the exploration of foods and herbs that support our personalized needs, we restore balance in areas that may need additional support.

Mind-Body Integration

 One of the clearest lessons from contemporary neuroscience is that our sense of ourselves is anchored in a vital connection with our bodies. We do not truly know ourselves unless we can feel and interpret our physical sensations. We need to register and act on these sensations to navigate safely through life. While numbing (or compensatory sensation-seeking) may make life tolerable, the price you pay is that you lose awareness of what is going on inside your body and, with that, the sense of being fully, sensually alive.

– Bessel Van der Kolk, *The Body Keeps the Score*

If you ever slammed on the brakes before realizing you nearly smashed into the car that suddenly stopped in front of you, you know the powerful connection between mind and body. Whether an argument or annoying email, anxiety about the future or replaying the past, our nervous system can react in the same way as if we were under physical attack, and we go into "fight, flight, freeze or fawn" mode. Our brains are wired to look for problems and detect threats, an evolutionary gain that kept our ancestors alive and able to detect and run away from predators or danger. Today those "saber-toothed tigers" are never-ending emails, being stuck in traffic or paralyzed with fear or anxiety of the unknown. We have to consciously work to bring our nervous system into balance, encouraging our "rest and digest" response, such as a slowing of the heart rate, a release of serotonin, a release of tension from our muscles and continued digestion.

As leaders, we face challenges like everyone else, but how we handle them and conduct ourselves has a ripple effect not only on ourselves, but also on our teams, businesses, partnerships, and family relationships.

Succumbing to our fight or flight response and sending that angry email could be a career-ending move. Lashing out at your partner or child because you've had it "up to here" magnifies and often worsens your own frustrations, and constantly losing sleep due to an overstimulated and out-of-balance nervous system puts you further on the path to burnout. It's critical to stay centered and keep our cool, but sometimes the rock that lands in our pond is so big the ripples throw us way off center and we drift away from ourselves.

The practices in this book invite us to integrate our mind and body so we learn to become literate in the language of our whole selves. We recognize the subtle signals of our body before they become health crises. We begin to view our mind-body as one united and integrated, breathing, leading being. The practices in the book expand our toolkit to know what will nourish and support us. The practices are designed to balance our nervous system, harnessing the power of movement and meditation to recharge, release and stay whole in our day-to-day. We explore a wide range of mind-body practices including yoga, meditation, dance, guided breathing, and tapping.

Rootsilience and the Chakras

We use the seven traditional Sanskrit chakras to organize the Rootsilience framework. The chakras offer us a lens with which to explore and understand the connections between our physical, emotional, and mental health. The chakra system has existed for thousands of years and comes from the same ancient texts that gave rise to yoga and meditation. The chakras, or "wheels of energy," run along the central column of the body, correspond to the nerve ganglion along our spine, and tie in with the neuroendocrine system of our bodies.

It is not the objective of this book to provide in-depth studies of the chakras, nor to prove or disprove the existence of chakras. Rather, we invite you to experience the chakras as a lens through which we can organize behavioral, physical, and emotional aspects of health and well-being. Additional reading resources on chakras to explore are provided in the Appendix.

According to the ancient texts, chakras hold a host of information about our physical, emotional, mental, and spiritual well-being. We are born with certain information pre-programmed into our chakras, just like our DNA carries the genetics of our ancestors. Chakras can be balanced, allowing energy to flow freely and with ease, or they can become restricted or blocked, or even "too open." When our chakras are in balance, we are healthy, able to cope naturally with the ups and downs of our day-to-day life. When our chakras are out of balance, there is "dis-ease" in the flow of energy through the system. We may have a tendency toward negative behaviors; we may even have chronic health conditions associated with this area of imbalance. If left unchecked, this "dis-ease" of the flow of our energy can lead to disease. According to the ancient texts, our chakras can get out of balance for a number of reasons, the primary factors being lifestyle, stress and diet. Detailed information on signs of balance and imbalance, along with tools to find ease, are included in each of the chapters in Section II.

This book includes leadership exercises based on each of the chakras for you to reflect on, including practices to embody those lessons and enable you to thrive as a more effective leader. You will learn how food and movement can be healing medicine for your body, and which practices you can prioritize based on your unique Rootsilience Leadership Map. (We will explain this a bit later in this chapter.)

Taking It from the Top and Clearing a Path to Our Roots

We have lost our ability to feel the Earth viscerally. Our receptors are numbed to the feedback the Earth has been offering us for decades, telling us time and again that she isn't happy or healthy ... we've been too focused on financial and material gain to heed those signs. We stopped caring about the Earth and instead viewed her as a set of resources to be used however we wanted.

– Richard Schwartz, *No Bad Parts*

The chakra system provides a framework to organize our exploration of practices and tools that clear a path to (re)connect us with our roots and to the Earth. While many chakra-based practices start at the bottom, from the Root Chakra to the Crown Chakra, Beyond Resilience to Rootsilience goes in the reverse, from the top down.

Many of us today are simply "talking heads on a screen," and we live our lives very much "in our heads," reacting to whatever gets thrown at us, further eroding our ability to connect to what grounds and centers us. Studies show that children between the ages of three and five can recognize five commercial brands, but they cannot name five types of plants or trees.[20] This separation of mind from body, of body from Earth, has led us to ignore, numb, or simply not recognize the signs of imbalance and dis-ease. We need to move down and in, into our connection with our whole selves, our planet and our roots.

Starting at the Crown Chakra, we explore our thoughts and connection with purpose. That thought and connection gives rise to a vision (Third Eye Chakra), which gives our thoughts and vision a voice (Throat Chakra). We stay motivated by this thought and vision through our passion (Heart Chakra), dedication (Solar Plexus Chakra) and creativity (Sacral Chakra), to ultimately manifest this reality in grounded actions at the Root Chakra. By starting at the top and working our way down, we rebuild our intrinsic connection with our whole selves and the Earth, finding balance at the physical, emotional, mental and behavioral levels.

Safety Note: Ancient texts advise that accessing the higher chakras should be performed only after grounding in the lower chakras. While this book starts in the higher chakras and works our way down, we are using the chakras as an organizational lens and part of a balanced and integrated framework. We approach each chakra with a grounding intention before starting the mind-body integration practices.

The Rootsilience Leadership Map

Your personalized Rootsilience Leadership Map helps you identify areas of focus to find balance and ease. This revolutionary tool maps the VIA Character Strengths to the ancient chakra system and highlights how our behaviors, as evidenced by the VIA Character Strengths – and our possible overuse and underuse of them – are connected at the physical, emotional and mental levels.

The VIA Character Strengths follow the principles of Positive Psychology and were developed in the early 2000s when American psychologists Christopher Peterson and Martin Seligman looked across history and cultures and asked questions such as: *What helps make a human being flourish? What is a strength?*[21] Positive Psychology is the study of positive traits, positive experiences, positive institutions, rather than viewing things from the negative, disorders, disease, conflict and other problems.

The VIA Character Strengths Survey is a short ten-minute questionnaire that identifies 24 elements of positive personality characteristics that are expressed alone and in combinations in characteristic ways by each individual. Character Strengths are the positive parts of your personality that make you feel authentic and engaged. You possess all 24 Character Strengths in different degrees, giving you a unique Character Strengths profile. Character strengths are different from other personal strengths, such as skills, talents, and interests, because they reflect who you are at the core. Each person's character strengths differ, giving everyone a unique profile. Each person who takes the VIA Character Strengths Survey is given a personalized report of their 24 Character Strengths, organized into a list with the top strengths categorized as "signature strengths" or "greater strengths" and the bottom strengths categorized as "lesser strengths."

In developing our Rootsilience Leadership Map, we developed a unique – and we think revolutionary – approach by mapping the 24 VIA Character Strengths into the seven chakras. By combining character strengths with the chakras, we begin to recognize the interconnectedness of our leadership behavior and our emotional, physical, and mental well-being. For example, someone with a greater strength of Zest, which we mapped to the Solar Plexus Chakra, may tend toward overuse. She may have a tremendous enthusiasm and ability to get things done, but when out of balance, she could tend toward craving sugar and sweets or caffeine, further fueling hyperactivity and leading to burnout, exhaustion, and possible digestive disorders. Similarly, a person with a lesser strength could have a tendency toward underuse, as in someone with a lesser strength of Honesty who is unable to speak her truth authentically and who often suffers from a sore throat or mucus build-up around the sinuses (all connected to the Throat Chakra).

The Rootsilience Leadership Map shows you which areas (or chakras) are more "vulnerable" and prone to getting out of balance. Each of the chapters in Section II provides tools to bring you into balance. When you have this holistic snapshot, you know where to look, and you become Rootsilient, able to bring yourself back to center rather than getting stretched beyond your limits.

Methodology for Mapping the VIA Character Strengths to the Chakras

At the start of the COVID-19 pandemic, when we were working through our own challenges of grief, burnout, and uncertainty, we first hypothesized that there could be a correlation between the VIA Character Strengths and the chakras. Samantha had extensively studied the VIA Character Strengths as part of her Functional Medicine Coaching Academy program, and also pursued deeper exploration of the work with Dr. Ryan M. Niemiec, Chief Science and Education Officer at the VIA Institute on Character, and Rimi had developed her own form of chakra yoga over the years.

Together, we created the first iteration of the Rootsilience Leadership Map mapping the VIA Character Strengths to the chakras. After running several pilot programs of our Rootilience framework and testing the Map with participants, we gained valuable insights and shifted a few of the character strengths to different chakras. We also referenced a 2013 PNAS study, a peer reviewed journal of the National Academy of Science on the correlation of emotions and physical sensations[22]. The VIA Character Strengths have been used with permission from the VIA Institute on Character.

During colleagues' reviews of our model and framework, there was some debate over which character strengths tied to which chakras and whether some character strengths spanned more than one chakra. Ultimately we decided, for simplicity, to map each character strength to one chakra and where there was debate, we chose the chakra that best matched the associated physical and emotional signs of imbalance from our participants in our programs. Ultimately, the key takeaway from this book is to help our reader make a connection between her unique signs of balance and imbalance, whether at the physical, emotional or behavioral level, and the Rootsilience Leadership Map serves as an illustrative framework to make these key connections.

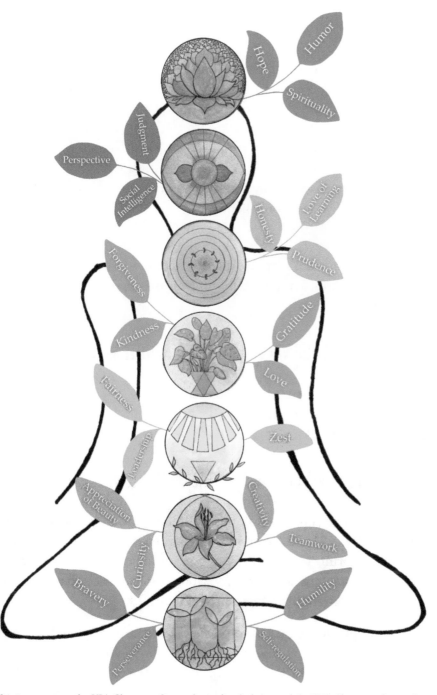

This image maps the VIA Character Strengths to the chakras, and the VIA Character Strengths are used with permission by the VIA Institute on Character.[23]

Exercise: Your Rootsilience Leadership Map

Now we're ready to dive in! We'll come back to your Rootsilience Leadership Map throughout the book so this is a critical exercise to complete. You'll need to set aside about 20 minutes to take the VIA Character Strengths Survey and then complete your Rootsilience Leadership Map.

You can access the online map at our book resources site (www.rootsilience.com/courses/beyond-the-book) or complete your map manually with the instructions that follow below.

If using the manual map, we'd like you to use two pens – preferably a green pen and a brown pen, but you can use any two colors that you have on hand.

Step 1: COMPLETE YOUR VIA CHARACTER STRENGTHS ASSESSMENT

As the first step, please register for an account and take the VIA Character Strengths Survey (give yourself 10 minutes to complete): https://rootsilience.pro.viasurvey.org/

Step 2: MAP YOUR VIA CHARACTER STRENGTHS TO THE CHAKRAS

Once you complete your VIA Character Strengths Survey, you'll receive a summary with the 24 Character Strengths ordered based on your unique results. Please print it out and save your summary report. Then, make note of your Top 5 "greater strengths" (those listed 1 through 5) and your Bottom 5 "lesser strengths" (those listed 20 to 24).

In the Rootsilience Leadership Map Worksheet on page 53, where you see the VIA Character Strengths listed, circle your Top 5 "greater strengths" (those listed 1 through 5) with a green colored pen and circle your Bottom 5 "lesser strengths" (those listed 20 to 24) with a brown colored pen.

Your map highlights your "greater strengths" in green (like the color of the leaves of a tree that is healthy and abundant) and your "lesser strengths" in brown (like the color of the roots you may need to nurture and solidify) next to each chakra.

Step 3: REVIEW YOUR PHYSICAL, EMOTIONAL AND BEHAVIORAL SIGNS OF IMBALANCE

Next, refer to the table of Physical, Emotional, and Behavioral Signs of Imbalance that begins on page 49. Check ✔ all the signs that apply for you and add up the number of checked boxes in each row.

Step 4: MAKE THE CONNECTION

Complete your Rootsilience Leadership Map by adding the number of "greater strengths" and "lesser strengths" you've circled in Step 2 together with the total sum of Physical, Emotional and Behavioral Signs of Imbalance from Step 3 for each chakra. The chakras with the highest total scores are the areas of focus for you to stay balanced.

Our revolutionary Rootsilience Leadership Map helps you answer these important questions:

- What are your unique signs of going out of balance?

- What connections can you make between your greater or lesser strengths and your emotional/behavioral and/or physical signs of imbalance?

We'll come back to these questions many times during this book so don't feel you need to have answers right away.

EXAMPLE: ROOTSILIENCE MAP LEADERSHIP WORKSHEET

Have a look at the example we've provided for guidance on how to complete your Rootsilience Leadership Map. In this example, Rimi has the following VIA "greater strengths" and "lesser strengths":

Greater Character Strengths: Love, Love of Learning, Gratitude, Curiosity, Zest

Lesser Character Strengths: Prudence, Judgment, Teamwork, Humor, Humility

Then, Rimi filled out her table of Physical, Emotional, Behavioral Signs of Imbalance as shown below, and added up her scores in the "Total Sum" row.

Chakra	Physical Signs of Imbalance	Emotional and Behavioral Signs of Imbalance	TOTAL SUM (sum of all checked in each row)
CROWN	☐ Addictions ☐ ADHD ☐ Amnesia ☐ Brain fog ☐ Early onset hair loss ☑ Extreme fatigue ☑ Insomnia and sleep disorders ☐ Seasonal Affective Disorder	☐ Alienation (feeling isolated or lonely) ☐ Depression ☐ Lack of purpose ☐ Lackadaisical, languid, lacking liveliness ☑ Overintellectualizing (head in the clouds) ☐ Pessimistic ☑ Poor sense of humor (taking things too seriously) ☐ Vague sense of values	4

THIRD EYE	☐ Alzheimer's Disease ☐ Chronic headaches ☐ Dementia ☐ Eye Infections ☐ Memory loss ☐ Migraines ☐ Pressure around the eyes ☐ Vision impairment	☑ Anxiety ☐ Biased decision making ☐ Difficulty concentrating ☑ Difficulty with discernment ☐ Lack of focus ☐ Migraines ☑ Mood swings ☐ Paranoia	**3**
THROAT	☐ Chronic ear, nose or throat infections ☐ Overwhelm from voices or sounds (misophonia) ☐ Sinus infections ☐ Sore throat, croaky voice ☐ Tinnitus (ringing in the ears) ☑ Thyroid imbalance ☑ Neck Pain/TMJ (temporomandibular joint) disorder ☐ Toothaches, periodontal disease	☐ Dishonesty ☐ Difficulty listening ☐ Difficulty expressing or speaking up ☐ Inability to make wise choices ☑ Overly talkative ☐ Phobia of public speaking ☐ Tendency to engage in or spread gossip or rumors ☐ Tendency to tell "little white lies" or half-truth	**3**

HEART	☐ Blockages and/or calcification in arteries ☐ Breast cancer or cysts ☐ Heart palpitations ☐ High/low blood pressure or high/low heart rate ☐ Lung or respiratory disease ☑ Poor circulation ☐ Rapid and shallow breathing or asthma ☐ Rosacea or flushing in the face	☐ Being a "doormat" (constantly putting yourself down) ☑ Difficulty receiving care and love ☐ Emotional overkill (sugary sweet behavior) ☑ Giving too much or people-pleasing ☐ Merciless and unkind ☐ Inability to forgive ☐ Repressed or stuck in grief and sadness ☐ Vindictive, vengeful and critical	**3**
SOLAR	☐ Constipation or Diarrhea ☐ Diabetes ☐ Gallbladder or Liver problems ☐ Heartburn ☑ Lack of energy and fatigue ☐ Muscle tension, particularly in the abdominal area and around ☐ the diaphragm ☐ Gastrointestinal issues (poor digestion and metabolism) ☐ Skin disorders, such as acne, rashes, or eczema	☐ Being a "control freak" and/or micromanaging ☑ Burned out ☑ Hypervigilance and focus on minutia ☐ Lack of self worth ☐ Low self-esteem ☐ Obsessiveness ☑ Rumination ☑ Tendency toward perfectionism	**5**

SACRAL	☐ Endometriosis ☐ Bladder and/or Kidney disease or infection ☐ Chronic hip or pelvic pain or tightness ☑ Chronic lower back pain ☐ Menstrual problems ☐ Ovarian cysts or PCOS (Polycystic Ovarian Syndrome) ☐ Reproductive and pelvic organ conditions (irregular or extremely heavy/scanty periods) ☐ Urinary tract infections	☐ "Bad endings" with ex-colleagues, partners, past lovers or friends ☐ Difficulty feeling joy and sensuality ☐ Difficulty thinking outside of the box, unimaginative ☐ Emotional instability ☐ Individualistic, "going it alone" or "I can do it myself" ☐ Lack of creativity ☐ Lost in groupthink ☐ Stuck in autopilot, unable to go with the flow	**1**
ROOT	☐ Bone injuries ☐ Feeling ungrounded ☐ Fight/flight/freeze/fawn responses ☐ Hemorrhoid ☐ Joint pain ☐ Muscle fatigue ☐ Out-of-balance nervous system, anxiety, stress, racing thoughts, panic ☐ Sciatica	☐ Cowardly or unwilling to face obstacles or challenges ☐ Decision making from fear ☐ Difficulty trusting ☐ Difficulty with commitment ☐ Fearful ☐ Giving up easily, lack of perseverance ☐ Poor and/or overly rigid boundaries ☐ Struggle creating and/or keeping a routine	**0**

Rimi's Rootsilience Leadership Map Worksheet results are shown below:

VIA Character Strengths: (Greater/ Lesser)	Hope Humor Spirituality	Judgment Perspective Social Intelligence	Honesty Love of Learing Prudence	Forgiveness Gratitude Kindness Love	Fairness Leadership Zest	Appreciation of Beauty Creativity Curiosity Teamwork	Bravery Humility Perseverance Self-Regulation
	CROWN	THIRD EYE	THROAT	HEART	SOLAR PLEXUS	SACRAL	ROOT
Sum of Physical, Emotional, Behavioral Signs of Imbalance	4	3	3	3	5	1	0
TOTAL SCORE	5	4	5	5	6	3	1

Based on Rimi's example, the Solar Plexus Chakra has the highest score with a "6", therefore she would benefit most from the practices, tips and tools presented in the Solar Plexus chapter to bring herself back into balance. She may also benefit from the practices, tips and tools presented in the Throat, Heart and Crown Chakras chapters, also with higher scores.

TABLE OF PHYSICAL, EMOTIONAL AND BEHAVIORAL SIGNS OF IMBALANCE

Note: This is a comprehensive, but not an exhaustive list.

Chakra	Physical Signs of Imbalance	Emotional and Behavioral Signs of Imbalance	TOTAL SUM (sum of all checked in each row)
CROWN	☐ Addictions ☐ ADHD ☐ Amnesia ☐ Brain fog ☐ Early onset hair loss ☐ Extreme fatigue ☐ Insomnia and sleep disorders ☐ Seasonal Affective Disorder	☐ Alienation (feeling isolated or lonely) ☐ Depression ☐ Lack of purpose ☐ Lackadaisical, languid, lacking liveliness ☐ Overintellectualizing (head in the clouds) ☐ Pessimistic ☐ Poor sense of humor (taking things too seriously) ☐ Vague sense of values	
THIRD EYE	☐ Alzheimer's Disease ☐ Chronic headaches ☐ Dementia ☐ Eye Infections ☐ Memory loss ☐ Migraines ☐ Pressure around the eyes ☐ Vision impairment	☐ Anxiety ☐ Biased decision making ☐ Difficulty concentrating ☐ Difficulty with discernment ☐ Lack of focus ☐ Migraines ☐ Mood swings ☐ Paranoia	

THROAT		
	☐ Chronic ear, nose or throat infections ☐ Overwhelm from voices or sounds (misophonia) ☐ Sinus infections ☐ Sore throat, croaky voice ☐ Tinnitus (ringing in the ears) ☐ Thyroid imbalance ☐ Neck Pain/TMJ (temporomandibular joint) disorder ☐ Toothaches, periodontal disease	☐ Dishonesty ☐ Difficulty listening ☐ Difficulty expressing or speaking up ☐ Inability to make wise choices ☐ Overly talkative ☐ Phobia of public speaking ☐ Tendency to engage in or spread gossip or rumors ☐ Tendency to tell "little white lies" or half-truth

HEART		
	☐ Blockages and/or calcification in arteries ☐ Breast cancer or cysts ☐ Heart palpitations ☐ High/low blood pressure or high/low heart rate ☐ Lung or respiratory disease ☐ Poor circulation ☐ Rapid and shallow breathing or asthma ☐ Rosacea or flushing in the face	☐ Being a "doormat" (constantly putting yourself down) ☐ Difficulty receiving care and love ☐ Emotional overkill (sugary sweet behavior) ☐ Giving too much or people-pleasing ☐ Merciless and unkind ☐ Inability to forgive ☐ Repressed or stuck in grief and sadness ☐ Vindictive, vengeful and critical

SOLAR			
	☐ Constipation or Diarrhea ☐ Diabetes ☐ Gallbladder or Liver problems ☐ Heartburn ☐ Lack of energy and fatigue ☐ Muscle tension, particularly in the abdominal area and around ☐ the diaphragm ☐ Gastrointestinal issues (poor digestion and metabolism) ☐ Skin disorders, such as acne, rashes, or eczema	☐ Being a "control freak" and/or micromanaging ☐ Burned out ☐ Hypervigilance and focus on minutia ☐ Lack of self worth ☐ Low self-esteem ☐ Obsessiveness ☐ Rumination ☐ Tendency toward perfectionism	

SACRAL	☐ Endometriosis ☐ Bladder and/or Kidney disease or infection ☐ Chronic hip or pelvic pain or tightness ☐ Chronic lower back pain ☐ Menstrual problems ☐ Ovarian cysts or PCOS (Polycystic Ovarian Syndrome) ☐ Reproductive and pelvic organ conditions (irregular or extremely heavy/ scanty periods) ☐ Urinary tract infections	☐ "Bad endings" with ex-colleagues, partners, past lovers or friends ☐ Difficulty feeling joy and sensuality ☐ Difficulty thinking outside of the box, unimaginative ☐ Emotional instability ☐ Individualistic, "going it alone" or "I can do it myself" ☐ Lack of creativity ☐ Lost in groupthink ☐ Stuck in autopilot, unable to go with the flow
ROOT	☐ Bone injuries ☐ Feeling ungrounded ☐ Fight/flight/freeze/ fawn responses ☐ Hemorrhoid ☐ Joint pain ☐ Muscle fatigue ☐ Out-of-balance nervous system, anxiety, stress, racing thoughts, panic ☐ Sciatica	☐ Cowardly or unwilling to face obstacles or challenges ☐ Decision making from fear ☐ Difficulty trusting ☐ Difficulty with commitment ☐ Fearful ☐ Giving up easily, lack of perseverance ☐ Poor and/or overly rigid boundaries ☐ Struggle creating and/ or keeping a routine

The Rootsilience Leadership Map Worksheet

VIA Character Strengths: (Greater/ Lesser)	Hope Humor Spirituality	Judgment Perspective Social Intelligence	Honesty Love of Learing Prudence	Forgiveness Gratitude Kindness Love	Fairness Leadership Zest	Appreciation of Beauty Creativity Curiosity Teamwork	Bravery Humility Perseverance Self-Regulation
	CROWN	THIRD EYE	THROAT	HEART	SOLAR PLEXUS	SACRAL	ROOT
Sum of Physical, Emotional, Behavioral Signs of Imbalance								
TOTAL SCORE								

How to Use This Book

This book is intended to be both inspiration, insight, and practical guide. We recommend that before continuing, you complete your Rootsilience Leadership Map to understand your unique signs of balance at the behavioral, physical and emotional levels. Keep your Rootsilience Leadership Map close by as you read this book and pay special attention to the chakra chapters where you have greater strengths and lesser strengths, as well as physical or emotional signs, to gain insight and practical tools to bring you into balance. Most important is that you begin to make a connection between your unique signs of ease and dis-ease, whether they be behavioral, physical, or emotional signs. The chakra system provides a lens through which we can organize and interpret our unique connections. The key here is you are decoding your behavior, body, and mind to recognize when you begin to become unrooted, and how to bring yourself back.

During the course of reading this book, we recommend keeping a journal and dating your Rootsilience Leadership Map at the start of reading this book, and then again when you have a chance to implement the practices and tools, to see how you may have changed. You can use your journal to complete the leadership exercises presented in each chapter, make notes on which recipes you've made and how they worked for you, as well as any notes on the movement practices along with the supplemental video recordings available to you online.

All the mind-body integration practice supplements for this book were filmed on São Miguel, Azores, a microcosm of all the chakra elements with waterfalls, volcanic geysers, black lava rock, and endless ocean vistas. You can access these supplemental mind-body practices on our website (www.rootsilience.com/courses/beyond-the-book). There you can engage with our online community, a private place to share insights, and connect to other readers around the world who are on this journey with you. It's also a place where we will be sharing supporting practices for the book and information on upcoming live events, retreats and courses.

Learning Objectives for Each Chakra

In Section II, each chapter explores the following learning objectives by chakra, based on the three branches of Rootsilience: conscious leadership, healing foods, and mind-body integration.

Crown Chakra:

- Learn how to find purpose and meaning.
- Understand what foods and herbs support sleep, circadian rhythm, and detoxification.
- Experience mind-body integration to clear the mind and enhance connection.

Third Eye Chakra:

- Learn how to set a clear vision and path.
- Understand what foods and herbs nourish your brain.
- Experience mind-body integration to expand your vision and perspective, and see the big picture.

Throat Chakra:

- Learn how to express your authentic voice.
- Understand what foods and herbs support listening to your body, and the importance of hydrating foods.
- Experience mind-body integration to find your voice, and hear and speak your truth.

Heart Chakra:

- Learn how to lead a life you love and nurture your whole self.
- Understand what foods and herbs support a healthy heart and lower stress.
- Experience mind-body integration to connect you to unconditional love, heart opening, and forgiveness.

Solar Plexus Chakra:

- Learn how to radiate your benevolent power.
- Understand what foods and herbs support healthy digestion and soothe the fire in your belly.
- Experience mind-body integration to balance your fire for rest and recharge.

Sacral Chakra:

- Learn how to be in creative flow and cultivate healthy partnerships.
- Understand what foods and herbs support hormone health.
- Experience mind-body integration to free your hips and pelvis, and invite in creativity and self-expression.

Root Chakra:

- Learn to lead with presence and trust.
- Understand what foods and herbs calm the nervous system and deeply ground and nourish you.
- Experience mind-body integration to access connective tissue and release fear and cultivate trust.

Let's get started on your path to Rootsilience!

Chapter Two

The Crown Chakra

Leading with Purpose
and Finding Connection

My first job after college was in New York City and I chose it based on the fact that it was in "the city" (as if no other city existed) and that it had the highest salary (yet I could still barely pay rent for my shared shoebox apartment!). I worked hard, was hired by a "big name" firm, and it wasn't until my mid-twenties, about five years into my career, that I actually wondered, "So what am I doing with my life?" It was a period of deep soul-searching that led me to question the kind of work I wanted to dedicate myself to. I began the business school application process and it was this essay question that stumped me: "What is most important to you and why?"

It took thirteen drafts of writing this essay, each time starting over from scratch and each time forcing myself to go beyond my ego-self, to write about what was truly essential and not just what I thought the admissions offer would be impressed by. I wrote about the pivotal experiences in my life that shaped me; a visit to India as an adult and reconnecting to a family I hadn't seen in decades, an impactful summer internship working as a camp counselor and living in nature. I wrote about the importance of connection.

The process of getting in touch with what was important to me helped me understand my values. Knowing my values served as a navigation tool in my life, like a "North Star," guiding me to live and lead with purpose and meaning. While over time my values evolved and changed, learning how to think about what is important to me has guided me to living a connected and purposeful life today.

– Rimi's Crown Chakra story

Crown

Hope ✦ Humor ✦ Spirituality

Traditionally, the thousand lotus petals symbolize infinity and the qualities of self-transcendence.

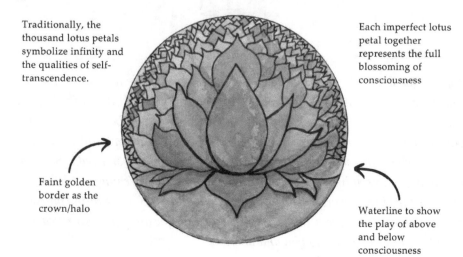

Each imperfect lotus petal together represents the full blossoming of consciousness

Faint golden border as the crown/halo

Waterline to show the play of above and below consciousness

Overview of the Crown Chakra

Rootsilience Symbolism of the Crown Chakra	Our Rootsilience Crown Chakra image represents blooming Consciousness. The lotus flower is a symbol for evolution and transcendence; the delicate lotus petals a representation of the infinite abundance available to us if we can lift ourselves out of the mud of materialism, ego and attachment.
	The lotus flower is both above and below the waterline, tenderly playing between the conscious and subconscious. Above, the crown is illuminated in a light gold, representing our glory and connection to oneness and all.

Key Themes	The Crown Chakra is known as the seat of the Higher Self, beyond all limitations of the mind and body. Fundamental to the Crown Chakra is our need to feel connected and have a sense of purpose and meaning. The Crown has also been called "the Spirit Chakra" – spirit of life force, vitality, chi, qi, and prana.
Key Leadership Challenges	• Lack of direction in life • Attachment to one's ego and outcomes • Pessimistic outlook on life
Key Physical Signs of Imbalance	• Addictions • Seasonal Affective Disorder • Sleep Disorders and Insomnia
Key Emotional and Behavioral Signs of Imbalance	• Alienated • Depressed • Lack of purpose
Location	The location of this chakra is found at the top of the head, the highest point of your skull, and is associated with the cerebral cortex – the part of our brain that is responsible for the high-order cognitive processing of the conscious mind.
Chakra's Body Functions	The Crown Chakra's body functions are found in the pineal gland, the small pinecone-shaped gland that sits inside the middle of the brain. This gland is responsible for brain activity and sleeping patterns. The pineal gland is affected by the cycles of the sun and is responsible for secretion of both melatonin and serotonin.

Element	The element associated with the Crown Chakra is Thought. Sometimes referred to as Consciousness, this is the awareness behind our mundane thoughts and behind our ego. It is the "Supreme Thought" and source of creation.
VIA Character Strengths	HOPE allows us to dream about our goals and objectives, expanding our possibilities. With hope, we optimistically believe that good things will come. When we cultivate HUMOR, we can more easily step into the role of the observer, taking a more lighthearted view than if we were attached to our ego. Humor enables us to recognize what is amusing in situations and can help us bring more playfulness into our attitudes, bringing levity to difficult situations. When we embrace SPIRITUALITY, we find ourselves connected to "that which is greater than us;" this can be as simple as feeling a sense of purpose beyond attachment or reward, or experiencing a connection to a higher dimension that reminds us we are never alone.
Color	Violet or white. On the rainbow spectrum of light, violet has the shortest wavelength and the strongest vibration of the colors.
Sanskrit	*Sahasrara*, translating to "thousand petals," and this chakra is symbolized as a lotus flower with 1,000 petals, representing our journey to infinite Consciousness.

Balanced Leadership in the Crown Chakra

 Know the Self as lord of the chariot,
The body as the chariot itself,
The discriminating intellect as
The charioteer, and the mind as reins.
The senses, say the wise, are the horses;
Selfish desires are the roads they travel.

– Katha Upanishad

What is Consciousness?

Take a moment to look up from this page and look around the room you're in. What's the first thought that comes to you? How do you become aware of it? Is it a voice in your head? Your voice? French philosopher René Descartes coined the term *cogito ergo sum*, or "I think therefore I am." He believed that thoughts are evidence that we exist. And for so many of us, we believe we *are* our thoughts. However, if we are aware of our thoughts, how can we *be* our thoughts? If we hear the voice in our head, are we not the awareness or consciousness behind that voice?

And so, who or what is the awareness behind our thoughts? This is the question philosophers and sages have explored for thousands of years. In the passage quoted earlier from the Upanishads,[1] the awareness behind our thoughts is known as the Self (with a capital "S"). It is this Self that exists in all living beings and is the same Self in you and me. It is this Self that is the Consciousness, or awareness behind our thoughts. It is the blue sky behind the clouds that float by. Too often we identify as the clouds. We get swept away and stuck in the clouds and forget to let go and embrace our infinite selves as the sky.

The ancient texts teach us that our attachment to our senses (specifically our attachment to pleasure and avoidance of pain) is what drives us away from this Self, forgetting that we are in fact this infinite being, here in this body temporarily, to experience what it is to learn to love and remember.

In the secret cave of the heart, two are
Seated by life's fountain. The separate ego
Drinks of the sweet and bitter stuff,
Liking the sweet, disliking the bitter,
While the supreme Self drinks sweet and bitter
Neither liking this nor disliking that.
The ego gropes in darkness, while the Self
Lives in Light.

– Katha Upanishad

The Perils of Ego and Attachment

When we attach ourselves to our senses, to our ego, or to the story we find ourselves in, we forget that we are able to step back into Consciousness itself. We forget that we can step back into the role of the observer and be the awareness or the Self behind our ego. We forget because we identify with our ego, the voice in our heads that tells us, "We can rest and be happy later, we just need to work every weekend until we get that promotion." Or, "We need to have that seven-figure home, then we know we've made it! Then we can live Happily Ever After." Or, "We must have a certain type of partner, marriage, family and lifestyle and we don't have it yet, so keep going, be skinnier, be prettier, work harder, DO MORE!"

So we chase those things and associate who we are with the *image* of who we are and who we want to be. That image can be based on what we own, what car we drive, what kind of phone we have, whether we have the "right" number of kids, what kind of stores we shop at, what school our partners or kids go to, etc. The image is not you, but rather a representation of you. When we look into the mirror, the reflection is not who we are. Literally, it's reversed! Maybe the mirror has dust on it, or the mirror is slightly slanted and it distorts us. We are not the image of who we are. But, we get attached to that image. We become so identified with the image of who we are, the image of who we think we ought to be, or the image of who we think other people think we are or ought to be. And we forget who we really are.

So who are we then?

The Parable of the Three Blind Men

In this ancient parable, the elephant is a mysterious being no one has ever seen or yet come to know. As three blind men approach this unknown thing, no one person can understand the whole. One man says, with his hand on the elephant's trunk, "Why it's a snake! It has a long, curved body." The other, with his hand on the elephant's tail, says, "No, it can't be a snake, it has a tail!" And the third, with his hand on the elephant's thick leg, says, "Rubbish, this is not an animal, it's a large, sturdy tree trunk."

The parable of the Elephant and the Three Blind Men brings to light the fact that "that which is greater than us" – be it "Consciousness," "God," "Universe," "Goddess," "Mother Nature," "my Wiser Self," "my heart," – is something beyond any one individual's comprehension. We cannot fully understand Consciousness (insert your word), but we can trust our own experience of it, in a way that encourages us to feel connected and to feel purpose. And maybe it is a spark of *this* that is our awareness behind the voice in our heads, or the Consciousness behind our thoughts.

In the parable, each man's experience is so different from the other that they start accusing each other of lying, and in some versions, their disagreement escalates into a deadly battle. Each one is adamant about his position and refuses to recognize the others' experiences or points of view. Sound familiar? Seems a fitting parable for the countless wars, genocide, oppression, and division that have resulted from disagreements on what "Consciousness" (or your word) is. Some of us were taught there is one God and "my God is the only god" and anyone who says otherwise is wrong or will go to "hell." Some of us grew up seeing our parents devoutly religious, reciting prayers and hymns day in and day out, but then living a life that was not entirely aligned with that devotion. So we shut down when we hear about Consciousness, Spirit or God. We think, "It has nothing to do with me", "It's not real", or "It's too out there."

Today, more than ever, we need to embrace Consciousness. Regardless of your beliefs, upbringing or religious orientation, we invite you to consider that everything is inherently connected, and as individuals, we influence the greater whole. We are the unique grains of sand that make up the beach of life. We are the individual water droplets that make up the sea. We can embrace Consciousness (or whatever word you prefer) in a way that doesn't alienate or trigger anyone, but rather enables all of us to see that everything is deeply connected and each action or cause has an effect. The importance of embracing Consciousness in leadership is realizing that it is not only your life that you're impacting, but the many interconnected webs and ripples that follow.

Purpose in Leadership

Over time, I discovered that "my purpose" wasn't something that existed on some silver platter I had to look outside of myself to find. Noticing where I thrived, where I naturally shared my talents, and in areas or projects that I loved, helped me to realize my purpose as a teacher and wisdom keeper. Knowing my purpose is acknowledging what I'm here to do at this time, and when I allowed myself to think outside the box of a defined career or label, I expanded more fully into my connected self.

– Rimi's Crown Chakra story (continued)

Purpose is not something you discover one day and then live happily ever after. It's not handed to you on a silver platter, and you don't need to do, achieve, or chase anything to get it. Connecting to your unique individual purpose is to harmonize the rich symphony of the Universe. Each one of our lives matters, each one of us has a place and purpose in this world, for however long we have. As leaders, we have many gifts and talents and thus pave the way for others to follow. Our grit, ambition, dedication and passion have the potential to move mountains and shape the world we want to lead.

Your purpose is at the intersection of what you love, what you thrive in and where you connect to Consciousness. When you do something that lights you up, that connects you to what enables you to thrive and what reminds you that everything is connected, you are living your purpose. The leadership exercises later in this chapter offer further guidance and ways for you to explore your purpose. When we lack a connection to what lights us up, to what makes us thrive, or to Consciousness, believing ourselves as separate from it, it's no wonder our purpose becomes an elusive theory that we're not quite sure how to reach or embody. When we are disconnected from a sense of purpose and meaning in our lives, we falsely assume that our happiness and success depend on external factors.

 When we let achievements and acquisitions determine our course, we're living in the illusion that happiness comes from external measures of success, but all too often we find that when we finally get what we want, when we find success, it doesn't lead to happiness.

– Jay Shetty, *Think Like a Monk*

The Elephant in the Room

When we have a bad day, we get into a big argument, lose a major business deal or our child won't stop throwing a tantrum, it's easy to lose sight of Consciousness and connection. When we are faced with the day-to-day challenges of having to hold it all together, sometimes we don't. And sometimes we fall down, we feel sad, we disconnect. We look for something that will make us feel better. We reach for a drink, go shopping, numb out with videos or binge-watch our favorite series. We all have our ways of coping, some of them admittedly less helpful than others. The elephant in the room is our dependency on these short-term coping behaviors that, in the long-term, prevent us from connecting to Consciousness and to ourselves.

Let's Talk About Alcohol

The word alcohol comes from the Arabic word *Al-kuhl* which means "body-eating spirit." Interestingly this word also serves as the origin for the English word "ghoul," an evil creature that could devour a human body. Alcohol is often referred to as "spirits," and it was believed that by drinking alcohol, your spirit would be extracted and consumed.[2] There is irony and relevance to these etymological connections. When we consume spirits in excess, we can black out and not remember what happens, often losing consciousness. Or worse, a version of ourselves we're not so proud of (our internal "ghoul") takes over and we are left making apologies the day after.

We are not here to harshly judge or criticize ourselves, but to enter into self-inquiry that gently brings us back into balance. Some of us can enjoy a drink socially or with a delectable meal, but sometimes we overindulge and give our ego a booze-infused adrenaline boost, getting even further away and clouded from our infinite Self. Today, alcohol is marketed and promoted in the media as something to consume for relaxation and enjoyment. Advertising specifically targets women to partake in "wine clubs" to relieve stress, and the prevalence of delivery apps makes it easier than ever to access alcohol on demand.

Despite the staggering profits and the nearly $1.65-billion-dollar alcohol market worldwide,[3] we now have a greater understanding of alcohol's significant deleterious effects. Because women absorb and metabolize alcohol differently than men, they are more susceptible to the negative physical consequences of alcohol, including liver disease, heart disease, and cognitive impairment. It is estimated that one-third of breast cancer cases could be prevented if women did not drink alcohol, were physically active, and maintained a healthy weight.[4] Additionally, alcohol use can negatively affect mental health. Women have twice the risk of men for depression and anxiety, and heavy alcohol use exacerbates depression, anxiety, and insomnia.[5]

During the start of the COVID-19 pandemic, there was a 54 percent increase in alcohol sales,[6] 60 percent of Americans reported drinking more during the lockdowns,[7] and the American Psychological Association found a quarter of Americans increased drinking to deal with pandemic-related stress.[8] Also during the pandemic, women increased their heavy drinking days (as evidenced by drinking more than 4 drinks within a few hours) by 41% compared to pre-pandemic drinking behavior.[9] Research has shown that the psychological stress related to the pandemic was associated with greater drinking for women, but not men.[10]

Alcohol is a central nervous system depressant that causes brain activity to slow down. The sedative effects of alcohol can be relaxing and initially help to bring on sleep, but the consumption of alcohol has been linked to poor sleep quality and duration as well as sleep disorders such as insomnia and sleep apnea.[11] [12]

Other Attachments

While alcohol is just one way we can lose sight of our connection to Consciousness, there are many vices that keep us from this deeper awareness of Self. It could be having to always be "busy," filling up your schedule with never-ending to-do lists so you never have to stop and feel what's really needing to be addressed within. Maybe it's over-exercising or always being on your phone. It could be watching TV or videos, or listening to audiobooks or podcasts incessantly to avoid being alone with yourself and your thoughts. It could be taking sleeping pills or CBD extracts every night because that's an easier crutch than actually slowing down in your life and giving yourself and your nervous system a break. It could even be having to always be around people because that distracts you from being with yourself, all of you. Notice as you were reading this if any of the above triggered a response in you. Deep breaths.

Stepping into the role of observer (and beyond ego) allows us to bring ourselves back into balance. Can we recognize the root thought or cause that leads us to overindulge? Are we seeking to numb ourselves from all the pain and loneliness we feel deep down inside? Or do we need some form of release from an intense day, week, year? Is there another way? Can you actually feel and sense your separation from Consciousness as you overindulge? How can you stay connected to your whole self?

This is certainly heavy and possibly uncomfortable stuff (so please don't forget one of our Rootsilience Character Strengths in the Crown Chakra: HUMOR!) and remember to pat yourself on the back (or the top of your head!), so you can remember this is all part of your journey and you're exactly where you need to be.

Take out your Rootsilience Leadership Map and review your results. Do you have strengths in the Crown Chakra? How do they show up for you?

When we are balanced in the Crown Chakra, we have clarity and meaning in our lives. We are not attached to a particular outcome, praise, or result. We are grateful for the abundance in our lives, not yearning for material things or "more." We have a strong sense of purpose and a connection to that which is greater than us.

When we are imbalanced in the Crown Chakra, we find ourselves attached to outcomes, or feel we can't be happy unless we have certain things or look a certain way. We get attached to success that is based on external praise or awards. We lose sight of our connection to Consciousness and become solely focused on chasing the dangling carrot, whether it be chasing titles, people, status or things.

Leadership signs of imbalance in the Crown Chakra:

- Close-mindedness

- Doubtful about meaning in life

- Feeling lackadaisical, languid, lacking liveliness

- Inability to see a brighter future

- Lack of direction and focus

- Loneliness, feeling isolated, "no one understands me"

- Nagging sense that life is without meaning or purpose

- Not being able to approach life and its challenges with a sense of curiosity

- Over-intellectualizing or "head in the clouds" and inability to find direction and make decisions

- Poor sense of humor, taking things too seriously

- Pessimistic, putting a damper on situations, not seeing the positive

- Tendency to addiction or attachment (alcohol, foods, activities, people, etc.)

- Tendency toward preachiness and rigidity in beliefs

- Vague sense of values

VIA Character Strengths Mapped to the Crown Chakra and Associated Overuse and Underuse[13]

VIA Character Strength	UNDERUSE	OPTIMAL	OVERUSE
HOPE	Negative / Pessimistic	Expecting the Best in the Future	Head in the Clouds / Unrealistic
HUMOR	Overly Serious / Stilted / Flat	Playfulness / Light-Hearted	Tasteless / Socially Inappropriate
SPIRITUALITY	Lack of Purpose or Meaning in Life / Disconnected from What is Sacred / Unaware of Core Values	Connected to Meaning	Preachy / Proselytizing / Fanatical / Rigid Values / Holier Than Thou

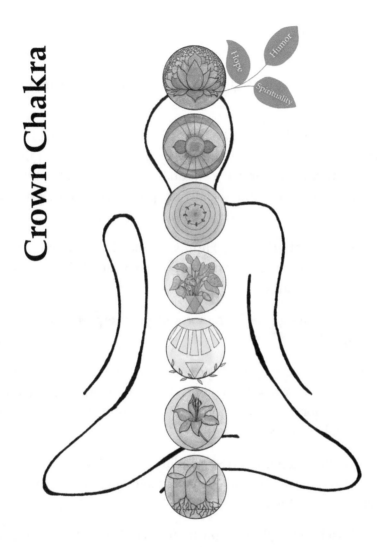

Crown Chakra

If your Rootsilience Leadership Map indicates that you have a greater strength in the Crown Chakra, you may have a tendency to overuse that strength. And if your map indicates a lesser strength, you may tend toward underuse. If you have neither a greater nor a lesser strength, it's likely you are in optimal use.

HOPE, used optimally, will allow for expansive possibilities. A leader using this strength can expect the best in themselves, others, and the future without letting prior setbacks cloud her vision for a brighter and more optimistic future.

- A greater strength of Hope could indicate a "head in the clouds" response to reality.

- A lesser strength of Hope could lead to negativism and being overly pessimistic.

A leader who effectively utilizes HUMOR maintains a sense of playfulness and lightheartedness despite challenges or triggers. They will find ways to poke fun at themselves and at a situation in order to lighten the mood or cut tension without being socially inappropriate or poking fun at another's expense.

- A greater strength of Humor could lead to inappropriate behaviors, such as tastelessness or even caustic jabbing without meaning to hurt.

- A lesser strength of Humor could be interpreted as stiltedness or rigidity.

A leader utilizing their optional strength of SPIRITUALITY will find ways to share their purpose with others, inspiring them to find their own path and take action. They are motivated to share their wisdom without being dictatorial or overly dogmatic.

- A greater strength of Spirituality could indicate a tendency toward preachiness or even proselytizing, trying to convince others to toe the line.

- A lesser strength of Spirituality could lead to a sense of disconnection and inability to find meaning or purpose in one's life.

Remember that if there are any greater or lesser strengths in this chakra, there may also be a tendency toward the physical / emotional / behavioral imbalances in this chakra or the one below it. Your objective is to recognize your unique signs of going out of balance and know how to bring yourself back to center.

Leadership Reflection Exercises to Lead with Purpose and Find Connection

The following exercises provide opportunities for you to reflect on the lessons of the Crown Chakra. Take some time to go through these at your own pace, and remember to connect with our online community to share your questions, comments, and "Aha" moments.

Exercise One:

Rootsilience Crown Chakra Image Meditation and Reflection

Take at least two minutes to gaze at this image while breathing deeply. Note how the lotus flower sits, suspended, on top of the water. Then ask yourself:

- What pushes you "below the line"? What pushes you into feeling lonely, isolated, feeling like others are out to get you, or some other emotion you don't like to admit you may sometimes feel?

- What pushes you "above the line"? What gets you back into a state of curiosity, compassion, and understanding?

Take some time to write down these responses. Now reflect on what you've written, and read it over a few times.

Exercise Two:

Going Beyond Ego and Exploring Values

Values are the guiding principles of our thoughts and beliefs. We obtain our values during the course of our upbringing and through life experiences, and our values can change over time. By exploring our values, we have an opportunity to step into the role of observer (stepping into expanded Consciousness) and can begin to see and work with our ego as an ally, rather than a bully or the one in the driver's seat. First, get out your journal and take a few deep breaths. Ask yourself:

- Where have you been most engaged in your personal and/or professional life? Where have you thrived?

- Where have you been most disengaged or challenged in your personal and/or professional life?

Take some time to write down your responses. What you've written can give you key insights into your values. The situations you just wrote about give you examples in which you are and aren't able to live in alignment with them.

Exercise Three:

Values and Purpose

Open a new page in your journal and create the following table:

Value / What's important to me	How am I living aligned with this value?	Where am I not aligned with this value?	Where am I overusing this or under-applying this value?

Take some time to fill in your table; what you wrote previously in Exercise Two can help you identify some specific values. Be as specific as you can; below is an example to get you thinking.

Value / What's important to me	How am I living aligned with this value?	Where am I not aligned with this value?	Where am I overusing this or under-applying this value?
EXAMPLE			
Accountability	I always do what I say I'm going to do, going above and beyond, and I don't let others down.	I often overcommit to projects and deadlines and sometimes I can't meet them all and feel terrible.	In order to meet the deadlines, I often need to work nights and evenings. I really hate letting people down. I tend to be hard on others when they don't do what they say they're going to do.

After completing the table above, make sure to put a date on it; we will be coming back to this exercise later in this book! Take some time to jot down any reflections. You may want to consider some automatic writing with the following journaling prompts:

- How do your values enable you to live with purpose and connection?

- Are these values you want to live by? What values do you need to tweak or release attachment to in order to expand your Consciousness and live with greater purpose?

Exercise Four:

Mind Map Exercise to Gain Clarity Around Purpose

The Mind Map is a powerful tool used to visually organize ideas and information. The Mind Map is built around a single idea, and associations that flow from that one concept are mapped out to see their relationship to the core concept. For example, when we create a Mind Map with the word "Garden," trailing out from that core topic are all the words associated with what you might want to do to plant a garden. So it might include activities like weeding and pruning to listing the items to purchase to create the garden like compost, a sprinkler, and gloves.

Before starting this exercise, close your eyes and think about your purpose or your calling. Think about what makes you thrive and where you feel a sense of connection with yourself and the world around you. Imagine that one thing that you feel called to do, perhaps even meant to do. This isn't necessarily the work you'll do forever, but for today, it's the one thing that you feel compelled to do. Once you have clarity, in the center of your Mind Map, write the one word that you feel is your core purpose. From there, allow the words to flow from that one word in the branches that extend from the center. Don't overly edit your thoughts as you draw on the page. Allow your thoughts to flow freely and see where they lead you.

THE CROWN MIND MAP

Exercise Five:

Crown Chakra Leadership Integration Exercise

Journaling prompts:

- How do you lead with purpose? Where do you feel aligned with that purpose? Where are you most connected? Where are you unsure or disconnected?

- How do you bring yourself back to alignment?

- What are your signs of being out of alignment with purpose?

- What insights did you gain from drawing your Mind Map?

- How do your attachments limit you from feeling connected and living your purpose?

- How could releasing attachments enable you to live your purpose?

- What assumptions drive you and/or your behaviors?

Exercise Six:

Meet Your Wiser Self (20-Minute Guided Meditation)

Head over to our online resources, found at www.rootsilience.com/courses/beyond-the-book, pop in some headphones, and prepare for a guided meditation to connect to your Wiser Self with Rimi. Think of your "Wiser Self" as having one foot firmly planted in your ego, who understands who you are, your life and all that you identify with and has one foot firmly planted in Consciousness, understanding the bigger picture and interconnectedness to everything. This meditation gives you a powerful way to connect with yourself and serves as a decision-making tool for life.

Reflection:

- How does your wiser self communicate with you? (Sounds, feelings, visions, etc.)

- Is your wiser self older or younger than you? (Note it can change each time you go into this meditation.)

- Describe the place of meeting your wiser self; what was it like to be there?

How the Crown Chakra Functions in the Body

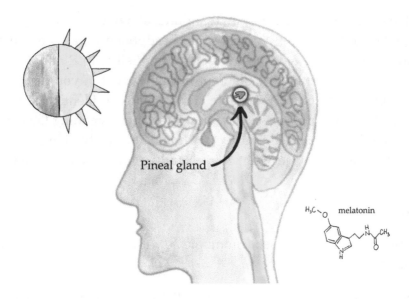

Pineal gland

H₃C–O   melatonin

We start our discussion of the Crown Chakra's function in the body with the pineal gland. The pineal gland, a small endocrine gland shaped like a pinecone and from where it gets its name, is located in the mid-brain behind the pituitary gland. As the Crown Chakra, in Sanskrit, *Sahasrara*, represents our journey to infinite consciousness through thought, the pineal gland is responsible for several important functions that help us sleep well and regulate our body clock. The pineal gland secretes hormones that regulate the body's endocrine functions, our nervous system's relationship with various endocrine signals, our circadian rhythms, and our sleep.[14] This gland is responsible for the production of melatonin, a hormone that modulates sleep patterns in both the circadian and seasonal cycles and helps us to distinguish between light and dark, day and night, sunlight and moonlight. The pineal gland is also responsible for producing serotonin, the hormone that provides a calm feeling of comfort and ease.[15]

Some chakra experts place the pineal gland in the Third Eye Chakra due to its sensitivity to light, however we place the pituitary gland in the Third Eye Chakra. Both the pineal and the pituitary glands are very close to one another in the center of the brain and we chose the pineal for the Crown Chakra due to its impact on seasonal affective disorder, depression, and sleep, all of which we associate with the Crown Chakra in this chapter.

With an imbalanced Crown Chakra, we may struggle with seasonal affective disorder (SAD), which is a depressive condition related to the changes in seasons. Headaches, dandruff, and other issues in the scalp and brain areas can be physical manifestations of imbalances in the Crown Chakra.

Other physical signs associated with an imbalance in the Crown Chakra may include:

- Addictions

- Amnesia

- Brain Fog

- Depression

- Difficulty concentrating or focusing resulting in scattered attention and thinking (ADHD)

- Early onset hair loss

- Extreme fatigue

- Insomnia and sleep disorders

- Nerve pain and neurological issues

Clear Thinking and Good Sleep

The term "circadian" comes from the Latin word *circa* which means "around" and the word *diem* which means "day." Circadian rhythms are the biological processes (or clocks) that occur in every plant, animal, and human over the course of a day. Each one of our cells contains one of these clocks, and each is programmed to turn on or off thousands of genes at different times of the day or night, which ultimately influences every aspect of our health. When we sleep well, we are healthier. In the morning we wake up feeling fresh and energetic. In the evening we're ready to go back to sleep without much effort. But when we aren't able to sleep well, for as little as a night or two, our circadian rhythms can't send the right messages to our genes, and our body and mind can't function properly. If this disruption continues for a few days, weeks, or months, we may become more susceptible to infections and diseases, from insomnia to ADHD, depression, anxiety, obesity, dementia, and even cancer.

About 70 million people in the United States suffer from sleep disorders, including insomnia, sleep apnea, narcolepsy, and restless leg syndrome.[16] Women are two times more likely to develop insomnia than men. One in four women reports some insomnia symptoms, such as trouble falling asleep, trouble staying asleep, or both.[17] It's no wonder so many are disconnected from a sense of purpose when we're tired, struggling to stay awake, reacting to the world through brain fog.

"Vitamin N" to the Rescue!

But luckily, it's easy to get back in sync with our circadian rhythms; we can restore our bodily rhythms by getting outside, spending time in nature, and surrounding ourselves in green spaces. We call this "vitamin N" for Nature. A study found that exposure to green space around one's home and surrounding neighborhood could improve processing speed and attention, as well as boost overall cognitive function.[18] When we are exhausted yet not sleeping well, it's even more important to make time for this simple activity.

Exposure to sunlight is key to establishing a healthy circadian rhythm. The sun provides a critical source of vitamin D which offers a host of immune-supporting properties. In addition to getting outside as much as possible, it is important to have enough *indoor* light to fully align our circadian rhythm. Poor daylight exposure reduces alertness, promotes depression, and affects all aspects of brain health.

Because the pineal gland is so sensitive to light, it is believed to play a role in seasonal affective disorder (SAD) – the depression that can occur from insufficient exposure to light during the winter. While light lamps can be used to combat the effects of SAD and support pineal gland functionality, if your pineal gland is exposed to white light at the wrong time of the day (during nighttime hours or counter to your circadian rhythm), it is counter-productive to sleep. Too much white light at the wrong time of day prevents the pineal gland from producing sufficient melatonin and our sleep can be disrupted. This white light can include light from screens and phones, hence the guidance to reduce our screen time in the evening to enable us to wind down.

Are We All Shift Workers?

The official definition of night shift worker is *anyone* who stays awake for more than 3 hours between 10:00 p.m. and 5:00 a.m. for more than 50 days a year.[19] That's just one night a week! Many of us surely find ourselves in that pattern. Shift work can include nurses, students, musicians, performing artists, new mothers, in-home caregivers, gig workers, weekend "social" short sleepers, and digital short sleepers who work across time zones. Just one night of shift work, or abbreviated sleep, can throw off your cognitive abilities for an entire week. And, the longer your circadian rhythm is out of sync, the greater the risk of developing a serious disease. That's why it's so important to find practices to enter into a quiet and calming sleep routine, such as darkening your room, removing blue light screens, or adding essential oils to your pillow.

A study in the journal *JAMA Psychiatry* found that going to sleep just one hour earlier could reduce a person's risk of major depression by

23%.[20] If someone who normally goes to bed at 1:00 a.m. retires, instead, at midnight and sleeps the same duration, she could cut her risk by 23%; if she goes to bed at 11:00 p.m., she could cut her risk by about 40%.

Healing Foods for the Crown Chakra to Support Clarity and Purpose

The Crown Chakra encourages us to think clearly, to gain clarity on our purpose and meaning, and we start our discussion of healing foods with fasting. Fasting, when done safely and in an intentional way, can be part of a clearing process to remove the "noise" that interferes with our system. With fasting, we can clear preservatives, toxins, or foods that disrupt our body's harmony and keep us from feeling clear. Emotionally and spiritually, we can clear the way to more focused thinking and being.

If you've fasted at least three hours before bedtime, your body has adequately digested, and your cells can go through a housekeeping process known as "autophagy."[21] The word autophagy, translated from Greek, means "self-eating." Autophagy is the body's way of cleaning out damaged cells which can improve your metabolism, your gut function, and brain health. It's a way for the body to recycle and reset in response to the stressors and toxins accumulated in the body. As Rootsilient women, we're looking to do this in a nurturing and wholesome way, and not as punishment or a way to control or abuse our bodies. Always approach fasting with a clear intention in mind, and check with your medical provider if you're unsure whether fasting is right for you.

There are several types of fasts depending on what you include and exclude and also the duration of the fast. One strategy for fasting is intermittent fasting (also called "Time Restricted Eating" or eating during specific windows of the day and fasting for the remainder). The idea behind intermittent fasting is that our bodies need food to restore and replenish, but they also need time to rest so the cells can revitalize and rejuvenate.

Crown Chakra balancing foods include *sattvic* foods, which come from Ayurveda and translate generally into foods that are "pure" and bring balance and harmony. Some of the foods to support the Crown Chakra happen to be white, one of the colors traditionally associated with this chakra.

Try out some of these foods to support your Crown Chakra, bringing this energy center into balance.

- Broth

- Dark leafy greens (Kale, Mustard Greens, Spinach, Swiss Chard)

- Fatty fish (SMASH fish = Sardines, Mackerel, Anchovies, Sardines, Herring)

- Lion's mane mushroom

- Macadamia nuts

- Olive oil

Reflection

1. What foods give you more clarity and which ones make you feel foggy?

2. What foods bring you into focus? What foods distract you?

3. What foods do you crave when you're feeling aimless, bored, or lonely?

4. What foods do you desire when you feel purposeful and with direction?

Herbs for the Crown Chakra

Addressing clarity imbalances with this chakra, you can experiment with several "Nootropics" – these are brain-boosting herbs that support cognitive health. Nootropics can help improve memory, concentration, focus and learning. They can also support mood, sleep, and mental health.[22]

{For any of these suggestions, please check with your doctor or healthcare practitioner to see if there are any contraindications for your health and any conditions you may have.}

BACOPA *(Bacopa monnieri)*

An herb that is a cerebral tonic and neuro-protective.[23] It helps support mental clarity, retention, and problem-solving. It's helpful for those who have trouble sitting and focusing.

GOTU KOLA *(Centella asiatica)*

A tonic for the nervous system, and it's a gentle nurturing herb for enhancing mental focus, functioning and memory.[24]

LAVENDER *(Lavandula)*

A mild sedative often used for anxiety, restlessness and insomnia. It is a gentle herb and can be used before bed in a relaxing bath (with a few drops of lavender essential oil placed in the water). Additionally, it can be used in an aromatherapy diffuser near your bed to promote ease and relaxation.[25]

LEMON BALM *(Melissa officinalis)*

Calming and supportive to the nervous system, while also increasing alertness. It helps us to re-center and can be uplifting, and helps protect the aging brain.[26] (It is not recommended for people living with hypothyroidism.)

ROSEMARY *(Salvia rosmarinus)*

A culinary herb that is wonderfully medicinal and nourishing for the nervous system, supporting cognition, memory and alertness.[27] You can use it in cooking or buy it as an essential oil to diffuse.

Try out some of the recipes that follow to support your Crown Chakra, bringing this powerful energy center into balance.

Crown Chakra Recipes

CROWN CHAKRA ENLIGHTMENT SMOOTHIE

Serves One

Ingredients:

1 cup coconut water

1 cup blueberries

1 banana

1 tsp protein powder (whatever kind you enjoy)

1/2 cup plain Greek yogurt

1 Tbsp honey

A handful of fresh mint leaves

Preparation:

1. Peel the banana and rinse the blueberries.

2. In a blender, combine the coconut water, blueberries, banana, protein powder, and Greek yogurt. Blend until smooth and creamy.

3. If the smoothie is too thick, add more coconut water until you reach your desired consistency.

4. Taste the smoothie and add honey as needed for sweetness. Blend again if necessary.

5. Add fresh mint leaves to the blender and pulse briefly to incorporate, leaving some mint pieces for texture.

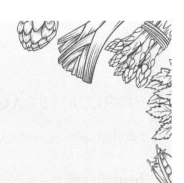

SUNSHINE SPIRIT WATER

Makes about 1 gallon

Ingredients:

1 gallon water

2 slices organic lemons

A handful of organic blueberries and strawberries

Preparation:

Put water and fruit in a large glass pitcher in sunlight for a few hours. Set an intention that this water will detox your body from whatever needs eliminating. Enjoy sipping!

SPIRIT EMBRACE BROTH

Serving: Makes enough to sip during a fast

Ingredients:

5 cups water

1 organic carrot

1 stalk organic celery, diced

½ cup cilantro, chopped

¼ ginger root, chopped

1 Tbsp fresh squeezed organic lemon juice

Sprinkle coarse sea salt

Preparation:

Boil water and add all ingredients. Gently simmer
for 30 minutes. Serve warm. Sip throughout the day
during a cleansing fast.

Mind-Body Integration to Clear Your Mind and Enhance Connection

The mind-body integration practice for the Crown Chakra embodies the qualities of Hope, Humor, and Spirituality. Supporting practices are available in our online resources (www.rootsilience.com/courses/beyond-the-book) and were filmed by a stunning waterfall and in a placed named the "Peace Forest." The focus here is on the area of the head and scalp as well as along the main channels of energy running along the center of the body.

Grounding Your Energy

Grounding our energy means taking moment to connect into the present "here and now." Start by standing and INHALE, draw energy and breath from the crown of your head down and then EXHALE, bring your energy and awareness down through the legs and into the Earth. Continue to breathe this way for a few breaths. Notice how you feel and what being grounded (or "centered" or "present") feels like to you.

As you stand, start to be aware of your entire central column, your spine, or your *Sushumna* channel, where all of your chakras and your central nervous system reside. Ground down into your feet by pressing your weight into your heels. As you continue to breathe, start to bring your awareness up from your legs to your tailbone. And now bring it up from your tailbone into the low back. And on your next breath, to the mid-back and back of the heart. Slowly bring your awareness up into the throat. On your next breath, bring your awareness into your forehead and then to the crown of your head. With every EXHALE, really feel that you are firmly supported, rooting down into the ground, pressing weight into your feet and legs. Take a deep INHALE here, standing tall, bringing your awareness to the Crown Chakra. And as you EXHALE, allow your awareness to drop down to your feet.

INHALE, bring your awareness all the way up and EXHALE, through the nose, bring your awareness all the way down. Two more breaths like that. What is your intention for bringing the Crown Chakra into balance?

Flushing the Microcosmic Orbit

Slowly, we're going to start to bring in some hand movement, sliding your hands up the centerline of the body along the front as you INHALE, hands come up and over the nose up to the crown of the head. And then as you EXHALE, they slide down the back (and you may need to kind of maneuver your way to continue all the way down). INHALE, with the backs of the palms touching together, sliding all the way up from the low belly up to the crown along your front body. EXHALE, the hands slide over the head and trace down the center of your back. On your INHALE, hands together as you slide them up, over lips, over nose, over crown, EXHALE, down the back of your head and down the back.

Let's do it two more times. Really feel what's happening here. We are tracing the microcosmic orbit backwards, so we are flushing or detoxifying the central meridian along your front, and the governing meridian along your back. Now stand still for a moment. Notice how you feel, notice your breath connection in your awareness to your crown. See if you can "touch" it with your awareness or with your breath.

Embodying Humor

This practice helps us clear the energy center at the top of our head and connects us to being in the role of the "observer" rather than being attached to our ego. If you have your hair pulled back, I invite you to take it out. Let your hair down! Make sure you have some space in front of you. Now INHALE, reach the arms straight up to the sky. EXHALE, "rain" (gently wiggle the fingers) as you bring the hands down onto the hair and fold forward (bend your knees if you need to).

You're going to hold your hair and gently pull your hair as you fold forward, and you're pulling your hair right at the top of your head. Gently pull it. And remember humor here. Sometimes something can be intense and we can choose how to respond, like someone's pulling our hair and it can feel like a threat until we realize we can laugh about it. We need humor to move beyond ego. Have a little humor here. Gently pull your hair as you shake your head and keep the knees soft, and stimulate the Crown Chakra.

Embodying Hope

Our scalp contains a host of neurovascular reflex points, which are points along the scalp that control blood flow between the brain and various organs.[28] These points have been found to connect into periarterial nervous fibers containing peptides and receptors involved in pleasure and pain.[29] In this practice, we open up these points for clear thinking and awareness. When we shake off what is blocking us (and clear the stagnancies in our heads), we can reconnect to hope, opening the channels for us to believe; to believe in ourselves, in the Universe or God or Consciousness, and in the connectedness that we are a part of.

Bring your hands to your scalp and like you were shampooing your head, gently press your fingers into your scalp and "shampoo," paying attention to places that feel sore (maybe you spend some extra time here). As you do this, INHALE through the nose and EXHALE through the mouth, slowly and deeply, about two to three times, shaking out your hands every so often to "clear" the energy.

Embodying Spirituality

Embodying Spirituality is a very personal practice. The objective is to recognize we're not alone and when we need to receive guidance, we can. Everything is connected.

We invite you to explore this guided meditation that offers a few different ways to connect to "Spirit" (or insert your word). You are invited to feel a connection in the most authentic way for you, and we offer a few suggestions below. You can download the guided meditation, filmed at a stunning waterfall in São Miguel, Azores, at www.rootsilience.com/courses/beyond-the-book.

Here are a few ways you'll be guided into embodying Spirituality. Notice what works for you, what resonates the most for you and what you feel. Stay in the role of observer, and as you do this, notice your body sensations, the quality of your breathing, any sounds, sights, smells or sensations of temperature.

Come into a comfortable seated position (can be in a chair, on the floor, hips supported, legs extended, etc., whatever works for you). Take a few deep breaths to center and ground. You can repeat the Grounding Exercise from above while seated.

- Connect with your heart: if the idea of Consciousness or Spirit still sounds "woo-woo" and isn't your thing, consider just calling in and connecting to your heart. Place your hands at the center of your chest and literally call upon your heart. Notice what you feel and experience. Take at least two to three minutes here. Notice what your skin and clothing feel like under your hands. Now bring your awareness to your chest and belly; what does it feel like from this place to feel the movement of breath, the weight of your hands? Notice how the energy is flowing.

- Connect with your "Spirit Team:" Some of us resonate with the belief that we all have a team, like a set of "guardian angels" that could be a mix of loved ones or even strangers who've passed on and agreed to be our guides. This team could even include people and pets from our life today. You can always call upon this team for support. Simply take a deep breath and say out loud, "I call upon my guides and spirit team to be with me now." You can also say something like, "I receive the blessings of my guides and spirit team and ask for your support, for the highest good at this time." There is no wrong way, so find what words work for you.

- Connect with those who inspire you: Calling in the "energy" of someone who inspires you or a mentor can help you to feel the presence of what you wish to cultivate in yourself. Who do you admire? Try calling them in or simply calling in the qualities they have that you admire. Take a deep breath and imagine this person. Visualize this person sitting beside you in your meditation. Feel his or her energy and radiance. You can even say, "I call upon the supporting energy and inspiration of (insert name)," and notice what you experience.

- Call in your loved ones: Many of us in times of crisis call out to loved ones (past and present), and this is no different as we're literally asking for their help. Don't be surprised if you suddenly receive a call from one of them saying, "I don't know why, but I had this feeling I needed to call you." Just like in the example above, you can imagine this person sitting beside you, meditating with you. Take some time to simply feel and be with them. You can also state out loud, "I call upon the supporting energy and inspiration of (insert name)," and notice what you experience.

Rootsilience Leadership Map Reflection

Review your Rootsilience Leadership Map results.

1. Do you have greater strengths in the Crown Chakra? What about lesser strengths?

2. Do you tend toward over or underuse in any of your greater or lesser character strengths?

3. Do you have physical, emotional, or mental challenges in this chakra?

4. What connections can you make between the physical signs of "dis-ease" (lack of ease), and how that connects to your emotions? To your state of mind? To your behavior?

5. What are the first signs you are out of balance?

6. What can you do to bring yourself back into ease and flow?

   • Character strengths I'm working to optimize include: _____

   • The practices, tools and foods that bring me back into balance are: _____

7. Reminders to myself to be a Rootsilient Leader: _____

See the Appendix for further readings and resources on the Crown Chakra.

Chapter Three

The Third Eye Chakra

Setting a Clear Vision
and Manifesting Your Path

"My word of the year is HEAL," I told Rimi, as we celebrated New Year's and shared our hopes and dreams for our lives in the coming year. "I want to live in a more natural setting and design a life that includes rest and restorative practices."

I set a goal and intention to heal, but had no idea exactly how to make it happen. What exactly did it mean to "heal"? I sat with it, dreamt about it, but it still felt elusive. Then I decided to create a vision board exploring the word "HEAL." I bought magazines and a large oak tag poster board and laid the materials on the floor. I started to play with the images, and my fingers began to assemble the pieces onto the large poster board. The words "plant" and "beginnings," "connected," "whole foods," and "eat the rainbow" filled the page, and bright colors and images of stairs called my attention. The vision board included healing natural elements, such as images of the sea, mountains, and doors to step through. I watched the piece unfold, mystically created as if my subconscious was sending me the information I needed to move forward.

I put the finished product on my wall for several months, and every day, I asked the question, "How can I live aligned with this vision?" Then, it came to me: I needed to leave New York City, the place I had lived nearly my entire life, and move to the country. A few short months later, we had made the decision to pack up and move to the Berkshire mountains in Western Massachusetts so that I could manifest my goal to heal.

– Samantha's Third Eye Chakra Story

● **Third Eye** Judgment ✦ Perspective ✦ Social Intelligence

Traditionally, the two lotus petals symbolize the ultimate duality: Self and Consciousness. They also represent the two hemispheres of the brain.

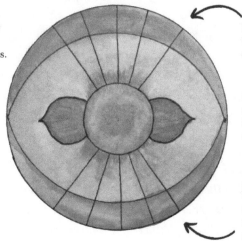

Rays upward (to Consciousness) and downward (to Self)

Center inspired by an eye – traditional interpretation of the energy center

Asymmetrical petals to show the constant fluctuation of perspective and connection

At an angle, the border can be an optical illusion (3D container) or to suggest an eye

Overview of the Third Eye Chakra

Rootsilience Symbolism of the Third Eye Chakra	Our Rootsilience Third Eye Chakra image represents the wisdom we can access when we see beyond the duality of self/ego and Consciousness, of the right and left brain, and of the constant fluctuation of perspective and vision. We simultaneously see and manifest our outer and inner world.
	This image and its two petals illustrate the interplay of intuition and discernment, inviting the viewer to see both the literal image of an eye in the center, as well as a three-dimensional representation of an orb.
	Rays shoot upwards to the Crown Chakra and Consciousness, and downwards toward manifesting our purpose and connection.

Key Themes	The Third Eye Chakra is known as the "seeing" energy center and is often referred to as the "Third Eye" because of its connection to expanding our vision and perception beyond our physical eyes. It is here we can interpret our dreams, lean into our intuition, and imagine and manifest what we choose to see. This chakra's energy helps you see yourself and the world.
Key Leadership Challenges	• Difficulty focusing • Doubting one's intuition and indecisiveness • Narrow-minded or rigid
Key Physical Signs of Imbalance	• Alzheimer's Disease and Dementia • Migraines • Vision impairment
Key Emotional and Behavioral Signs of Imbalance	• Anxiety • Difficulty concentrating • Paranoia
Location	The location of this chakra is found between the eyebrows and the front of the brain. It's often referred to as the "Third Eye" as it sits above our physical eyes in the center of the forehead.
Chakra's Body Functions	The Third Eye's body functions are found in the brain, balancing the duality of the "right brain" of creativity and "left brain" of logic and reasoning.

Element	The element associated with the Third Eye is light, illuminating our path forward and enabling us to see clearly.
VIA Character Strengths	When we cultivate JUDGMENT, we arrive at a decision based on a clear understanding of the situation relying on both logic and intuition. We can discern facts from emotion or opinion, and see clearly to make a decision without getting lost or delayed. When we embrace PERSPECTIVE, we expand into new ways of seeing, creating space for getting "out of our heads" and into a more expansive outlook on life. SOCIAL INTELLIGENCE provides us with greater understanding of ourselves and those around us. It helps us "read" the room, sense what people need, and gives us clarity about what is driving our motivations.
Color	Indigo blue or purple, a deep and rich color that represents wisdom, intuition, and spiritual awareness. The indigo color symbolizes the opening and activation of this Third Eye energy center, allowing for heightened intuition, expanded awareness, and connection to higher realms of consciousness.
Sanskrit	*Ajna*, translating to "perceive" or "to command" is represented by a lotus flower with two petals, associated with intuition, inner wisdom, clarity, and insight. Considered a gateway to accessing expanded states of perception, Ajna helps us transcend ordinary reality and tap into deep inner knowing.

Balanced Leadership in the Third Eye Chakra

Beauty derives from the light of consciousness that is irradiated through objects. It is never really contained in any object. Hence beauty can never pass away but merely has manifold forms for its revelation. The light of beauty we see in things is thus the light of our own awareness.

– David Frawley, *Tantric Yoga and the Wisdom Goddesses*

Seeing – From the Outside In

Take a moment and look up and around you. Take a deep breath as you slowly look around the room, taking in the colors, textures, and objects around you. While you're using your eyes to take in this information, it is actually your brain that makes sense of all the sensory input. The light in your room is bouncing off the objects you are seeing, and it is the reflected light that enters your eye. Since the area of your eye that receives the reflected light is quite small in comparison to the area you are observing, your retina, located at the back of the eye, receives an upside-down image of what you actually see. It is your brain that converts the upside-down image into information sent back to you to perceive the world as you see it. But are you really seeing what is around you? You're seeing an inverted image of reflected light. Are you seeing things as they really are?

> *It is not matter that we perceive, but light. When we look at the world around us, we think that we see objects, but what we are really seeing is the light reflected by these objects – we see what they are not, we see the spaces between them, the spaces around them, but we cannot see into the actual objects.*
>
> – Anodea Judith, Ph.D., *Wheels of Life: A User's Guide to the Chakra System*

Humans can only see a small portion of the electromagnetic spectrum. Honeybees can see light in the ultraviolet range, and some snakes can detect infrared radiation.[1] There is far more happening around us than meets the eye. Since vision is primarily a brain event, and much of the time we aren't really seeing what is around us, the question is, what do we *choose* to see? Our brains are wired to look for problems and detect threats, an evolutionary gain that kept our ancestors alive and able to detect and run away from predators or danger. This inherent "Negativity Bias" is why we are more likely to focus on an insult amidst a stream of compliments or to dwell on a small failure in a career full of successes. We have to work harder to see the world through rose-colored glasses.

Seeing – From the Inside Out

> *You'll see it when you believe it.*
>
> – Wayne Dyer, *You'll See It When You Believe It: The Way to Your Personal Transformation*

Imagine: You walk by a friend and wave from afar. She ignores you. You spend the next hour wondering why she didn't acknowledge you, and proceed to spend an inordinate amount of time overthinking your last conversation and have now concluded that you've upset her with that last comment about … and now she's ignoring you. Turns out the sun was in her eyes and she didn't even see you. Our childhood experiences, the way we were raised, any traumas and patterns of being shape our subconscious mind, which is responsible for 90-95% of our brain activity.[2]

Think of it like the hard drive of our computer. In the first seven years of our lives, that hard drive gets recorded into our brains. We learn to decipher all the big and small things around us. In addition to the things we are taught, our subconscious records all our observations in those first seven years; how our mother speaks to us as a child and how it's different from how she speaks to our father; and how she speaks to our father is different from how she speaks to the shopkeeper. We take in so much information, and that hard drive gets written into our brains, shaping the way we see and experience the rest of our lives.[3]

Our conscious mind is the part of our brain that enables creativity, thoughts and conscious decision-making, whereas the subconscious mind plays out the program on the hard drive. Some of those programs are useful, like keeping our heart beating or our digestion going, but some of the programs keep us from living our dreams or recreate limiting behaviors from our past.

Maybe you were yelled at as a kid or told you weren't good enough, or nothing you did could keep your mother or father happy. So now you see everything you do as somehow "not good enough." Maybe you watched your parents fight as a kid and felt that it was somehow your fault, so now you tend to take on everyone else's problems. Maybe you learned good habits, but maybe you also took on habits you wouldn't necessarily choose for yourself. The good news is that while the subconscious brain has been hard-wired to shape your reality, with intentional repetition and the creation of new habits, you can change it. We can choose how to see the world, and this choice enables us to manifest that reality. When we know where we are headed, we find a way to get there. If we're stuck seeing the world through fear, anxiety, or always reacting to other people and situations, we can lose sight of our path. But if we have a clear sense of our dream, of where we want to be going, of who we are and how to get there, then we can begin to make our dreams a reality.

Seeing Beyond – Harmonizing our Inner and Outer Worlds

As we recognize negative subconscious patterning as simply a fog or blemish on our lens of reality, we can work to create an inner world to see things as they really are, and even as we wish them to be. We can clear our lenses to allow the light of a more purposeful, connected and beautiful reality. Visualization is used among healthcare professionals to reduce stress, amongst sports athletes to boost confidence and performance, and is used by many who wish to see a brighter future for themselves. Studies show that visualizing movement in certain parts of the body trains the muscles just as much as the actual movement.[4] While visualization involves creating imagery in our minds, we can use other senses to shape the vision of our inner world.

The following table provides an overview of how to shape a reality you wish to manifest in your mind. Whether it's creating an internal map of how you want your day to go, or an important meeting, to where you see yourself in ten years, this gives you a sense of how to create that inner world.

Sense	Tools to create your inner world
Visual	What colors are present (or black and white)? How bright is it? What are the shapes? Is it in 3D or 2D? What's the contrast like? Is it a moving picture or a photograph in your mind?
Auditory	What do you hear? What is the volume, pitch, tone and rhythm? What sounds harmonious, what sounds dissonant?
Kinesthetic	What do you feel? Where is it in your body? What's the texture and shape? Is there movement? Is there pressure or lightness? What is its temperature?

By taking the time to create a clearer sense of our inner world, we can expand our senses to take in more than just what we see in our outer world. The Third Eye Chakra is closely linked with our intuition and psychic abilities. Each one of us has the capacity to cultivate our intuition and see beyond our eyes alone. By enhancing these additional senses, we fine-tune our perception and can tap into a greater depth of wisdom, perspective and social intelligence, enabling us to make wiser and clearer decisions. The table on the next page outlines the "five Claires," or ways of seeing beyond, based in our five primary senses. We are naturally stronger in one or two of these, but all can be cultivated just like we can strengthen, lengthen and train a specific group of muscles.

"Claire" or Sense Perception	Examples
Clairvoyance	Seeing images, colors, and/or shapes either during meditation or while awake. Seeing symbols or images or vivid dreams.
Clairaudience	Suddenly tuning into the words of the song on the radio and receiving an important "Aha" or message. Hearing your or someone else's voice or suddenly being tuned into a sound.
Clairolfaction	We can become aware of a smell, even one that may have no obvious connection to what's around us. Our sense of smell can connect us to memories and events from the past.
Clairsentience	Physical sensations in the body, often experienced by "empaths," where you may, for example, be feeling what others around you are feeling. A "gut feeling" or sudden sensation, like a tightening in the chest, butterflies in the stomach or a tingling in the crown.
Claircognizance	A "knowing," without a rational explanation, just a feeling or sensation that you *know* something.

In addition to these five ways of seeing, *interoception* – the body and brain's ability to understand and process internal sensations – is another way we can intuitively connect to our physical body.[5] This includes understanding hunger, thirst, fatigue, and temperature. Interoception also includes digestion, respiration, heart rate, and emotions. Knowing when we're hungry or thirsty, or need to use the bathroom, is a biochemical interaction between our internal organs, muscles, and skin communicating with the brain, using receptors, to process the information from outside and inside the body.[6]

Take out your Rootsilience Leadership Map and review your results. Do you have strengths in the Third Eye Chakra? How do they show up for you?

When we are balanced in the Third Eye Chakra, we can discern between reality and illusion. We see where we are going, trust and cultivate our intuition, and are balanced in our moods and how we see the world. We have a vision for what guides us so we're able to stay focused on our intention. We are equanimous, observing a situation before automatically reacting, and have an ability to "see" the big picture.

When we are imbalanced in the Third Eye Chakra, we lack vision and perspective. We may overly focus on a particular viewpoint and fail to see another side. We may distrust, devalue, or even disconnect completely from our intuition, relying entirely on our own rigid set of beliefs and viewpoints. We can become victims of anxiety or intense emotional states, carried away by the pendulum of our emotional ups and downs and reacting to the warped way we may see the world when gripped by our moods.

When there is ease and uninterrupted flow between the Third Eye Chakra and the Crown Chakra above, we receive a clear connection to Consciousness, and know we are part of something bigger. While we may still experience feelings of isolation, loneliness, or anxiety, we're able to move past these challenges knowing we're never alone and that we can trust in this deeper connection. Our vision for our future is driven not only by ego but also by connection and consciousness.

Leadership signs of imbalance in the Third Eye Chakra:

- Anxiety

- Biased decision making

- Difficulty with discernment

- Inability to see the big picture

- Inability to see other perspectives

- Lack of focus

- Lack of vision

- Myopic focus or seeing the world "through blinders"

- Moody and overly reactive to emotions

- Paranoia and belief that others are out to get you

VIA Character Strengths Mapped to the Third Eye Chakra and Associated Overuse and Underuse[7]

VIA Character Strength	UNDERUSE	OPTIMAL	OVERUSE
JUDGMENT	Illogical / Closed-Minded	Critical Thinking / Observing All Sides	Narrow-Minded / Cynical / Rigid / Indecisive
PERSPECTIVE	Shallow / Superficial	Wisdom / Taking Big Picture View	Overbearing / Arrogant
SOCIAL INTELLIGENCE	Socially Naive / Emotionally Insensitive	Awareness of Motives and Feelings of Self and Others	Overly Analytical / Overly Sensitive

Third Eye Chakra

If your Rootsilience Leadership Map indicates that you have a greater strength in the Third Eye Chakra, you may have a tendency to overuse that strength. And if your map indicates a lesser strength, you may tend toward underuse. If you have neither a greater nor a lesser strength, it's likely you are in optimal use.

JUDGMENT, used optimally, will offer critical insight leading to decision-making that is precise and balanced between what is fact-based and sensed through intuition. A leader with Judgment examines a full spectrum of opinion, advice, and evidence rather than spontaneously jumping to conclusions.

- A greater strength of Judgment could indicate you may tend toward being rigid and narrow-minded or indecisive.

- A lesser strength of Judgment suggests you may tend toward being illogical or close-minded.

A leader with optimal use of PERSPECTIVE can see the "big picture" in situations and has the ability to observe holistic systems, taking into consideration multiple points of view in making a wise decision.

- A greater strength of Perspective could indicate you may tend toward being overbearing and pushing your viewpoint on others.

- A lesser strength of Perspective suggests you may easily jump to conclusions based on shallow or superficial evidence, or as a result of a strong emotional attachment.

A leader who effectively utilizes SOCIAL INTELLIGENCE will have an innate sense of what motivates their team members, intuitively tapping into others' feelings, emotions, and desires. A person with this strength not only has greater social awareness about others, but they also understand what to do with that awareness, treating colleagues with respect and dignity.

- A greater strength of Social Intelligence could indicate you may tend toward being overly analytical or hypersensitive, unable to separate seeing the whole from being mired in the details.

- A lesser strength of Social Intelligence suggests you may tend toward being naive or insensitive, unable to take in the often non-verbal cues that come with understanding others.

Remember that if there are any greater or lesser strengths in this chakra, there may also be a tendency toward the physical / emotional / behavioral imbalances in this chakra or the one above or below it. Your objective is to recognize your unique signs of going out of balance and know how to bring yourself back to center.

Leadership Reflection Exercises to Set a Clear Vision and Manifest Your Path

The following exercises provide an opportunity for you to reflect on the lessons the Third Eye Chakra offers. Take some time to go through these at your own pace, and remember to connect with our online community to share your questions, comments, and "Aha" moments.

Exercise One:

Rootsilience Third Eye Chakra Image Meditation and Reflection

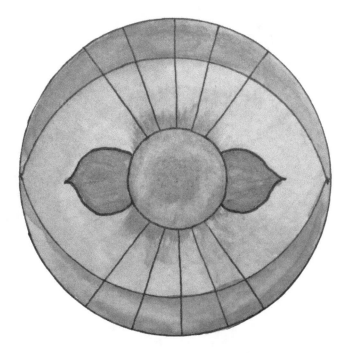

Take at least two minutes to gaze at this image while breathing deeply. Then ask yourself:

- What vision from your "inner world" (based on your upbringing and subconscious programming) could you be projecting into your day-to-day reality?

- What are you not fully "seeing" from your outer world?

- What would happen if your inner and outer world perceptions aligned?

Take some time to write down these responses. Now reflect on what you've written, and read it over a few times.

Exercise Two:

Rootsilience Vision Tree

Take out your journal and draw an image similar to the above, a tree with roots, a trunk, branches and leaves (and remember, it doesn't have to be perfect!). This exercise has four parts:

1. Think about an important vision or intention you'd like to bring to life. It could be a vision for what kind of leader you want to be, manifesting your ideal career, a balanced work and family life, an

ideal home, a vision for how you see yourself in three to five years, etc. Write that vision across the roots of your tree.

2. Next, the trunk is what lifts your vision and intention up. Identify and label along the tree's trunk your support, resources, and skills to strengthen your vision.

3. The branches are your connections and collaborations. Who are the people and organizations who can help you grow and spread your vision? Draw and label them along the branches.

4. The leaves represent what will blossom when you manifest this vision. What are the "fruits" of your dream?

Take some time to write down these responses. Now reflect on what you've written, and read it over a few times. Then consider the following and journal on these prompts:

- What "season" is your tree in? Consider the below and allow yourself to write and reflect for another few minutes.

  - Is it in Winter, lying dormant, hibernating until it's time to emerge?

  - Is it in Spring, growing and blooming?

  - Is it in Summer, full and abundant?

  - Is it in Autumn, shedding its leaves after the harvest and preparing for rest?

- Label and date your tree and come back to this as you work through this book and in manifesting your vision!

Exercise Three:

Creating a Map for Your Inner World

If we are unable to see ourselves as truly happy or successful, our subconscious programming will keep us stuck in reliving our old programs. Creating this map of our inner world helps bring more color, sound, and texture to what we want to manifest.

Have another look at your Vision Tree. You can work with the intention you set in the Vision Tree exercise or choose another intention or something you'd like to manifest. It could be a simpler intention, such as how you'd like to see an important meeting go, or how you'd like to see yourself having a balanced and fulfilling day, a trip away with your partner, etc.

- What is your intention (what are you creating an internal map for)?

- How will you know when you've got it?

  - What will you see?

  - What will you hear?

  - What will you feel?

  - What will you taste or smell?

  - Reflect back on the table from page 111 and use as many of the visual, auditory and kinesthetic descriptives you can use.

- Where, when, and with whom do you want this?

- What resources do you need to get this?

- What boundaries do you need to have or maintain to reach your intention?

- We'll have a chance to return to this exercise[8] in the next chapter, the Throat Chakra, where we'll have the opportunity to voice this vision.

Exercise Four:

Expand Your Perspective

Think about a challenging professional experience you've had, for example, a situation where you felt deeply upset or offended, perhaps by a colleague or a manager, or a business partner.

- Write out what happened from your perspective; remember to breathe deeply and feel your feet on the ground, knowing that you're reflecting in order to gain perspective.

- Now, take a moment to see yourself from the offending party's perspective. And see if you can do this from an intention of compassionate understanding (as opposed to wanting to be "right"). Now write out what happened from this other point of view. How is the story different?

- Has your judgment or perspective about the situation changed?

- If a similar situation were to arise again, how do you see yourself? How do you want to see yourself?

How the Third Eye Chakra Functions in the Body

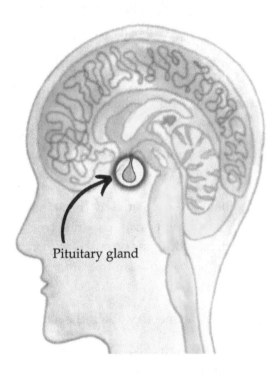

Pituitary gland

The Third Eye Chakra is connected to, as its name suggests, the eyes. The Sanskrit word, *Ajna*, is translated to "perceive," and this chakra allows us to view the world, see our surroundings, and translate that perception into our goals, decisions, and beliefs.

In the body, the Third Eye Chakra is connected to the pituitary gland, the brain, neurotransmitters and the eyes.[9] The pituitary gland, a small endocrine organ, lies between the two halves of the brain, behind the bridge of the nose. It is small and oval-shaped, and it is known as the "master gland" because its main function is to produce hormones and then secrete them into your bloodstream, regulating and controlling the rate at which other glands release their hormones and the timing of the release. The pituitary gland runs the show in your body!

The Brain as a Neurological Engine

The brain is a biochemical gem. Composed mostly of fat and powered by electricity, the brain processes thoughts, feelings, perceptions and sensations. It is constantly communicating with all of the organs in our bodies, making sure we are breathing, digesting, and our hormones are active. The brain is the body's most complex organ, with around 86 billion neurons, all of which are in use at any given time.[10] The brain sends and receives chemical and electrical signals throughout the body. Different signals control different processes, and your brain discerns what is required, interpreting the information and making decisions, both consciously and unconsciously. Modern science has revealed quite a bit about the brain's functions, and yet, women's brain health is one of the most underrepresented areas of medical research. According to the WHAM (Women's Health Access Matters) Report, only 12% of the $2.4 billion 2019 National Institute for Health's budget for Alzheimer's Disease went to women-focused research, while women make up nearly two-thirds of those affected by the disease.[11]

So, What is the Difference Between Men's and Women's Brains?

In part, that difference can be found in the pituitary gland and the hormones it controls. Hormones keep our brains energized and youthful, our bones strong, our gut active, and our sex life vital. Hormones influence every aspect of our body, and when they're out of whack, you'll start to feel it everywhere, from your joints to your thoughts. While all hormones are important in this regard, there's one – estrogen – that is considered to be an important driver of women's brain health.[12] Estrogen keeps brain cells active and healthy and is responsible for brain activity in the regions that regulate memory, attention, and planning. It's also "neuro-protective" – playing an important role in boosting the immune system and protecting our brains.

Research is now evolving that suggests that male and female brains age differently, in part, because of the changes in the amount and quality of estrogen available in women's bodies as we age. As we approach perimenopause and menopause, the hormonal changes which can cause hot flashes, night sweats, disturbed sleep, and memory loss actually originate in the brain itself – previously these changes were thought to originate in our ovaries and the changing reproductive system. Research is now discovering that the ebb and fall in estrogen may cause the loss of a key protective element in the female brain, weakening our neurons and making our brains more susceptible to symptoms of aging.[13]

Alzheimer's Disease affects close to 6 million people in the United States, and two-thirds of those diagnosed are women.[14] Women in their 60s are about twice as likely to develop Alzheimer's as they are to develop breast cancer. So, there's a real imperative to catch up and learn more about women's brains. But, interestingly, Alzheimer's doesn't just appear one day; it's progressive and begins in the brain two to three decades before the first symptom. It's important to note: perimenopause and menopause do not "cause" Alzheimer's Disease, but with decreased levels of estrogen, the brain needs to work more efficiently to adjust to these shifts in hormone levels. As Dr. Lisa Mosconi, Director of the Alzheimer's Prevention Program at Weill Cornell Medicine/New York-Presbyterian Hospital writes in XX Brain, "As an event, menopause is more like a trigger in which the superpower of estrogen and its companion hormones is revoked, and the brain has to find new ways to perform efficiently."[15]

Anxiety as a Pandemic

In 2019, an estimated 301 million people worldwide were living with an anxiety disorder.[16] The term "anxiety disorder" refers to specific psychiatric disorders that involve extreme fear or worry, and includes generalized anxiety disorder, panic disorder and panic attacks, social anxiety disorder, and specific phobias. Women are nearly twice as likely as men to be diagnosed with an anxiety disorder in their lifetime and the prevalence of any anxiety disorder is higher for females (23.4%) than for males (14.3%).[17]

In today's social-media-saturated world, we're deluged with a lot of new and unfamiliar information that we're not quite sure how to interpret or even trust. As a result, there's an increase in a focus on the future, on controlling the future, or having the desire to control specific future outcomes. Indeed, the rise in anxiety in society over the past decade is tied to more of us "waking up" to signs we can no longer ignore in our intuition. Many of us simply need more tools to understand this new "language of seeing."

Physical signs associated with an imbalance in the Third Eye Chakra may include:

- Alzheimer's Disease and dementia

- Anxiety, mood swings, depression

- Memory loss

- Migraines, chronic headaches, ocular headaches

- Pressure around the eyes

- Vision impairment

Healing Foods for the Third Eye Chakra to Nourish Your Brain

The Third Eye Chakra encourages us to tap into our vision and set a path, so we start our discussion of healing foods with cognitive-boosting nutrition to enable clarity and lucidity. Despite what we've heard about Alzheimer's Disease as a fatal and irreversible disease, there is growing understanding that this diagnosis does not need to be a death sentence. A diet that includes flavonoid-rich fruits and vegetables such as berries, kale, red cabbage, fresh fish, healthy fats, and whole grains has been shown to reduce cognitive decline and help the brain regulate energy.[18]

Flavonoids – which help to open up blood vessels, lowering blood pressure and inducing relaxation – are compounds that are found naturally in many fruits and vegetables. Flavonoid-rich foods significantly reduce anxiety[19] and may help with cognitive decline.[20] They work in similar ways to the class of medicinal relaxants called benzodiazepines, such as Valium.[21] Low-glycemic and low-sugar meals also support brain health and cognition. A mildly ketogenic (low in carbohydrates), highly nutritive, predominantly plant-based diet, combined with nightly fasting of at least 12 hours, and ceasing eating three hours before bedtime also has been shown to reverse and prevent cognitive decline.[22]

Sometimes hormonal changes – such as the beginning of our menstrual cycle or as it begins to wind down – lead us to crave certain foods, most likely as an effort to balance out a deficiency or an excess. However, we can also use foods to elevate our moods. Blue-purple foods, like berries and grapes, also have remarkable power to sharpen memory. These blue and purple fruits support cognitive function, playing an important role in helping the cells respond to inflammation.

A recently published small clinical trial in older adults with mild cognitive impairment indicated that those individuals who ate relatively higher amounts of anthocyanins in their diet (from blue, purple, and red plant foods) performed better on memory tests compared with the group taking in lower amounts of dietary anthocyanins.[23] Chocolate also has a remarkable effect on our mood, calming our nervous system, and it is a powerful psychoactive food that has an ameliorative impact on mental processes and cognition.[24] Chocolate contains magnesium – a mineral many are deficient in – which also supports brain functioning. The chemical compounds in the cocoa plant help protect both brain matter and the cardiovascular system.

Caffeine can also have numerous beneficial effects – though too much can make you jittery, so be mindful of the appropriate amount for you. Each of us is unique, so use your intuition and listen to your body's signs to see how much is right for you. Caffeine sourced from whole food and herb sources, like green tea[25] or raw cacao,[26] includes a bundle of protective antioxidants.

Try out some of these foods to support your Third Eye Chakra, bringing this energy center into balance.

- Acai berries
- Bilberries
- Blackberries
- Blueberries
- Carrots
- Cherries
- Cacao beans

- Cocoa, unsweetened
- Concord grapes
- Cranberries
- Elderberries
- Kumquats
- Plums

Reflection

1. What foods "catch your eye"?

2. What foods help you feel alert and give you perspective to hone in on your path?

3. What foods make you feel "blah" and detract from your focus?

4. What foods do you crave when you're depressed or anxious?

5. What foods do you desire when you feel clear and sharp?

Herbs for the Third Eye Chakra

To stay balanced in this chakra, you can experiment with several neuro-protective herbs to support brain health. Refer back to the herbs mentioned in the Crown Chakra chapter for additional resources on "Nootropics" – brain-boosting herbs that also support cognitive health.

{For any of these suggestions, please check with your doctor or healthcare practitioner to see if there are any contraindications for your health and any conditions you may have.}

GINGER (*Zingiber officinale*)

The antioxidants in ginger defend the brain against damage and may improve memory loss after a stroke. In addition, ginger shields glial cells in the brain from damage. These glial cells act as antioxidants helping to preserve neurons and remove metabolic debris and toxins in the brain which contribute to Alzheimer's Disease.[27]

GINKO (*Ginkgo biloba*)

Ginko supports circulation to the brain, and also used in the treatment of memory problems.[28] It also works synergistically with Gotu Kola, an herb mentioned in the Crown Chakra chapter.

ROSEMARY (*Salvia rosmarinus*)

Known for inducing memories and even cited in Shakespeare's *Hamlet* when Ophelia says, "Rosemary is for remembrance," the culinary herb rosemary has been used for centuries to sharpen focus and aid memory retention.[29]

RHODIOLA (*Rhodiola rosea*)

Rhodiola is the root of a plant that is adapted to high altitudes, and is a gently stimulating herb to improve focus as an alternative to caffeine. Rhodiola is an herb that is highly protective of the brain,[30] and its use has been documented to temporarily relieve symptoms associated with stress, fatigue, and exhaustion.[31] Take care where you source this plant because it is native to fragile mountain ecosystems that are in danger of overharvesting.

PASSIONFLOWER (*Passiflora incarnata*)

This flower, the precursor to passionfruit, can be consumed as tea or tincture to help calm mental chatter so that you can better listen to your internal wisdom. Combines well with Skullcap (*Scutelleria lateriflora*) which is a mint family plant with similar properties.

Try out some of the recipes that follow to support your Third Eye Chakra, bringing this powerful energy center into balance.

Third Eye Chakra Recipes

VERY BERRY SLUSH

Serves One

Ingredients:

1 cup water

2 cups frozen mixed berries (blueberries, raspberries, blackberries)

1 ½ cups organic nut milk/regular milk (whatever kind you enjoy)

1/4 cup grape or pomegranate juice

Preparation:

Combine mixed berries, nut milk, and juice in a
blender until smooth. Drink as a smoothie or freeze if
you prefer to drink cold.

BERRY ORACLE DELIGHT COBBLER

Serves Four

For the Berry Filling:

2 cups fresh or frozen blueberries

1 cup fresh or frozen raspberries

1 cup fresh or frozen strawberries, sliced

½ cup granulated sugar

2 Tbsp cornstarch (gluten-free)

1 Tbsp fresh lemon juice

Zest of 1 lemon

½ tsp vanilla extract

For the Gluten-Free Cobbler Topping:

1 cup gluten-free all-purpose flour

½ cup granulated sugar

1½ tsp gluten-free baking powder

¼ tsp salt

½ cup unsalted butter, cold and cubed

¼ cup boiling water

¼ cup milk (use a dairy-free alternative if desired)

½ tsp pure vanilla extract

Preparation:

1. Preheat oven to 375°F. Mix berries, sugar cornstarch, lemon juice and zest, and vanilla in a medium-sized bowl. Gently toss until berries are coated.

2. Place in a greased 9-inch baking pan. In a separate bowl, combine gluten-free flour, sugar, gluten-free baking powder, and salt. Add the cold, cubed butter to the dry mixture and use a pastry cutter or your fingers to cut the butter into the dry ingredients until the mixture resembles coarse crumbs.

3. Pour liquid mixture into the dry mixture and stir.

4. Bake 35–40 minutes or until slightly browned. Cool a bit before serving – it's best served warm.

CABBAGE AND APPLE SLAW WITH DIJON-MAPLE DRESSING

Serves Four

Ingredients for the Slaw:

1/2 medium red cabbage, thinly sliced

1 large apple, julienned

1/2 cup shredded carrots

1/4 cup chopped fresh cilantro

For the Dressing:

3 Tbsp mayonnaise

2 Tbsp Dijon mustard

2 Tbsp maple syrup

Salt and pepper to taste

Preparation:

1. In a large bowl, combine the thinly sliced cabbage, julienned apple, shredded carrots, and chopped cilantro.

2. In a small bowl, whisk together the mayonnaise, Dijon mustard, apple cider vinegar, and maple syrup. Add dash of salt and pepper.

3. Pour the dressing over the cabbage, apple, and carrot mixture, and toss the slaw.

4. Cover the bowl and refrigerate for at least 30 minutes to allow the flavors to blend.

Mind-Body Integration for Clarity and Insight

The mind-body integration practice for the Third Eye Chakra embodies the qualities of Judgment, Perspective, and Social Intelligence. Supporting practices are available in our online resources (www.rootsilience. com/courses/beyond-the-book) and filmed in one of Portugal's seven wonders, Sete Cidades, and provide stunning views and "eye candy." The intention for the practice is to strengthen and stretch the eyes and brain and explore some variations on simple balance poses.

Grounding Your Energy

Grounding our energy in the Third Eye Chakra means we use visualization to connect us down into the Earth. You can start seated with your palms together at the heart. If sitting in a kneeling position as shown is not accessible, you can sit up on a book or block, or sit on a chair.

Take a few breaths to arrive. Notice the movement of breath. What does it look like when you imagine it moving inside? What does the inhale look like, and where does it go? What about the exhale? Is there a color associated with it? A texture? What about the temperature? Is it warm or cool?

Now, INHALE and send your awareness downward, seeing your breath as a cord of light moving from your nostrils down into your chest, and further into your belly; EXHALE, see this cord of light running down both legs, both feet and down into the Earth. INHALE and see your breath as a light expanding from your nostrils down your throat, into your body, and EXHALE, see this light grow out of both feet and whatever is touching the ground, into the Earth. INHALE and sit up a little taller, feeling each cell of your body full of this beautiful light, and EXHALE, feel this light expanding, like roots reaching down further and further into the ground. INHALE and allow this light to start emanating in all directions as it moves downward, and EXHALE, visualize this light touching the center of the Earth, and wrapping around the center. Feel and see your brilliant light expanding, grounded and rooted into the center of the Earth and able to expand in all directions. See yourself in this bright, beaming light and notice how you feel, sense and see.

Embodying Perspective

Endless screen time is destroying our vision, keeping us from seeing the big picture. It's not our brains that lose the ability to see, but the lack of strength and elasticity in and around our eye muscles, so here we can stretch and strengthen the eyes and the muscles around them for enhancing our Perspective, so we can see things as they really are.

You may want to take your glasses off if you have them (contacts are okay), as we'll do a bit of shifting our vision between near and far. Sit comfortably with your toes curled under as pictured (this allows a "passive" toe stretch, but if it doesn't feel so passive, you can lean forward or use a block for support). Bring the thumb of one hand to eye level about a foot (or 20 cm) in front of you or a distance where you can comfortably focus on the nail of your big thumb. In this exercise, you will keep the thumb *exactly where it is* and move the head and chin to stretch the eyes in the following movements. Always keep the thumb in focus.

INHALE and while keeping the thumb in focus, lift your chin and head up, as you look down over your chin at your thumb. EXHALE and lower your chin as you now gaze up over your eyebrows at your thumb. Do this two more times.

Now for lateral movements: INHALE, turn your head to the left while gazing out the corner of your right side of your eyes at your thumb (don't move the thumb!), and EXHALE, turn your head the other direction, maintaining your gaze at the thumb. Repeat two more times.

Now for diagonal movements: INHALE and move your chin and head up and to the left diagonal, and EXHALE, move your chin and head to the right diagonal, continuing to gaze at your thumb. Now change the diagonal: INHALE, chin and head move to the up and right diagonal, and EXHALE, chin and head move to the lower left diagonal. Return to center.

Release your toes (if you haven't already!) and sit any way you like. You can repeat the same exercises above while keeping your chin and head still and moving your arm (up/down, side-to-side, and on the diagonal).

Embodying Social Intelligence

Our Third Eye Chakra rules over our senses and is located right in the center of our brain where the limbic system resides, helping us to process input from what we see, hear, and sense. Sometimes we can feel like we are taking so much stimulation and it all feels "too much" (like an overuse of the Social Intelligence VIA Character Strength), and sometimes we are blocked. This practice incorporates a simple cross-over pattern, which is key to balancing this powerful energy center.

Lie down on your belly and place your elbows under your shoulders. If there is any back pain or pinching in the lumbar spine, you can walk your elbows forward or do this from your chair with your elbows resting on a desk.

With your left hand, pinch the nose bridge (where your nose meets your eyebrows) with your thumb and first two fingers and slide your right palm between your face and your left arm and press the right palm into the left temple. You have a cross-over in your arms (see photo). Now INHALE and squeeze the nose bridge, press the right palm into your temple, and EXHALE through the mouth. Repeat this two more times. You can take a few breaths in sphinx pose (releasing both forearms to the ground) before switching sides. Notice how you feel. Come into child's pose to unwind.

Embodying Judgment

When we judge ourselves or others, we can block our ability to see; it's like putting blinders on, and suddenly, we are seeing through the lens of our bias. Here we practice balance and explore *closing our eyes* (yep!) to find center without relying too heavily on sight alone, and by falling out (literally!) of judgment to be present with what is.

Stand comfortably with your feet hip-width distance apart. You can start by placing your weight into your right foot and lifting your left heel to rest up on your ankle. This is a modified tree pose, and you may choose to stay here, or lift the left leg higher up (anywhere except on the knee; can be on the inner thigh or lower calf). Notice your balance here, slow down your breath. INHALE and lengthen up tall, EXHALE and press the left foot into the standing leg. Now, after a few breaths, and when you feel steady, start to lower your gaze. If it feels safe, close your eyes. You may want to return to an easier version of the pose and come back if you fall out. Take some time here, notice what you take in when you're not focusing with your sight alone. Can you sense your foot on the ground, can you find center, can you lengthen up and out of your spine like a tall and strong tree? Experiment over a few breaths and then change sides.

Strengthen Your Brain: The Color Test (best done with a friend!)

Say the COLOR (not the word) listed below as fast as you can.

RED	GREEN	BLUE	YELLOW	PINK
ORANGE	BLUE	GREEN	BLUE	WHITE
GREEN	YELLOW	ORANGE	BLUE	WHITE
BROWN	RED	BLUE	YELLOW	GREEN
PINK	YELLOW	GREEN	BLUE	RED

Body Brain Teasers[32]

These are great to get you out of habitual patterns and strengthen your corpus callosum, the part that connects the two hemispheres of your brain, plus they are generally just fun to do. Bring one arm out in front of you and trace a circle in the clockwise direction. Keep going. Now take your other arm in front of you and trace a square in the counterclockwise direction. Breathe and have fun. You can do any movement with the right side (arm/leg) and vary the direction or shape with the other. With practice, it does get easier!

Palming

This is such an easy practice we can do (especially after staring at a computer screen for hours on end!). Rub your hands together to create some friction, take a few deep breaths in and out. Then gently palm each hand over your eyes. Feel the warmth, feel a soothing sensation, and allow your eyes to rest.

Rootsilience Leadership Map Reflection

Review your Rootsilience Leadership Map results.

1. Do you have greater strengths in the Third Eye Chakra? What about lesser strengths?

2. Do you tend toward over or underuse in any of your greater or lesser character strengths?

3. Do you have physical, emotional, or mental challenges in this chakra?

4. What connections can you make between the physical signs of "dis-ease" (lack of ease), and how that connects to your emotions? To your state of mind? To your behavior?

5. What are the first signs you are out of balance?

6. What can you do to bring yourself back into ease and flow?

   - Character strengths I'm working to optimize include: _____

   - The practices, tools and foods that bring me back into balance are: _____

7. Reminders to myself to be a Rootsilient Leader: _____

See the Appendix for further readings and resources on the Third Eye Chakra.

Chapter Four

The Throat Chakra

Leading with Truth and Expressing Your Authentic Voice Fearlessly

In my lower-middle-class neighborhood full of broken homes, I was the brown one, the one that people asked, "So where are you from?" in a way that made me feel like someone from outer space. I wasn't white, I wasn't black, and so what was I? And my name, oh how I hated my name, it was so different than everyone else's. I often lied and said my name was "Lisa" on the playground just to blend in.

A fake name, my parents' messy divorce, and living with an alcoholic parent led me to flee further from my truth and who I was. I was thirteen years old when I joined a gang, smoked dope and other things, and was on a first-name basis with the local police. Meanwhile, I was earning straight A's at school in spite of the fact that I came to school "high" every single day.

An intervention from my parents, moving into a stable home, and being in a new high school that truly challenged me put me on an entirely new path. I felt supported, and that enabled me to be honest about how I felt and what I was going through. Rather than acting out, I asked for help. I learned to be truthful with my parents and with myself, and I learned to make wiser choices.

From being a delinquent who was nearly expelled from middle school, I went on to graduate Magna Cum Laude from an Ivy League university, worked my way "to the top" on Wall St., and got an MBA from one of the top business schools in the world. Against all odds, I rewrote my story. I honored my truth and my name.

My surname, Chakraborty, as I later learned, is a well-known and honored name of those from the spiritual caste of India who are the teachers and wisdom keepers. And how fitting that I now work as a teacher and healer, the very framework for my wisdom being the chakra system on which my name is based. Today I shout my name from the top of volcanic mountains and I live my Truth.

– Rimi's Truth story

Throat

Honesty ✦ Love of Learning ✦ Prudence

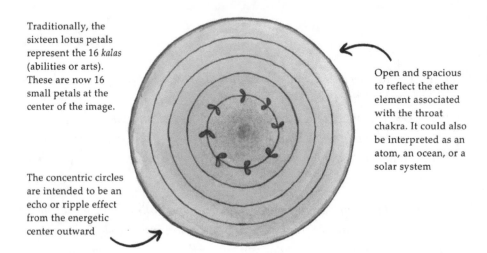

Traditionally, the sixteen lotus petals represent the 16 *kalas* (abilities or arts). These are now 16 small petals at the center of the image.

Open and spacious to reflect the ether element associated with the throat chakra. It could also be interpreted as an atom, an ocean, or a solar system

The concentric circles are intended to be an echo or ripple effect from the energetic center outward

Overview of the Throat Chakra

Rootsilience Symbolism of the Throat Chakra	Our Rootsilience Throat Chakra image represents spacious vibration and the undulation of harmony. This image illustrates our pure expression of Truth at the center, expanding through echo, ripples and waves. We are invited into this authentic expression by being true to ourselves, accepting our own uniqueness, and living in alignment with our true selves, gently held in the spaciousness of our own authentic being.

Key Themes	The Throat Chakra is all about expressing our truth, in how and what we communicate, and also in how we listen. The Throat Chakra ebbs and flows, like the ocean. Sometimes we express ourselves outwardly, through our voice. Sometimes we express our truth in the ways we turn inward, pausing to listen and allow space between thoughts and words. And often, we express our truth through the choices we make.
Key Leadership Challenges	• Difficulty speaking up or deeply listening • Inauthenticity • Lying, dishonesty, or sharing false or "half" truths • Poor communication skills
Key Physical Signs of Imbalance	• Neck and/or jaw pain and difficulty hearing • Thyroid imbalance or disease • Sinus infections
Key Emotional and Behavioral Signs of Imbalance	• Dishonesty • Inability to express • Overly talkative
Location	The location of this chakra is found at the throat and is connected to the area of the neck, jaw, ears, nose and throat.
Chakra's Body Functions	The Throat Chakra's body functions are found in the thyroid gland which acts as a communicator throughout our body. This chakra also oversees hearing, smelling, and tasting.

Element	The element associated with the Throat Chakra is ether, space or sound (vibration). The capacity to speak our truth requires space, with sound waves traveling through ether.
VIA Character Strengths	HONESTY is about truth and authenticity. When we are honest, we honor the truth with sincerity, speak with integrity and are consistent in being honest with others and ourselves. A LOVE OF LEARNING is a passion for learning, motivated by the desire to expand one's knowledge. A person with this strength goes deep into a topic, soaking in the richness of the material, expanding one's knowledge base and trusting oneself to make prudent, honest choices with the wisdom gained. PRUDENCE helps us to know when and how to effectively exercise caution. With this strength, we are able to consider our options, weighing the consequences of our actions, not saying or doing anything that would cause concern or regret.
Color	Aquamarine blue or turquoise. Blue is often seen as a calming and soothing color, symbolizing clarity, truth, and openness.
Sanskrit	*Vishuddha,* translating to "pure" or "purification," is represented by a lotus flower with sixteen petals, and is associated with communication, self-expression, and authenticity. It serves as a center for speaking one's truth, listening actively, and expressing oneself clearly.

Balanced Leadership in the Throat Chakra

To be a hill, to be a sandy beach, to be a Saturday, all are possible verbs in a world where everything is alive. Water, land, and even a day, the language a mirror for seeing the animacy of the world, the life that pulses through all things, through pines and nuthatches and mushrooms. This is the language I hear in the woods; this is the language that lets us speak what wells up all around us.

– Robin Wall Kimmerer, *Braiding Sweetgrass*

What is Your Truth?

Truth is your authentic expression of living in alignment with your values. You can live your truth, be your truth and communicate your truth through what you say and how you listen. You can live and be your truth by making choices that enable you to realize your vision. For example, if your vision is to live a balanced and fulfilling life, you can't say "yes" to every request or opportunity that requires your time and attention. You need to make choices that enable you to live your truth, turning away from what is distracting or depleting.

You can listen and hear truth around and within you, noticing the words and type of language you use with yourself and others. Truth is honoring your word and having integrity in your actions. Truth is about doing the right thing, even when no one is looking. Truth is your expression of your Purpose, or of Consciousness coming through your voice, choice and decisions.

What Keeps Us from Truth?

Many of us say what we think others want to hear to "be nice," or "fit in," or to avoid being stamped as the "B!tch boss." The technical term for this is "fawning," a trauma response of "pleasing and appeasing" rather than holding true to our beliefs and desires. But when we slip into that "little white lie," the expression of our inner truth is strangled and warped. What little white lies do you tell? To yourself? To others?

In a culture of face time and never leaving before the boss leaves, Rimi used to tell her colleagues she was headed out to a meeting when she was really off to the gym for a yoga class. Samantha would refrain from telling the hard truth about her burnout and exhaustion, believing that a health and wellness coach needed to be always "on" for her clients.

Maybe you've prepared for a difficult employee performance review where you need to deliver a tough message, but when face to face with this employee, your important but tough message is lost between a sandwich of pleasantries and people-pleasing. In a culture of smiles and "How are you's" (but I really don't want to know if you're anything but "fine"), how are we to speak our truth?

When we aren't able to get our message across clearly, there are consequences to not speaking our truth. That employee may leave the performance review thinking she's doing a great job and because there wasn't clarity in communication, the problems go unaddressed. When we avoid having an uncomfortable conversation, we need to consider the consequences of *not having* the conversation. We can't ignore, pretend or beat around the bush when we know something is wrong.

You can speak your truth by being "impeccable with your word,"[1] doing what you say you'll do, and recognizing the power and weight of your words. When we speak, we weave our reality, plucking the chords of the fabric of life and vibrating our vision into the world. If you say, "Great, I'll call you tomorrow!" or "I'll get you that report next week," do you really call? Do you get that report out the following week? If you want to lead in a way that uplifts humanity and inspires the best and brightest to lead purpose-driven businesses, do you go on and on complaining about how awful the world leaders are, or do you inspire with your words of commitment to the kind of world you want to be co-creating? What you give voice to is what you're vibrating into reality. Rephrasing what you say and how you say it to align with truth has the power to reshape your world.

Tough Decisions

Let's say you know it's time to change direction in your career and you need some time to process and brainstorm before making that next leap or having another job opportunity lined up. Suddenly your boss tells you what a great job you've been doing and you're being considered for promotion. It's a considerable increase in salary (and responsibility). Great news, right? You're tempted to take the job because, why not?

Living your truth means you take the time to listen (to yourself, to your mentors or trusted friends) and make a decision that aligns with your values and vision. Living and being connected to your truth doesn't necessarily mean you turn down the job offer, but it could mean that after inquiring within (asking yourself how this role aligns or not with what's important to you) and inquiring of your manager (key questions you have for him/her), you are able to make a well-informed, wise decision that enables you to live aligned with your purpose and path. Just because someone invites you to the party doesn't mean you have to go.

Wait, I Can't Hear My Truth

We are living in the "Age of Overstimulation," bombarded with more messaging platforms, advertisements, and increasing demands on our attention than ever before. While the amount of stimulation the average person takes in today has increased exponentially compared with our hunter-gatherer ancestors, our nervous system remains largely the same. The signals that turn on our fight/flight/freeze/fawn or our rest/digest response are the same today as they were hundreds of thousands of years ago, and so it's no wonder we are faced with total overwhelm, stress and exhaustion in the face of these epic levels of information inundation. Studies find that instead of being better equipped to make decisions with the plethora of information at our disposal, we are trapped by it.[2] How are we to distinguish what is important from what is unnecessary? How to know what is enough or just too much? How do we know right from wrong?

Ancient texts speak about the power of silence in connecting to truth; taking small or longer periods of silence is known as the sacred practice of *mouna*. Going on silent retreat may seem daunting or inaccessible, however, a modern-day *mouna* could mean designating weekends without devices, or dedicating one morning a week, or month, to block time and have nothing planned but simply allowing yourself to be. Silence can look like going for a solo walk in nature without your headphones and just being present to the sounds, smells, colors and textures all around you. Silence can mean spending time with yourself without a plan, agenda, or distraction.

It is in these periods of decreased stimulation that we engage the Default Mode Network[3] of the brain, where the communication between various regions of the brain helps us to solidify the learning we've made, create memories, and enable us to make decisions more effectively.

A wandering mind unsticks us in time so that we can learn from the past and plan for the future. Moments of respite may even be necessary to keep one's moral compass in working order and maintain a sense of self.[4]

– Ferris Jabr, *Scientific American*, Oct. 2013

Knowing When to Speak Up

As we become aware of hearing, living, and being our truth, knowing when and how to express it is key. A helpful decision-making tool is recognizing whether what you're saying (to yourself or to others) is based in fear or anger, or some other "ego-based" emotion. For example, if you feel you need to interrupt a business meeting to make a point that is based in "I need to show that I am right" (regardless if it's helpful to finding a solution), then you may need to pause and see if you can dig deeper to find the root of your message. If it's important to share a critical point that you observed but that others are overlooking, then your message isn't based on "needing to be right," but rather highlighting important information to align on a solution. If in doubt, remember that the best decisions, words, and wisdom come when you are firmly aligned on your vision (Third Eye Chakra) and clearly communicating from a place of compassion (Heart Chakra). The flow between the chakras always brings ease and balance.

Take out your Rootsilience Leadership Map and review your results. Do you have strengths in the Throat Chakra? How do they show up for you?

When we are balanced in the Throat Chakra, we speak authentically and with confidence. Our voice carries a resonance and depth that is heard and felt because we are deeply connected to our truth. We listen and hear clearly and are able to give space to others and to ourselves. We can be comfortable in the pauses, in the spaces between words and conversations, mindfully bringing ourselves back to the breath and back to truth.

When we are imbalanced in the Throat Chakra, the expression of truth is strangled or warped. We may tend to speak out of fear or don't speak up at all. Or we may dominate a conversation and have trouble listening. Imbalance in the Throat Chakra can start with a small white lie that turns into a habit of saying what we think people want to hear. We can lower our vibration through gossip or even start rumors. We restrict the expansion of truth within us.

When there is ease and uninterrupted flow between the Throat Chakra and the Third Eye Chakra above, our ability to "see clearly" (our vision or reality) translates into clear communication. When we are clearly seeing and manifesting our path, we have the ability to communicate that vision. We can listen deeply and tune into what is true and shape that vision and perspective with our words, decisions, and communication in how we choose to see the world.

Leadership signs of imbalance in the Throat Chakra:

- Difficulty listening

- Difficulty speaking up

- Dishonesty or lack of authenticity

- Disassociation and disconnection from what is true

- Dominance in a conversation or speaking over others

- Easily influenced and coerced into choices by others

- Inability to make wise choices

- Phobia of public speaking

- Repression of other voices or shutting down others' feelings or opinions

- Tendency to engage in or spread gossip or rumors

- Tendency to tell "little white lies" or half-truths

VIA Character Strengths Mapped to the Throat Chakra and Associated Overuse and Underuse [5]

VIA Character Strength	UNDERUSE	OPTIMAL	OVERUSE
HONESTY	Inauthentic / Lacking Integrity	True to Oneself / Authenticity	Self-Righteous / Rude
LOVE OF LEARNING	Smug / Uninterested	Mastering New Skills	Know it All / Elitist
PRUDENCE	Reckless / Thrill-Seeking	Careful / Cautious	Rigid / Passive / Prudish

Throat Chakra

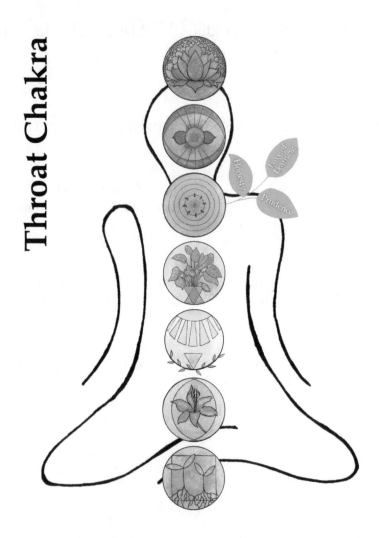

If your Rootsilience Leadership Map indicates that you have a greater strength in the Throat Chakra, you may have a tendency to overuse that strength. And if your map indicates a lesser strength, you may tend toward underuse. If you have neither a greater nor a lesser strength, it's likely you are in optimal use.

A leader with optimal use of HONESTY is true to herself and knows when she is authentic and aligned with her truth.

- A greater strength of Honesty could mean that you may be so truthful that you can come across as "self-righteous," or the timing of your honesty could be viewed as being "rude" and lacking tact.

- A lesser strength of Honesty suggests you may tend toward being inauthentic or find yourself being coerced into decisions that you know aren't right, i.e., saying what you think others want to hear and people-pleasing.

LOVE OF LEARNING, used optimally, can enable you to master new skills and expand your knowledge base and trust in yourself to make prudent, honest choices.

- A greater strength of Love of Learning suggests you may tend toward being a "know it all" or get lost in so much learning you never feel you truly know anything, chasing certifications and training without standing in your authentic truth, knowledge, and power.

- A lesser strength of Love of Learning could mean you may tend toward being uninterested or complacent, not venturing outside what you already know.

A leader who effectively utilizes PRUDENCE will know how to be cautious and make a careful or wise decision, tempered by rational decision-making.

- A greater strength of Prudence suggests you may tend toward being so rigid you're stuck and unable to make a decision, or you have a hard time taking in other points of view.

- A lesser strength of Prudence could mean you tend toward being reckless and you make decisions that are for thrill-seeking purposes, or you may be easily coerced into decisions you don't respect, and follow others.

Remember that if there are any greater or lesser strengths in this chakra, there may also be a tendency toward the physical / emotional / behavior imbalances in this chakra or the one above or below it. Your objective is to recognize your unique signs of going out of balance, and know how to bring yourself back to center.

Leadership Reflection Exercises to Express Your Authentic Voice Fearlessly

The following exercises provide an opportunity for you to reflect on the lessons the Throat Chakra offers. Take some time to go through these at your own pace, and remember to connect with our online community to share your questions, comments, and "Aha" moments.

Exercise One:

Rootsilience Throat Chakra Image Meditation and Reflection

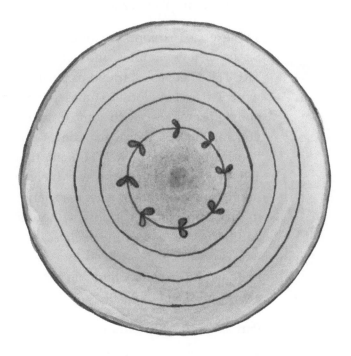

Take at least two minutes to gaze at this image while breathing deeply. Then ask yourself:

- How can you articulate your vision (from Chapter Three's Vision Tree exercise)?

- How can you honor your truth?

Take some time to write down these responses. Now reflect on what you've written, and read it over a few times.

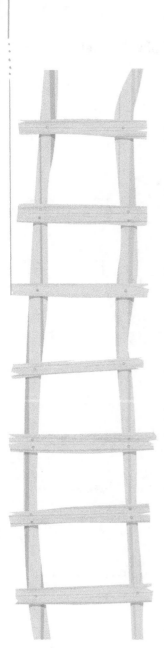

Exercise Two:

Truth Ladder Exercise

Part 1: Create Your Truth Ladder

This exercise explores creating a ladder of words.[6] Sit for a few minutes and reflect on the word TRUTH. Then, ask a friend or partner to read the word TRUTH out loud 20 times (or you can record yourself saying it), with some time in between so you can write a word that comes up for you as you hear the word TRUTH. Each time you hear TRUTH, write whatever word comes to your mind, calling forth whatever association you bring to that word. Just let it flow without stopping or editing. At the end of the exercise, you'll have 20 words on the page arrayed in a vertical pattern, like a ladder. You may find that some are repeated a few times, and that's okay.

Part 2: Truth Affirmation

Sit quietly with your ladder of 20 words, allowing them to sink into you. Slowly, gradually, start to piece them together in a composition of an affirmation statement. Start with the phrase "I believe," "I am," "I will," or "I do," and then weave the words together. Don't feel obligated to try to use every word on your ladder, but play with using whatever words resonate as you craft your affirmation statement.

Look at your truth statement. Maybe you decide to design a beautiful affirmation and hang it on your mirror or someplace you can see it often. Now, how can this affirmation help you to have the tough conversation you may have been avoiding?

- Why is the conversation uncomfortable? What thoughts are based in fear or rejection?

- What are the implications of NOT having the uncomfortable conversation?

- What are the communication styles of the other(s) involved and how could you best get your message across, i.e., in-person meeting vs. written, vs. phone call?

Exercise Three:

Voicing Your Vision

For this exercise, you can work with the vision you set in the Vision Tree exercise in Chapter Three (Third Eye Chakra) or choose another intention or something you'd like to give voice to. Try using the voice memo function on your phone to record and capture your thoughts.

- Take a few moments to read about your vision from the Vision Tree Exercise in Chapter Three.

- While it may not be true just yet, this is a truth you're bringing to reality now. You're going to tell a story about this vision exactly as you wrote it, but *as if it already happened.*

- Review your story and think about it as if it's true and you're reflecting back on it: What was your intention (intended Truth)? How did you know when you realized it?

  - What did you see?

  - What did you hear?

  - What did you feel?

  - What did you taste or smell?

  - Where, when and with whom did you realize this?

  - What resources helped you get there?

  - What boundaries were you successfully able to have/maintain that helped you reach your intention?

- Now, HIT RECORD! Tell this story. Tell it loud and clear. Sing it even! This is a recording just for you. Be as authentic as you can.

- Keep the recording on your phone and make a point to listen to often, especially if you're feeling doubtful or out of alignment with this truth.

Exercise Four:

Vulnerability Exercise – Asking for Help

Identify a challenge you're currently facing in your personal or professional life.

- What would be helpful? Realistically helpful for you?

- Who could you ask for help? Even if it's something small and simple…

- Why might that person/group be able to help? Or not?

- Consider how you could best ask this person for help. Is it an email or conversation?

- How can you be clear and direct in your ask for help?

- Set a date to make the ask. Remember, even if the person is not able to help or declines, by simply asking, it's a huge win in speaking up for yourself.

- If you're thinking, "Oh, I always ask for help and I never get it!" then think again about how you're asking and if you already believe you're not going to get it when you initiate the energy to ask.

- Consider practicing using visualization and sounding similar to the above exercise.

Exercise Five:

Speaking the Truth Exercise

Notice what you say and how and when your actions are aligned with your words. Pay particular attention to the phrases, "I'll try" and "maybe." See the difference in the statements below:

Examples of ambiguous vs. clear communication:

Compare this phrase... (AMBIGUOUS)	With this phrase... (CLEAR)
"I'll try to create a daily routine for self-care because I know it's good for me."	"I will start my regular routine for self-care, even if it's just 1–2 times a week. AND I've already calendared it in for the next 2 weeks, just 15 minutes a day!"
Can you come to my annual summer party this July? Would love to have you! "Yeah sure, maybe I can make it."	*Can you come to my annual summer party this July? Would love to have you!* "I'd love to, but I need to check the kids' summer schedules and coordinate with... When do you need to know by?

(Coordinating an important meeting amongst senior colleagues at work)	(Coordinating an important meeting amongst senior colleagues at work)
"Maybe we can do the 12th, or maybe we can do the 14th? Or maybe we can meet sometime on the 15th? What does everyone think?	"I suggest the following three dates and times. • April 12, 12:30–2 p.m. • April 14, 3–4:30 p.m. • April 15, 10–11 a.m. Please message me by 5 p.m. tomorrow so I can get a calendar invite out to all."
(Colleague/peer asks you for help and you're really overwhelmed and busy on another project but are the right person to help)	(Colleague/peer asks you for help and you're really overwhelmed and busy on another project but are the right person to help)
"Sure, I'll try to get you that information ASAP."	"I can help but after Tuesday of next week, does that timing work for you? And I'll need to review XYZ with you so I'm sure I'm getting you what you need."

Notice the differences in the above examples? The more you fine tune your words, speaking with intention, vision and purpose, the more powerful an instrument you have for expressing and manifesting this truth as reality.

Part 1: What are the ambiguous phrases you have a habit of saying? Your "maybe"s, or "I'll try"s? Have a look at the table above for reference. Create a list of the ambiguous phrases or statements you tend to say and see how you can rephrase them to be clear and aligned with your vision.

Part 2: What white lies do you tell? Make a list of all of them, and notice any themes. What is at the root? Is it fear? People-pleasing? Wanting to fit in? Consider what you could say or do instead of saying the white lie. How can you align with your truth?

How the Throat Chakra Functions in the Body

The Throat Chakra, known in Sanskrit as *Vishuddha*, translates to "pure" or "purification. It is associated with communication, self-expression, and authenticity. The Throat Chakra is associated with the neck, jaw, ears, nose and throat, including vocal cords and the thyroid gland.

The Throat Chakra's gland is the thyroid, an organ shaped like a small butterfly and found in the lower neck. It produces thyroid hormones, primarily thyroxine (T4) and triiodothyronine (T3), which play a crucial role in regulating various bodily functions. The secretion of thyroid hormones is controlled by the pituitary gland through the release of thyroid-stimulating hormone (TSH).

The thyroid gland (governed by the pituitary or "master gland" we discussed in the chapter on the Third Eye Chakra) releases hormones that impact your metabolism, breathing, heart rate, nervous system, weight, body temperature, and energy levels.[7] A healthy thyroid gland encourages positive well-being, metabolism, and energy levels. When thyroid hormone levels are low, a condition known as hypothyroidism, it can lead to a variety of symptoms, including fatigue, weight gain, depression, constipation, and feeling cold. Conversely, when thyroid hormone levels are high, a condition known as hyperthyroidism, it can cause symptoms such as weight loss, increased appetite, anxiety, and rapid heartbeat.[8]

Imbalances in the Throat Chakra can include sore throats and laryngitis, coughs and hoarseness, a feeling of a lump in the throat when expressing important or difficult information, sinus problems, and neck stiffness and pain.

Physical signs associated with an imbalance in the Throat Chakra may include:

- Chronic ear, nose or throat infections
- Globus hystericus or global pharyngeus (lump in the throat)
- Hiccups
- Mouth breathing at night
- Overwhelm from voices or sounds (misophonia)
- Sore throat, croaky voice
- Tinnitus (ringing in the ears)
- TMJ (temporomandibular joint) disorder or chronic jaw soreness
- Toothaches, periodontal disease

Thyroid Disease: A Widespread Condition Impacting Millions Across the Globe

Thyroid disease affects about 30 million Americans, and almost 90% of those affected by thyroid disease are women.[9] On a global scale, 200 million people have problems with their thyroid, and about 50% or so are undiagnosed, meaning they experience symptoms of thyroid problems, but the underlying root cause has not yet been identified.[10]

Hypothyroidism occurs when your thyroid gland doesn't produce enough of thyroid hormones, slowing the metabolism. It can be impacted by elevated blood sugar and can be connected to insulin resistance, a condition in which your body does not respond as it should to insulin.[11]

Symptoms of an underactive (hypothyroid) include:[12]

- Constipation
- Depression
- Dry skin
- Elevated blood cholesterol level
- Heavier than normal or irregular menstrual periods
- Hoarseness (of voice)
- Impaired memory
- Increased sensitivity to cold
- Muscle aches, tenderness and stiffness
- Muscle weakness
- Pain, stiffness or swelling in your joints
- Puffy face
- Thinning hair
- Sleep issues
- Slowed heart rate
- Weight gain

When the thyroid is overactive, causing hyperthyroidism, symptoms may include:[13]

- Changes in bowel patterns, especially more frequent bowel movements
- Changes in menstrual patterns
- Difficulty sleeping
- Enlarged thyroid gland (goiter), which may appear as a swelling at the base of your neck
- Fatigue, muscle weakness
- Fine, brittle hair
- Increased sensitivity to heat

- Increased appetite

- Irregular heartbeat (arrhythmia)

- Nervousness, anxiety and irritability

- Rapid heartbeat (tachycardia)

- Pounding of your heart (palpitations)

- Sleep issues

- Sweating

- Skin thinning

- Tremor or trembling in your hands and fingers

- Unintentional weight loss, even when your appetite and food intake stay the same or increase

Many food triggers can cause thyroid disorders and chronic inflammation. These foods include dairy, soy, gluten, and sugar. When our bodies are exposed to a virus or bacteria, or any other foreign substance that causes a disease, we mount a defense by memorizing the structure of the protein of that virus or invading bacteria. Food triggers can cause a similar physical reaction; for example, gluten can be problematic because the proteins in gluten look very similar to the thyroid gland. This process is called "molecular mimicry," turning a defensive immune response into an autoimmunity."[14] If we have a sensitivity or allergy to gluten, the body triggers a breakdown of not only the gluten proteins but also the thyroid itself, causing inflammation and, for some, it can cause an autoimmune condition called Hashimoto's disease.[15] By eliminating gluten, the body can relax, calming the inflammation response, and allow the body to heal.

The Connection Between the Jaw and Pelvis

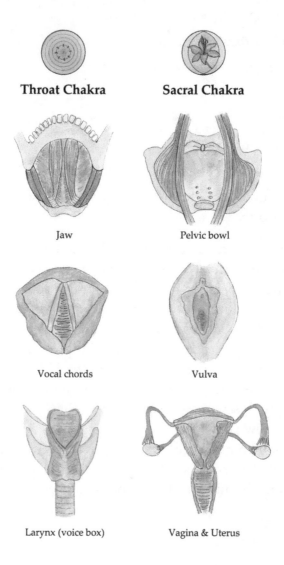

Throat Chakra **Sacral Chakra**

Jaw Pelvic bowl

Vocal chords Vulva

Larynx (voice box) Vagina & Uterus

The chakra system is an interconnected system of spinning disks or "wheels" of energy. It is common to see aspects of one chakra flow into another, and to see connections between them. Notably, the Throat Chakra and Sacral Chakra are aligned in their relationship between the jaw and pelvis.

Each of these body parts shares similar attributes in terms of their anatomy and structure as illustrated in the image on the previous page. There is connective tissue between the jaw and pelvis that originates in the womb, one part of the tissue forming the mouth and jaw, and the other forming what becomes the reproductive system.[16]

Our vocal cords mimic the appearance of the vulva and pelvic floor, analogous in structure as well as connected in their function. How we breathe and speak effects our pelvic floor, and vice versa. Tightness in our vocal cords and/or our throat, chest, and diaphragm can restrict movement through the pelvic floor. Indeed, high-pitched vocalizations or shallow breathing can slow vaginal birth, and tightness or weakness in the pelvic floor can restrict dynamic movement of the breath (which is one reason pelvic floor therapy can be beneficial to singers).[17]

These body parts are our corridors for expression. We give birth through the pelvic floor and birth canal, and through our larynx and vocal cords we express our needs, desires, and wants.[18] The Sacral Chakra is all about emotion and creativity and the Throat Chakra is all about expressing those feelings and creativity.

We'll return to the pelvic area in our chapter on the Sacral Chakra, but it's worth mentioning here the integration and flow of the chakras throughout our bodies, and how when one is affected or imbalanced, there are implications of imbalance on another.

Healing Foods for the Throat Chakra to Support Expression and Listening

To help balance the Throat Chakra, take the time to eat mindfully and avoid distractions such as eating while sitting in front of a computer or looking at a smartphone.

Foods to support our Throat Chakra include sea vegetables (plants derived from the sea) that provide minerals like iodine. Iodine is necessary for your thyroid gland to function properly and can help support the regulation of your metabolism. When you do not have adequate iodine in your diet, goiter, excess sweating, weight loss, insomnia, and other symptoms can occur. However, if you have a thyroid disorder such as Hashimoto's disease, you'll want to take caution and not consume too much iodine as it can aggravate a thyroid condition.

Some sea vegetables to try:

- Arame— an edible brown algae that has a mild, sweet, and slightly briny flavor.

- Dulse— a coarse red seaweed often used as a food condiment.

- Hijiki— a brown sea vegetable rich in dietary fiber.

- Kelp— large brown algae that can be found in flake form.

- Nori— edible, dried preparation of red algae often pressed into sheets and used as a wrapper for sushi.

- Wakami— a seaweed with a distinctive strong flavor and texture.

Selenium and Zinc contain minerals and nutrients that support thyroid function. Brazil nuts are high in Selenium (note: just one Brazil nut can provide the daily recommended adult allowance of 55 mcg), and pumpkin seeds are high in Zinc.

Reflection

1. What foods "soothe your voice"?

2. What foods help you feel you can express yourself with authenticity?

3. What foods or beverages do you eat/drink when you want to slow down, bringing awareness into your dining experience?

4. Time yourself eating and see how long it takes you to finish a meal. Could you eat more slowly next time?

Herbs for the Throat Chakra

The Throat Chakra is about expression and communication. Water and hydrating foods allow communication and transport to occur in the body. When considering herbs to support the Throat Chakra, we invite you to create a mindfulness practice of tea preparation, sitting quietly with a steaming cup, pausing to listen and allow space between your thoughts and words.

{For any of these suggestions, please check with your doctor or healthcare practitioner to see if there are any contraindications for your health and any conditions you may have.}

BUTTERFLY (OR BLUE) PEA FLOWER (*Clitoria ternatea*)

Butterfly Pea Flower has a long history of use in Ayurveda and has recently been popularized (and appropriated) in the West due to its stunning indigo blue color when infused in water. A popular addition to teas or mocktails/cocktails, the flower (and Latin name) bears a striking resemblance to the anatomy of a vulva. Research has shown that

Butterfly Pea Flower increased the functional properties of food with its antioxidant and antimicrobial properties.[19]

COMMON SAGE *(Salvia vulgaris)*

Common (culinary) sage has long "throated" purple flowers and, on closer inspection, there are small reddish spots along the inside of the flower tube. Sage has a long history of use as an antiseptic and tonic for the throat and as a remedy for sore throats due to its antibacterial properties[20] Sage-infused honey is wonderfully soothing to clear the throat and congested nasal passages.

SPILANTHES *(Acmella oleracea)*

Native to northern Africa and a close relative of Echinacea or Purple Coneflower, Spilanthes is also known as the "Toothache Plant."[21] The tiny blossoms of Spilanthes are rich in anti-inflammatory compounds called alkylamides[22] which are antimicrobial and also stimulate the body's immune system[23] and salivary glands creating an overall healing and moistening effect in the mouth.[24] The blossom can be chewed fresh, dried, or infused into a mouth rinse for oral and throat health.

Try out some of the recipes that follow to support your Throat Chakra, bringing this powerful energy center into balance.

Throat Chakra Recipes

INTO THE SEA MISO DULSE SOUP

Serves Two

Ingredients for the Soup:

1 Tbsp of white or red miso

1 small yellow onion, sliced thin

1 inch of ginger, minced

4 cloves garlic, roughly chopped

6 cups of water

Tamari to taste

1 package of rice vermicelli noodles (or whatever kind you prefer)

1 bunch of broccoli

1 large carrot

1 cup of shiitake mushrooms, chopped

1/3 cup of dulse leaves

For the toppings:

Bunch of fresh cilantro

2 radishes, sliced thin

Tamari sauce

Preparation:

1. Combine the onion and garlic in a soup pan, on simmer. Cook until translucent.

2. Mix ginger, dulse leaves, miso and water in the pan, and bring it slowly to a boil. (Include tamari, optional.)

3. Then place the rice vermicelli (or whatever noodles you prefer), broccoli, carrot, and shiitake mushrooms in the broth to soften for 10–15 minutes.

4. When the vegetables are soft, take off the heat.

5. Ladle into bowls and add the toppings ingredients.

6. Serve warm, allowing the liquid broth to nourish. Take your time mindfully enjoying the soup.

OCEAN SLAW

Serves Four

Ingredients:

2 cups shredded red or green cabbage

1/3 cup chopped green pepper

¼ cup apple cider vinegar

1 tsp honey

1 tsp sesame seeds, toasted or pumpkin seeds, toasted

¼ tsp salt

Preparation:

1. In a large bowl, combine the cabbage and green pepper.

2. Whisk the vinegar, honey, sesame seeds and salt.

3. Pour over cabbage mixture; toss to coat.

4. Cover and refrigerate until serving.

THROAT SOOTHING CHICKEN SOUP

Serves Eight

Ingredients:

1 whole chicken (about 3–4 pounds), cut into pieces

8 cups organic chicken broth

1 onion, diced

3 carrots, peeled and sliced

3 celery stalks, sliced

2 cloves garlic, minced

1 bay leaf

1 tsp dried thyme

1 Tbsp dried sage

Salt and pepper to taste

Preparation:

1. In a large pot, combine the chicken pieces, chicken broth, onion, carrots, celery, garlic, bay leaf, thyme, sage, salt, and pepper.

2. Bring the pot to a boil over medium-high heat.

3. Reduce the heat to low, cover the pot, and let the soup simmer for about 1 to 1 ½ hours, or until the chicken is cooked through and tender.

4. Remove the chicken pieces from the pot and set them aside to cool. Once cooled, remove the meat from the bones and shred it into bite-sized pieces.

5. Return the shredded chicken to the pot and discard the bones.

6. Taste the soup and adjust the seasoning with salt and pepper as needed.

7. Continue simmering the soup for an additional 30 minutes.

8. Remove the bay leaf from the pot before serving.

Mind-Body Integration to Free Your Neck and Voice

The mind-body integration practice for the Throat Chakra embodies the qualities of Honesty, Love of Learning, and Prudence. Supporting practices are available in our online resources (www.rootsilience.com/courses/beyond-the-book) and were filmed by the ocean blue at the far west side of São Miguel Island in an energetic hotspot known for connecting us to Truth. The focus here is on the neck, jaw, throat, and the muscles around the shoulders. The connection between the Throat Chakra and the Sacral Chakra in the pelvis is emphasized in this practice through some standing postures and lunges.

This practice brings our Throat Chakra into balance through mantra and various sounding techniques as well as neck, jaw, and shoulder-opening practices.

Embodying Honesty

The neck and shoulders are chronically tight for leaders who often spend most of the day hunched over desk or device. Feeling "the weight of the world" on your shoulders can lead the best of us to exaggerate or lie, keeping us from cultivating honesty. Neck stretches can help us release the weight of the world and be authentic in our speech, thought, and action.

Standing tall, interlace your hands behind your back and reach them behind you for a shoulder stretch. Now bring your wrists to the outside of your left hip, and feel a stretch along the right side of your shoulders. Roll the left shoulder back, and bring the left elbow in line with your shoulder. Keep both elbows pointing behind you and the spine long.

Now, INHALE, lengthen up through the spine, and EXHALE, gently release your left ear to your left shoulder. Keep your heart open and chest lifted (avoid rounding in the upper spine). INHALE, lengthen down through your feet, and EXHALE, keep the tailbone tucked and allow the scalene muscles on the right side of your neck to stretch. Take a few more breaths here.

Now, on your next INHALE, slowly shift your chin down toward the left shoulder, and on your next EXHALE, slowly lift your chin up, toward the sky, gently releasing all the sticky spots along the right side of your neck. Repeat two or three times, taking extra time in any sticky spots to unlock and release any tension along the neck or shoulders. Just let it roll off your back and shoulders.

Release just your left hand and place it on the side of your head. On your next EXHALE, keeping the neck relaxed, gently lift your head with your hand, using only the strength of your arm. Once you align your head over your heart, notice the difference between sides.

Repeat the sequence on the other side.

Embodying Prudence

The practice incorporates a lunge sequence, i.e., a deep hip-opening sequence, combined with neck stretches and side body lengthening, emphasizing and strengthening the connection between jaw and pelvis.

Low lunge: Starting in downward facing dog (*adho mukha svanasana*), INHALE, lift your left leg (maybe just a bit, maybe a lot) and EXHALE, bring the knee to nose and step the foot toward the front of your mat. You can also gently walk the left foot forward and pad the underside of the right knee with a folded blanket or mat. If you need support under your hands, use a block or thick book. Allow your hips to gently lower to the ground and make sure the front knee is directly aligned over the ankle. INHALE, press your front foot into the Earth, and EXHALE, press the back leg into the Earth, and feel the gentle opening around the pelvis and Sacral Chakra.

Now bring your left arm on your left thigh, and INHALE, bring your right arm up to the sky, EXHALE, lean to the left, getting a deep side bend from the right leg and hip up to the pinky finger on the right hand.

Breathe here, engage the low belly, keeping the lumbar spine long, and press your legs into the Earth.

Now interlace both arms behind you (just like we did in the Embodying Honestly practice). Bring your wrists to your left hip.

Take three breaths here, allowing the head to soften toward the left shoulder. Feel the opening in the hips and in the jaw, throat, neck and shoulders. Slowly, release the left arm, place it on the side of the head and lift the head back to center with your arm. INHALE, bring both arms up, and EXHALE, lower the hands down, return to downward facing dog (*adho mukha svanasana*) and repeat on the other side.

Embodying Love of Learning

We are unable to take in new information or learn when our nervous system is under stress or in "survival mode." This mudra (hand position) helps to calm the sympathetic nervous system response, a.k.a. the "fight or flight" response.

From a standing position, gently press your thumbs into the sternum and thymus gland while also pressing the index fingers into the throat notch (an important acupressure point to calm the triple warmer meridian, associated with our stress response). INHALE, soften the throat, jaw and neck as you press the thumbs and index fingers into the points as shown. EXHALE through the mouth, clearing away any stress. Repeat three times.

Throat Chakra Mudra + Mantra

A Throat Chakra practice would not be complete without mantra and sound! In the practice, we use the *bija* (seed sound) of the *Vishuddha* (Throat) Chakra along with opening and closing the arms, to expand and vibrate the mantra around our throat, neck, and shoulders. Later in the practice, we open the jaw using vowel sounds. Using our voice for the sake of vibration is a unique way to "tune" and balance this powerful chakra.

For a guided practice for *bija* mantra in the Throat Chakra, go to our online resources found at <u>www.rootsilience.com/courses/beyond-the-book</u>.

Rootsilience Leadership Map Reflection

Review your Rootsilience Leadership Map results.

1. Do you have greater strengths in the Throat Chakra? What about lesser strengths?

2. Do you tend toward over or underuse in any of your greater or lesser character strengths?

3. Do you have physical, emotional, mental challenges in this chakra?

4. What connections can you make between the physical signs of "disease" (lack of ease), and how that connects to your emotions? To your state of mind? To your behavior?

5. What are the first signs you are out of balance?

6. What can you do to bring yourself back into ease and flow?

   • Character strengths I'm working to optimize include: _____

   • The practices, tools and foods that bring me back into balance are: _____

7. Reminders to myself to be a Rootsilient Leader: _____

See the Appendix for further readings and resources on the Throat Chakra.

Chapter Five

The Heart Chakra

Leading a Life You Love
and Nurturing Your Whole Self

My father died of a heart attack on a warm sunny afternoon in April 2001. He was 59, seemingly healthy, vibrant in body and mind. Earlier that morning, he took my 18-month-old son for a swim and from the photos taken that day, as they played in the water together, splashing and dunking, one never could have imagined his passing just a few hours later.

I was his partner in our family business, and his death left an empty void not only in my personal life but also professionally. I closed the business shortly after he died and pivoted to work in a new sector, helping nonprofits develop revenue-generating business strategies.

While I tried to rise up from my grief and explore a new professional path, a heavy sadness permeated my life with pain. His death was a huge blow, creating an empty hole that consumed my body until there was hardly anything left.

Meanwhile, I numbed out with alcohol and busyness to distract myself from the pain, while leading an intense home life raising three small children, rarely stopping for a moment to pause, feel, or think. It felt too overwhelming to open my heart to the loss. So I clamped down hard, compartmentalizing the pain into a container under lock and key.

Over the years, this had an immense impact on my health. I had been carefully monitored by a cardiologist in the years after my father passed, and as I entered the decade that he died, in my 50s, we saw plaque starting to grow on my heart. The years of numbing, distracting, and hardening to the pain had caught up with me.

I recognize that this "armor" had protected my heart, but it had also prevented me from truly healing and growing. As we go through life, we all experience pain, hurt, and trauma. It is a natural part of the human experience. But when we don't process these experiences, they can linger in the form of emotional scars and cause us to build up defenses that prevent us from truly connecting with others and ourselves.

Removing the armor from my heart has been a daunting task. It required bravery, vulnerability, and a willingness to face my pain head-on. But it is so worth it. By doing so, I am giving myself the chance to grow and live a more fulfilling life.

It is time to heal, soften, and take the armor off my heart, not for anyone else, but for myself.

~ Samantha's Heart Chakra story

Heart

Forgiveness ✣ Gratitude ✣ Kindness ✣ Love

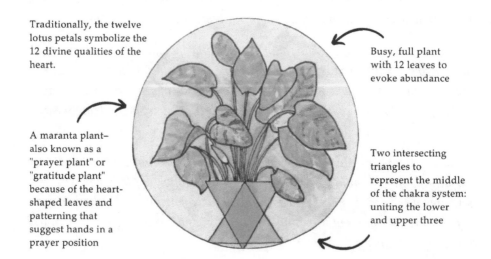

Traditionally, the twelve lotus petals symbolize the 12 divine qualities of the heart.

Busy, full plant with 12 leaves to evoke abundance

A maranta plant— also known as a "prayer plant" or "gratitude plant" because of the heart-shaped leaves and patterning that suggest hands in a prayer position

Two intersecting triangles to represent the middle of the chakra system: uniting the lower and upper three

188

Overview of the Heart Chakra

Rootsilience Symbolism of the Heart Chakra	Our Rootsilience Heart Chakra image represents the divine portal to our soul essence as a blossoming bouquet of gratitude growing out of the vase of unity. The prayer plant (*Maranta leuconeura*), who folds her leaves nightly in a gesture of thanks, has 12 leaves, each of which represents the traditional 12 qualities of the human heart: bliss, peace, harmony, love, understanding, empathy, clarity, purity, unity, compassion, kindness, and forgiveness. The rich green color represents the life-force energy of unconditional love that is within and all around us, and the two intersecting triangles that form a six-pointed star represent the unity that exists at the heart. The upward pointing triangle represents the three chakras above, our connection to Source/Spirit and to masculine energy; the downward pointing triangle represents the three chakras below, our connection to the Earth and feminine energy. Regardless of the "mud" of pain, grief and hardship, this blossoming green abundance is at our core, situated in the deep well of our heart.
Key Themes	The Heart Chakra is the energy center where we learn our most important lessons as humans: What really is love? Is there a love that is deeper and more profound than that between lovers or even between a mother and child? It is here we learn our greatest life lessons around forgiveness and letting go. When we can find balance between how much we give and how much we receive, we learn to truly love ourselves and expand into our infinite essence.

Key Leadership Challenges	• Giving too much or people-pleasing • Difficulty receiving or poor self-care • Inability to forgive or stuck in grieving and holding onto past
Key Physical Signs of Imbalance	• Breast cancer • Heart disease • Lung or respiratory disease
Key Emotional and Behavioral Signs of Imbalance	• Stuck in grief or sadness • Unable to forgive • Vindictive
Location	The location of this chakra is found in the center of the chest, behind the sternum, at the center of our thoracic spine.
Chakra's Body Functions	The Heart Chakra's body functions are found in the heart, thymus gland, lungs, breast, shoulders, arms, and through the circulatory and respiratory systems.
Element	The element associated with the Heart Chakra is air, allowing for expansion of breath and the circulation of our blood, as well as our infinite capacity to love.

VIA Character Strengths	A person with the strength of FORGIVENESS is able to let go of being hurt, and when appropriate, can accept and forgive situations due to others' or one's own shortcomings. We heal when we can forgive, growing from rather than being stuck in and attached to the pain.
	GRATITUDE involves both feeling thankful and also expressing that sensibility to others. It is defined as appreciation for somebody or something, a sense of goodwill toward others, as well as a positive disposition flowing from that sense of abundance.
	When we nurture KINDNESS, we are compassionate, generous, and caring. There is no expectation of mutual reciprocity – being kind stands on its own as a gesture of intrinsic goodness. You simply care and want others to feel that warmth and connection.
	When we experience LOVE as a character strength, we are connected to others in deep relationships. We value that closeness, embracing it in warm and kind ways and we experience balance between giving and receiving.
Color	Green represents harmony, balance, and a deep connection to nature and the natural world. Green also signifies love and the ability to give and receive love openly and unconditionally.
Sanskrit	*Anahata,* translating to "unstruck" or "unhurt," meaning that love is our essence and we cannot be separated from it, existing in a state of unity, balance, healing, calmness and serenity.

Balanced Leadership in the Heart Chakra

> *... Life is giving you a gift, and that gift is the flow of events that takes place between your birth and your death. These events are exciting, challenging, and create tremendous growth. To comfortably handle this flow of life, your heart and mind must be open and expansive enough to encompass reality. The only reason they're not is because you resist. Learn to stop resisting reality, and what used to look like stressful problems will begin to look like the stepping-stones of your spiritual journey.*

– Michael Singer, *The Untethered Soul*

What is Love?

There's always at least one woman in the room uncomfortably fidgeting in her chair or having to suddenly go to the restroom when we ask the group to reflect on "What is Love?" A few women in the group start to share: "Love is the spark between two lovers" or "that electric feeling." "It's the nurturing mother who always has enough to give to those in need" or the "unexplainable force behind the warrior strength a mother has in saving her child from a dangerous situation." During the discussion, nearly every woman shares a definition of love that is based on the love given by another (i.e., a partner, spouse, parent, or child). It's no wonder someone is left fidgeting and uncomfortable, as there's always someone who is currently single or doesn't have children, or has recently lost a loved one, or didn't have a nurturing mother or father.

When we speak about the enormous, loaded and quite often "esoteric" concept of "Love," it's helpful to jump right into a game: have a look at these nine dots below. Use your finger and see if you can connect all nine dots without lifting your finger and make only three straight lines. Go ahead, give it a try.

Problem

Notice if you're having a hard time, how do you feel? Are you feeling "stuck" or frustrated? Where do you feel this in your body?

Consider this: Love is not something you find in a box. Love cannot be grasped, divided, parceled out or limited in any way. Love is our essence, it's the core of who we are, and like the Heart Chakra element, air, it's all around us. Does this give you a hint? *Think outside the box.* (Solution found in the Appendix.)

Regardless of the kind of childhood you had, the kind of parents you had, the types of romantic partnerships you've experienced and whether or not you've had children, love is your natural state and you don't have to do, have, or be anything to get it. It is the essence of who you are.

What Keeps Us from Love

We've all had experiences in life where we've been deeply hurt, betrayed or let down. While it's natural to want to avoid the pain and move on, numbing or avoiding can inadvertently lead to shutting off a part of ourselves, and like Samantha's heart plaque, we can solidify our "armor" and further separate from our essence.

Maybe we confided in a friend our deepest secret, only to find out she's used it to mock us, and we learned to lock up who we really are, never trusting or sharing our deepest secrets with anyone ever again. Maybe we let a romantic partner fully "see" us, where we were completely and authentically ourselves, but when the relationship didn't work out, we felt rejected and blamed our "inappropriate parts" for pushing this partner away and never opened up in the same way again. Over time the expansive space of our heart becomes a maze of walls (parts of us we want to hide or exile) or a minefield (deep-seated resentment and anger ready to explode). While it may seem at first like they are protecting us, these barriers are blocking us from feeling the expansiveness of this powerful energy center.

Pain is Inevitable, Suffering is Optional

During our lives, we will experience both ups and downs. Our hearts expand with the joy of falling in love, having a child, winning an important project, getting promoted, or simply enjoying a breathtaking sunset on a perfect summer day. We also experience heartbreaks during our lives, whether they be the loss of a loved one, a rejection from a friend or lover, a betrayal, or experiencing feelings of isolation and loneliness. The saying "pain is inevitable, suffering is optional" is an old Buddhist maxim that illustrates that pain (and joy) are part of life, but it is the story we tell ourselves and get attached to that contributes to and continues our suffering.

Let's say you were deeply betrayed by someone you loved. The thought of this person brings back painful memories and even anger and frustration. Grief is often accompanied by physical and emotional pain as we mourn the loss of possibilities with this person. While the sting of such a loss can take time to heal from, we have a choice in holding onto our pain or finding healthy ways to let it go. Holding onto pain can look like continuing to define ourselves by the loss, long after we've had time to speak about and process it. Holding onto pain can look like constantly ruminating over what happened, or putting energy into hurting the person who hurt us, or purposefully making their life difficult.

A wound takes time to heal from and a scar is a necessary component for healing. When the wound is raw or deep, a scar can take longer to form and will be vulnerable and sensitive. While it's necessary to feel the pain in order to heal it, there's a delicate balance between giving time and space to heal and consciously choosing to accept and let go. Remember that letting go and forgiving is not about forgetting or condoning what happened, but rather allowing for and accepting our own and others' shortcomings. Letting go and cultivating forgiveness allows us to release our pain and anger. It was hard enough to go through the painful experience, why allow it to eat at us from the inside? Remember that we each have our own healing journey and it's important not to rush, force, or compare your healing with anyone else's.

A powerful way to let go of the pain, when you're ready, is to consider what lessons the person or experience has taught you. You can also ask yourself what you're ready to forgive. How can we learn and evolve to truly understand love without having something or someone to forgive? Take a moment and consider: Is it possible to look at the person who betrayed you and shift beyond anger and resentment to gratitude for helping you learn a powerful lesson? Consider, who was it that was betrayed? The individual you (ego), or the infinite you (Consciousness)?

The major experiences, or even the traumas in our life, guide us on a path of learning and evolution, to know ourselves and to remember our essence as infinite and expansive love. Note too, that it's important to forgive ourselves if we're not ready to forgive or see the lesson or value in the painful experience or betrayal.

The Cause of Suffering is Attachment

When we attach ourselves to what happened to us, we get stuck in ego. We forget that we're here to learn, or we get stuck in the repetitive thinking of, "This or that happened to me," and we can even subconsciously recreate these scenarios to reinforce our attachment or belief. Remember the lessons of the Crown Chakra? Who are you if you're not your thoughts or the image of who you are? And remember the lessons of the Third Eye Chakra? Our "inner landscape" shapes how we see the world.

The path to liberation, then, is taking down the walls and clearing the minefields; it's opening the doors to the parts of ourselves we've locked away or exiled, and in a safe and grounded way, bringing ourselves back to our whole selves. It's important to clear the expansive space of our heart, but not at the expense of negating or "spiritually bypassing" the sensitive and vulnerable parts that are still grieving over the hurtful experience. We'll explore ways to do this in the Leadership Reflection Exercises, and we also offer resources in the Appendix to safely explore deeper traumas or painful experiences.

Why Self-Love Isn't Selfish

The world is lonely for comfort, and for the hips and breasts of women. It calls out in a thousand-handed, million-voiced way, waving to us, plucking and pulling at us, asking for our attention.

– Clarissa Pinkola Estés, *Women Who Run With the Wolves*

One of the safest and most effective ways to take down the walls and clear the minefields of the heart is to cultivate compassion and love for yourself. However, women have been programmed for centuries to believe we need to do and give to everyone else first before we (ever) get to ourselves. Our culture even celebrates women "martyrs," or those who sacrifice themselves for their children, work, parents or partners. We may convince ourselves that "we just need to finish (insert "urgent" To Do here) and then we can take a break," or "I'll take a Me-Time vacation when the kids are older," or "I am here to serve and help others, so any time I'm spending on myself is being wasted where I could be serving others." Maybe subconsciously we are simply finding excuses not to be with our whole selves. Deep down there could be a lack of nurturing for ourselves because somewhere along our lives, we didn't receive the nurturing we needed.

Rimi shares:

In my late teens and early 20s, I had a deep-seated sense of loneliness. I am an only child and my parents divorced when I was 12. I was always looking for "the one," the partner who would "complete me." When I did start a relationship, after the initial honeymoon period there would inevitably be problems because I always found something wrong with them and picked and picked at it like a scab I would scratch raw. I couldn't stand to see weakness in my boyfriends and I called them out on it, even bullied them for it.

It wasn't until I started doing my own personal and psychological work that I realized just how hard I was on myself. I couldn't stand others' weaknesses because I couldn't stand my own. Once I started forgiving myself for not acing every test or breaking the school hurdle record every time I raced, and started to lower the extremely high bar I set for myself, I saw a drastic improvement in my relationships. I also found that when faced with bouts of loneliness, I began to befriend, appreciate, and learn to be with all of me. And I learned that none of us is ever alone.

The journey to loving ourselves is a lifelong journey, but finding ways to be compassionate with yourself enables you to connect with and experience the real unconditional love that you are. Being compassionate with ourselves is about finding balance between how much we are giving and how much we are receiving. Think of your day as spirals of energy. The amount of time and energy you experience putting yourself out there and being "on" needs to be balanced by the ways you come back and spiral into yourself. Otherwise, you're an overextended slinky that just falls over, having lost its bounce and shape. When we give to ourselves, it's far more than "treating ourselves" to a mani-pedi or a decadent dessert (while those things may be nice). Giving to ourselves is balancing our giving and receiving in a way that enables us to stay whole. We have a powerful leadership exercise ahead in this section for you to explore this spiraling analogy.

Take out your Rootsilience Leadership Map and review your results. Do you have strengths in the Heart Chakra? How do they show up for you?

When we are balanced in the Heart Chakra, we give generously, without expectation, and without overextending or compromising ourselves. We strike a balance between giving and receiving, receiving openly from others as well as ourselves. We live in joy, full of gratitude for what we receive and all that we offer to the world. We embrace love and cultivate caring relationships without fear of rejection or dismissal. We are, quite literally, heart-centered, leading from a place of genuine warmth and kindness. When balanced at the Heart Chakra, we learn from past hurts and traumas in a way that expands our heart rather than building barriers or closing down. We forgive what we're ready to, healing and returning to wholeness in ourselves and in our heart.

When we are imbalanced in the Heart Chakra, we give to the point of exhaustion, or leave unhealed scars from past wounds to fester, inhibiting us from giving or receiving, or both. We may struggle to offer care and affection or hold onto grievances, finding it difficult to forgive. Worse, we may act out of anger or desperation and consciously put energy into making the lives of others difficult or unpleasant. Loneliness and resentment are features of an imbalanced Heart Chakra and can lead to a type of leadership based in defensiveness. When defensive, one is primarily focused on survival and protection, literally walling off the expansive potential of the heart.

When there is ease and uninterrupted flow between the Heart Chakra and the Throat Chakra above, the Truth that we share is an unobstructed expression of the love and passion centered in our hearts. We are fueled by what we want to expand into rather than cowering away in fear or defensiveness. Our choices, words and actions stem from a place of connectedness and compassion, even when we experience pain or difficulty.

Leadership signs of imbalance in the Heart Chakra:

- Being a "doormat" or constantly putting yourself down

- Difficulty receiving or poor self-care

- Disconnected from others, feeling isolated or profound loneliness

- Emotional overkill (sugary sweet behavior)

- Giving too much or people-pleasing

- Inability to forgive or stuck in grieving and holding onto past

- Merciless and unkind

- Repressed grief, resentment or anger that triggers emotional outbursts

- Vindictive, vengeful and critical or oppressive of others

VIA Character Strengths Mapped to the Heart Chakra and Associated Overuse and Underuse [1]

VIA Character Strength	UNDERUSE	OPTIMAL	OVERUSE
FORGIVENESS	Vengeful/ Merciless/Easily Triggered by Others	Mercy/ Accepting Shortcomings/ Letting Go of Hurt	Permissive/ Doormat/Too Lenient or Soft
GRATITUDE	Entitled/ Unappreciative/ Self-Absorbed	Thankful/ Feeling Blessed	Ingratiation/ Contrived/ Profuse/ Repetitive
KINDNESS	Indifferent/ Selfish/Uncaring to Yourself/ Mean-Spirited	Nurturance/ Compassion/ Doing For Others	Compassion Fatigue/ Intrusive/Overly Focused on Others
LOVE	Isolating/ Cut Off from Others/Afraid to Care/Not Relating	Genuine Warmth / Close Relationships	Emotional Overkill / Misaligned with Others' Needs / Sugary Sweet / Touchy-Feely

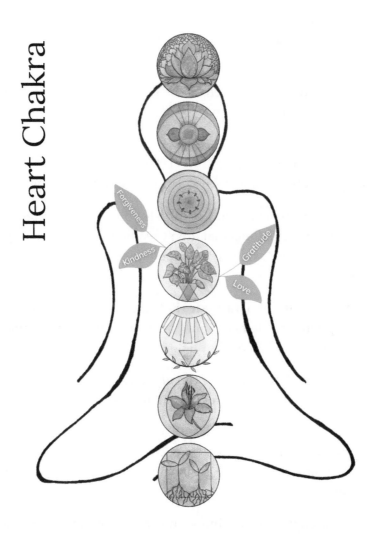

Heart Chakra

If your Rootsilience Leadership Map indicates that you have a greater strength in the Heart Chakra, you may have a tendency to overuse that strength. And if your map indicates a lesser strength, you may tend toward underuse. If you have neither a greater nor a lesser strength, it's likely you are in optimal use.

FORGIVENESS, used optimally, can enable you to let go of pain and hurt. Note that this is not about forgetting or disassociating from pain, but rather allowing for acceptance of people's shortcomings, including your own.

- A greater strength of Forgiveness could mean you allow people to treat you like a doormat, and allow those who hurt you to continue to do so.

- A person with a lesser strength of Forgiveness may tend toward revenge when triggered, and harbor anger and lots of explosive minefields.

A leader who effectively utilizes GRATITUDE will feel thankful for their blessings and is aware of and acknowledges the contributions of others.

- A greater strength of Gratitude suggests you may have a tendency to "bypass" tough situations that aren't really okay, but you're profuse with your gratitude as a way to people-please that can be contrived or inauthentic.

- A lesser strength of Gratitude indicates you may tend toward self-absorption, entitlement, and being unappreciative, unable to recognize the abundance around you.

A leader with KINDNESS, used optimally, is nurturing and compassionate, and does for others in equal measure to what they're given.

- A greater strength of Kindness suggests you may be overly focused on others' opinions and compassionate to the point of being intrusive and exhausting yourself.

- A lesser strength of Kindness indicates you may tend toward indifference and selfishness, or even be mean-spirited.

A leader with an optimal use of LOVE cherishes warm and close relationships and is balanced between giving and receiving, living in harmony with herself and others.

- A greater strength of Love indicates you may lay it on thick with sugary sweetness, offering too much or not being authentic in what you're giving.

- A lesser strength of Love suggests you may tend toward isolation when triggered and stressed, shifting into defensiveness and protection.

Remember that if there are any greater or lesser strengths in this chakra, there may also be a tendency toward the physical/emotional/behavioral imbalances in this chakra or the one above or below it. Your objective is to recognize your unique signs of going out of balance and know how to bring yourself back to center.

Leadership Reflection Exercises to Lead a Life You Love and Nurture Your Whole Self

The following exercises provide an opportunity for you to reflect on the lessons the Heart Chakra offers. Take some time to go through these at your own pace, and remember to connect with our online community to share your questions, comments, and "Aha" moments.

Exercise One:

Rootsilience Heart Chakra Image Meditation and Reflection

Take at least two minutes to gaze at this image while breathing deeply. Then ask yourself:

- How can you experience unconditional love?

- What walls or minefields are you ready to clear in order to expand your Heart Chakra?

Take some time to write down these responses. Now reflect on what you've written, read it over a few times.

Exercise Two:

Love Letter Exercise

Part 1: Get out a piece of nice stationery. Start with the date and "Dear (your name)."

Start writing yourself a love letter. Some of you won't need any prompts for this, but we include a few below just in case this is a challenging exercise, which it can be for many!

Consider:

- (Your Name), thank you for being... (What qualities about yourself do you love?)

- (Your Name), I love that you... (What can you highlight that you love about yourself?)

- (Your Name), remember when... (What memory reminds you about how special you are?)

- (Your Name), I'm sorry that... (What are you ready to forgive yourself for)?

- (Your Name), don't ever forget that you... (What do you want to always remember?)

Part 2: Find a friend or loved one and ask them to read you your letter. Receive it fully. (And consider having them do this exercise too and read them theirs.)

Exercise Three:

Balancing Giving + Receiving Exercise

Get out a piece of paper and have some colored pens, pencils or crayons around. Think about a beautiful tree. Maybe it's one from your imagination, maybe it's one you remember as a kid, or it could also be your favorite tree that you may see or visit quite often.

Now think about your day-to-day life right now, in this season, or this time period of the last three months or so. Think about all the different roles you play. You have professional roles in your life as well as personal ones. Now, start to draw each role you play as a branch on your tree. A larger or thicker branch represents a bigger role in your life, as in one that requires more of your time and energy. A smaller role in your life is represented by a shorter or thinner branch. Take a few moments and label your branches.

Now think about your day-to-day life right now, in this same time period, and consider all the people and things in your life that feed and nourish you, and all the ways you nourish yourself. What are the activities, people, or ways you are nourished? Go ahead and draw these in as your roots. Just like with the branches, draw your roots longer or thicker based on how much time you spend in them. It's natural to have some aspects of your life that are both roots and branches, i.e., your role as a mother is also deeply fulfilling, but consider drawing the size of the trunk and the size of the root commensurate with the amount of energy you spend giving and receiving in that role. Also, be honest about what you are *actually feeding yourself with*, not just what you *wish* you were doing.

Now, take a moment to look at your tree. Is it healthy? Turn your image upside down. Does it still look like a tree? Did you know that the roots of a tree take up about three times as much space as the branches and foliage? The roots are MUCH larger than the branches for most trees. How are yours?

Now ask yourself:

- Where could you be more balanced?

- How can you "prune" some branches on your tree?

- How could you solidify or strengthen your roots?

Remember to save your tree drawing, date it and feel free to spend time coloring or adding detail. This is a powerful exercise to do as the seasons change and you think about how to stay balanced.

This practice is offered as a guided meditation and journaling exercise you can follow along with online at: www.rootsilience.com/courses/beyond-the-book.

Exercise Four:

Gratitude + Forgiveness Exercise

Gratitude is a superpower and when we experience gratitude, we raise our vibration, bringing our heart and body into coherence. When we are full of gratitude, we are more capable of clearing and forgiving the blocks in our hearts.

1. Make a list of 108 things you're grateful for. (A list of 10 is easy. A list of 20 gets you to start thinking. We choose 108 because it is an auspicious and sacred number and has mathematical significance.[2]) Now, read over your list – feel the expanded state of abundance you are in.

2. Now make a list of 10 people, situations, or moments in time with yourself that you are willing to forgive. The key word here is willing to forgive. One of your items can be forgiving yourself for what you're not yet *willing* to forgive.

3. Now prepare to repeat the Ho'oponopono (ancient Hawaiian forgiveness prayer) for each item on your list. Say out loud, slowly, "I am sorry. Please forgive me. Thank you. I love you." Say it to each person or experience on your list. Notice how you feel after saying it.

4. Reread your gratitude list to close off this exercise.

Exercise Five:

In Times of Loneliness, Ask for HELP Exercise

If and when you feel overwhelmed and are experiencing utter darkness and loneliness (yes, we have been there too!), consider this:

- Hello

- Eternal

- Loving

- Presence

See if you can repeat the above out loud, remember you are not alone and you can ask for HELP.[3] Just recognizing that love is all around you, within you and the essence of our very being can remind us to drop back into a state of compassion, peace and harmony. Try it when you need it most.

How the Heart Chakra Functions in the Body

Anahata is the "Still Center Point" with its "triangles representing the descent of the spirit into the body and the ascent of matter rising to meet spirit."

– Anodea Judith Ph.D., *Wheels of Life: A User's Guide to the Chakra System*

Anahata, the Sanskrit name for the Heart Chakra, sits in the middle of the body, at the center of the seven chakras. Like a divining rod, the Heart Chakra represents the area in our bodies where our physical and non-physical aspects meet. *Anahata* means "the sound that is made without any two things striking" and it also means "unhurt," "unstruck," and "unbeaten,"[4] meaning it can't be separated and exists in a state of unity, balance, healing, calmness and serenity.

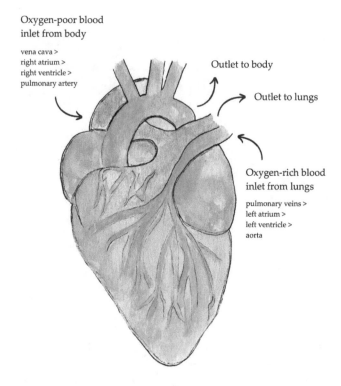

Oxygen-poor blood
inlet from body

vena cava >
right atrium >
right ventricle >
pulmonary artery

Outlet to body

Outlet to lungs

Oxygen-rich blood
inlet from lungs

pulmonary veins >
left atrium >
left ventricle >
aorta

The Heart Chakra represents not only the heart but also the lungs and breasts and controls breathing, circulation and oxygenation. Its color is green, a cooling color, the color of healing and expansion. Through breath, we carry in oxygen and transport nutrients throughout our bodies to heal and make ourselves whole. The heart pumps blood to all parts of the body. Blood provides oxygen and nutrients to the body and removes carbon dioxide and wastes. Oxygen-poor blood—blood that doesn't have much oxygen in it — comes back to the heart through two main tubes called the superior vena cava and inferior vena cava. It enters the top part of the heart, called the right atrium. From there, the oxygen-poor blood moves through a door-like structure called the tricuspid valve, and goes into the lower part of the heart, called the right ventricle. The right ventricle pushes this oxygen-poor blood through another door called the pulmonary valve into a big tube called the main pulmonary artery. Then, it travels through smaller tubes into the lungs.

In the lungs, the blood gets fresh oxygen when we breathe in, and it gets rid of carbon dioxide when we breathe out. This oxygen-rich blood flows from the lungs to the top part of the heart, called the left atrium, through four tubes called pulmonary veins. It then moves through another door, the mitral valve, into the lower part of the heart, the left ventricle. The left ventricle pumps this nice oxygen-rich blood through another door, the aortic valve, into a big tube called the aorta. The aorta is like the main highway that carries the oxygen-rich blood to all parts of our body.[5]

When we experience stress, our hearts beat faster, our blood pressure rises, and our stress hormone, cortisol, rises. When we are balanced, we're calm, joyful, our hearts pump at a healthy rhythm, and blood moves through the arteries at a healthy pressure.

Women and Heart Disease

Heart disease is the leading cause of death for women in the United States, representing about 1 in every 5 female deaths.[6] Worldwide, 8.6 million women die from heart disease each year, accounting for a third of all deaths in women.[7] Heart attacks for women under the age of 50 are twice as likely to be fatal as compared to men. Women's symptoms of heart attack (often flu-like nausea, weakness and fatigue without the classic chest pains) differ from men's, often leading to delayed diagnosis and treatment. The breasts are also located in the Heart Chakra, and breast cancer is the second leading cause of death among women worldwide, following heart disease.[8]

Physical signs associated with an imbalance in the Heart Chakra may include:

- Blockages and/or calcification in arteries

- Cold hands and a slow circulation

- High blood pressure

- High or low heart rate or heart palpitations

- Personal or family history of breast cancer or cysts

- Rapid and shallow breathing or asthma

- Rosacea or flushing in the face

- Sleep apnea (restricted nighttime breathing)

Healing Foods for the Heart Chakra to Nourish the Body with Kindness and Compassion

As noted above, the heart acts like a pump moving blood throughout the body, and requires flexibility to effectively perform this task. The lungs play an important role in moving air through the body, providing oxygen to the arteries, expanding blood vessels and amplifying circulation. To provide the heart with the necessary nutrition for its important job, green leafy vegetables offer nutrients such as chlorophyll, which gives the foods their green color and acts as an antioxidant and blood purifier, promoting robust circulation to give us a healthy glow and skin coloring. These leafy green vegetables contain important phytonutrients (plant-based nutrition) that open our circulation, detoxify, and aid in the expansion of our blood vessels.

The recommended number of daily servings of vegetables is between 9 and 13 servings. However, only 1 in 10 Americans eat the daily recommended amount.[9] 33% in the European Union reported not consuming any fruit or vegetables daily and only 12% of the population consume 5 or more portions daily. On average, over half of the EU population (55%) say they eat between 1 and 4 portions of fruit and vegetables daily.[10]

Green foods also contain an essential nutrient known as folate. This nutrient, along with vitamins B6 and B12, is needed to lower levels of a compound known as homocysteine in the blood, which is correlated with heart disease, stroke, and deep vein thrombosis.[11] Other vitamins and minerals provided by green foods include vitamins A, C, and K and minerals of calcium, magnesium, and potassium. Increasing your green food intake will help to reduce levels of "bad" (LDL) cholesterol and will enhance your heart health,[12] balance estrogen,[13] and calm your mood.[14]

The old adage, "an apple a day keeps the doctor away" turns out to be true! Apples contain natural chemicals that can protect the heart, fight cancer, boost memory, help hair grow, heal burns, keep your mouth healthy, and prevent skin problems caused by certain medicines or the sun. Apples also are antioxidative, helping to protect the vascular endothelium and reduce blood lipids.[15]

Try out some of these foods to support your Heart Chakra, bringing this energy center into balance

- Apples
- Artichokes
- Arugula
- Asparagus
- Avocado
- Beet greens
- Bok choy
- Broccoli
- Broccolini
- Chard

- Collards
- Green tea
- Kale
- Lettuce
- Olive oil, extra virgin
- Onions
- Pomegranate
- Salmon
- Spinach
- Tomatoes

Reflection:

1. What foods calm your heart?

2. What foods help you feel you're caring for yourself?

3. What foods do you enjoy being made for you?

4. What foods do you enjoy eating with your loved ones and friends?

Herbs for the Heart Chakra

To stay balanced in the Heart Chakra, you can experiment with several cardioprotective herbs to support heart health.

{For any of these suggestions, please check with your doctor or healthcare practitioner to see if there are any contraindications for your health and any conditions you may have.}

BITTER MELON *(Momordica charanti)*

This vegetable can be consumed in capsule form if you cannot source it fresh, and it has been shown to decrease cholesterol levels, specifically the "bad" LDL cholesterol and high triglycerides.[16] Bitter herbs in general support the liver's ability to process cholesterol and other blood lipids, protecting the heart and arteries and preventing heart disease.

HAWTHORNE *(Crataegus spp)*

Hawthorne has been used for millennia to treat heart and cardiovascular symptoms, particularly in the European herbal tradition. It dilates the arteries that supply the heart muscle itself with blood, oxygen, and fuel and can steady the heartbeat. It can increase blood flow and strengthen the heart muscle.[17]

MOTHERWORT *(Leonurus cardiaca)*

Motherwort preparations were first used in medical practice as cardiotonic agents regulating the heart activity rhythm, in angina pectoris, cardiovascular neuroses, and the initial stages of hypertension.[18] It is bitter and grounding, reconnecting the rhythm of our heartbeat to the heartbeat of Mother Earth, and is specifically indicated if anxiety shows up as occasional heart palpitations.

WILD BEACH ROSE (*Rosa rugosa*)

The vibration of the aroma of rose petals invites our heart's electromagnetic frequency into a vibration of coherence and harmony, and a heart in harmony is energetically contagious, inviting other hearts in their vicinity to join the same frequency. Rose petals are a gentle remedy for the emotional heart, opening hearts that are bitter and closed, or astringent hearts that are too open resulting in poor boundaries or frequent, overflowing tears.[19]

Try out some of the recipes that follow to support your Heart Chakra, bringing this powerful energy center into balance.

Heart Chakra Recipes

WALNUT-KISSED ARUGULA & BROCCOLI SALAD

Ingredients:

4 cups fresh arugula, washed and dried

2 cups broccoli florets, blanched

1 cup walnuts, toasted

1/4 cup extra-virgin olive oil

2 Tbsp balsamic vinegar

1 Tbsp honey

Salt and pepper to taste

Preparation:

1. Wash and dry the arugula thoroughly.

2. Blanch the broccoli florets in boiling water for 2-3 minutes, then transfer them to an ice bath to stop the cooking process. Drain and set aside.

3. Toast the walnuts in a dry skillet over medium heat until they become fragrant. Stir frequently to prevent burning. Once toasted, let them cool.

4. In a large salad bowl, combine the arugula, blanched broccoli, and toasted walnuts.

5. In a small bowl, whisk together the extra-virgin olive oil, balsamic vinegar, and honey until well combined.

6. Season the dressing with salt and pepper to taste.

WARMTH FROM WITHIN SPROUTS

Serves Four

Ingredients:

1 lb fresh Brussels sprouts, washed and cut in half

1 clove of garlic, peeled and sliced

1 Tbsp olive oil

Dash sea salt and pepper

2 Tbsp freshly grated Parmesan cheese (optional)

Preparation:

1. Steam Brussels sprouts for 2–3 minutes or until bright green and tender.

2. Saute garlic in 1 Tbsp olive oil until translucent.

3. Add steamed Brussels sprouts and the remaining olive oil.

4. Toss, sprinkle with salt and pepper to taste, and drizzle salad with dressing.

5. Add salt and pepper to taste, and Parmesan if desired.

HEART-OPENING GREEN SMOOTHIE

Serves One

Ingredients:

1 cup spinach or kale (or a combination)

1 ripe banana

1 cup fresh or frozen mango chunks

½ cup fresh or frozen pineapple chunks

1 Tbsp chia seeds

1 cup coconut water or almond milk

A sprig of fresh mint leaves (optional)

A few ice cubes (optional)

Preparation:

1. Wash the spinach or kale leaves thoroughly.

2. Place all the ingredients into a blender.

3. Blend until smooth and creamy, adjusting the consistency with coconut water or almond milk as desired.

4. If desired, add a few ice cubes and blend again for a chilled smoothie.

Mind-Body Integration to Open Your Heart

The mind-body integration practice for the Heart Chakra embodies the qualities of Forgiveness, Gratitude, Kindness, and Love. Supporting practices are available in our online resources (www.rootsilience.com/courses/beyond-the-book) and were filmed by emerald green lakes in the verdant green and fertile region of Furnas. The focus here is to expand the area around the chest and to cultivate gratitude and forgiveness by connecting to our breath and opening space around the heart.

Embodying Love

Find yourself a comfortable seated position (sit bones supported by a blanket, block or cushion) and find a straight spine. Take a couple of breaths and place your hands over the heart with one palm over the other at the center of the chest on the Heart Chakra. Drop your awareness into this space and really feel your expansiveness of breath, INHALE, feel the spaciousness around your heart, and EXHALE, notice the movement of your ribs, the muscles between your ribs. Take a moment over the next few breaths to set an intention for the experience of love; love that doesn't depend on anyone or anything; love that is universal, unconditional and infinite. Take another breath and breathe your intention to experience love through your body.

Slowly, bring your arms out to your sides, parallel to the ground. Spread your fingers so your wrists are in line with your arms, your middle finger in line with your wrists. Now internally rotate one arm and externally rotate the other, in other words, flip the right palm up and feel the upper right arm rotating externally away from the shoulder joint, and the left palm down, with the upper left arm internally rotating toward your ribs. Keep your shoulders level with one another. INHALE, spread your arms apart and then switch as you EXHALE, switch, i.e., flip the left palm down and the right palm up. If your shoulders are comfortable, you can continue the rotation on the left palm so the left thumb starts to open the palm face-up again. INHALE, extend through the front of the heart and arms here, spreading the fingers, and EXHALE, switch. INHALE, extend through the back of the heart and arms, EXHALE, switch. Our hands formed from the ganglion of our heart, so our hands are directly connected to the heart. Take a few more breaths and feel your heart extending into your hands with each breath. When you're ready, release both palms to the center of your heart again, and breathe deeply, feeling the expansiveness of your breath, your heart energy, and experiencing the spaciousness of your Love.

Embodying Gratitude

We embody gratitude through a somewhat intense pose, also a form of an inversion, i.e., where the heart is above the head. It is often in times of intensity that we can grow and evolve the most, and when we are ready, we can cultivate gratitude for the learnings and openings we received.

Dolphin pose (ardha pincha mayurasana): Come onto all fours (hands under your shoulders and knees under your hips). Come down onto your elbows and measure the distance between your elbows by gently clasping your hands around the opposite elbows. This is "shoulder width" apart and it's important to measure every single time as we'll be putting weight into our arms. Now clasp your hands together in front of you and press your forearms into the Earth.

INHALE, press the forearms down and at the same time, lift the shoulders up and away from your arms and relax your head (note that your head should not be touching the floor in any part of this pose). EXHALE, lift the hips up to the sky (like downward facing dog but on your forearms). Walk your feet a few baby steps in toward your arms so your hips start to align over the shoulders. Most of us will need to bend our knees a lot here, which is fine, but keep the spine long.

INHALE, press into the Earth with the strength of your arms and shoulders, EXHALE, lengthen your hips up to the sky by pressing your feet into the ground and lifting up out of the shoulders. Feel gratitude for your strength, the reality of being alive, feeling your breath big and expansive while in this intense inversion. Keep the head relaxed, take three to five breaths here and after your last EXHALE in the pose, lower into a child's pose with the arms by your sides.

*Modification is to keep the knees on the ground and as you INHALE, press your forearms into the Earth and lean your chin over your fists, EXHALE, come back into modified dolphin with your knees and forearms on the mat.

Embodying Forgiveness

In order to forgive, we need to create space in our hearts. We do this by breathing into the various parts of our rib cage. By using deep breath and gentle side and back bends, we cultivate a space for forgiveness.

Spinal flexion and extension: From a comfortable seated position, place your palms face down on your knees. INHALE, press your hands into your knees and lengthen your spine (spinal extension), opening your heart and creating an opening along the front of your rib cage. EXHALE, and round your spine, bringing your chin to your chest. Keep the awareness and movement in the thoracic spine as much as possible. Continue for three more breaths.

Lateral side bends: Keeping both sit bones on the ground, cushion or padding, and hands on the knees, shift your torso to the left. Now notice if your right shoulder dipped down, and bring it up level with the left so the movement is opening the left rib cage in a lateral or side opening movement. INHALE, expand breath into the left side ribs, and EXHALE, shift the body to the right (keep the shoulders in the same line). Stay here, INHALE into the right ribs and side body, EXHALE, shift to the other side. Notice that both sit bones stay grounded and both shoulders stay in one line; you can practice this in the mirror. Repeat three times.

Circling: Now we bring the above movements together. INHALE, open the heart (spinal extension), EXHALE, shift to the right side (lateral opening on the right). INHALE here, EXHALE, round the spine (spinal flexion), INHALE to the left (lateral opening on the left), and EXHALE, return to center. You can repeat a few times each direction to really isolate each movement. Then, when you know you are moving the thoracic spine (and not the hips or shoulders), you can smooth out the movements, taking a full circle on INHALE, and a full circle the other direction on EXHALE.

Embodying Kindness

Kindness is a natural outpouring of your Heart Chakra energy, and when you can be kind because it is your nature, it opens doors and removes walls that keep us from Love. In this pose, we press our arms and remove the walls that block us from being kind.

INHALE, expand your arms, spread your fingers, feel the palms of your hands wide open. EXHALE, let your shoulders come down away from your ears. Stay here for two more breaths. INHALE, spread the fingers, spread the arms, and EXHALE, keeping your neck long, pulling the chin in to extend the back of the neck. INHALE, expand around the heart, feeling into genuine kindness, and EXHALE, press away any walls that keep us from being kind. Staying here, one more breath, INHALE, lengthen the spine, and then EXHALE, gently release your arms by your sides. Feel the energy around your heart center.

The supporting practice for the Heart Chakra is a Heart Chakra Salutation – a standing series embodying the themes of the Heart Chakra can be found at www.rootsilience.com/courses/beyond-the-book.

Rootsilience Leadership Map Reflection

Review your Rootsilience Leadership Map results.

1. Do you have greater strengths in the Heart Chakra? What about lesser strengths?

2. Do you tend toward over or underuse in any of your greater or lesser character strengths?

3. Do you have physical, emotional, or mental challenges in this chakra?

4. What connections can you make between the physical signs of "dis-ease" (lack of ease), and how that connects to your emotions? To your state of mind? To your behavior?

5. What are the first signs you are out of balance?

6. What can you do to bring yourself back into ease and flow?

   • Character strengths I'm working to optimize include: _____

   • The practices, tools, and foods that bring me back into balance are: _____

7. Reminders to myself to be a Rootsilient Leader: _____

See the Appendix for further readings and resources on the Heart Chakra.

Chapter Six

The Solar Plexus Chakra

Leading with Balanced Power

COVID hit our home, not unexpectedly, as Omicron was raging throughout New York City at the height of the holiday season in 2021. Throughout the pandemic, I had done everything possible to protect my family from getting sick, being vigilant about our activities, regularly testing, and limiting guests in our home. I had held it all together so tightly for so long, and that vigilance had taken a toll.

Suddenly, everything fell apart. My bout with COVID totally knocked me out. It was January, the beginning of a new year when I wanted to remain focused and energized by my work and important projects, but I couldn't get going. I couldn't focus. I couldn't make my brain work the way I needed it to. I had crushing fatigue, disorienting brain fog, and loss of smell and taste. I was gripped by a debilitating depression that hung over me like a wet blanket. For weeks, I would break out into tears from the slightest issue, lost in an unfamiliar cognitive confusion. When colleagues asked for status reports on my work product and deliverables, I felt embarrassed and guilty for not having done more.

I desperately needed the rest that my illness ironically offered. I learned first-hand that I can't just give lip service to rest. I learned how important slowing down is to my mind, body, and spirit; and how I should share my pain with my loved ones so they can offer help and love.

~ Samantha's Solar Plexus Chakra story

Solar Plexus

Fairness ✦ Leadership ✦ Zest

Traditionally, the ten lotus petals symbolize the 10 *vayus* that are regulated by the Solar Plexus Chakra.

Sun and rays to show life and zest

Symmetrical design for discernment, fairness

10 olive leaves inspired by a wreath to symbolize fairness and peace

Inverted triangle to represent connection to root / base chakras

Overview of the Solar Plexus Chakra

Rootsilience Symbolism of the Solar Plexus Chakra	Our Rootsilience Solar Plexus Chakra image shows the sun radiating from above, the powerhouse of energy that feeds every living being on our planet, and represents our fire and power within. An olive branch sits on the circle's edge, representing fairness and justness, reminding us to use our power responsibly. A downward pointing triangle represents the fuel for our power, based in trust and partnership, and balance in the lower chakras.
Key Themes	The Solar Plexus Chakra is all about power – your self-esteem and belief in your power, your use (or abuse) of that power, and your ability to balance and restore your energy levels to have the willpower to take action toward the causes you believe in.

Key Leadership Challenges	• Inability to rest and recharge, resulting in burnout • Misalignment with power resulting in self-serving or manipulative behavior
Key Physical Signs of Imbalance	• Diabetes • Gastrointestinal issues • Heartburn
Key Emotional and Behavioral Signs of Imbalance	• Burned out • Lack of self-worth • Low self-esteem • Obsessiveness
Location	The Solar Plexus Chakra extends from just below the sternum down to the navel and presides over our bodies' ability to create and store energy.
Chakra's Body Functions	The Solar Plexus Chakra's body functions are found in the liver, pancreas and stomach which work together to regulate digestion. These organs break down and distribute the nutrients in our food, and energy is then created from these nutrients in the cells.

Element	The element associated with the Solar Plexus is fire. It is our digestive fire that metabolizes food into fuel, and our inner fire that lights us up to go after what we believe in. In this chakra, we work to cultivate our digestive and energetic fire, but in a way that keeps us healthy, motivated and balanced, without burning the house down or burning out. The Solar Plexus is energy in motion, and this element of fire can also relate to emotions that may be difficult to transmute and metabolize.
VIA Character Strengths	We all have a gut feeling around FAIRNESS, about what is right and what is wrong. What is fair is not always black and white, and so it's important to access a deeper connection with our bellies (our gut) to attune to and give space to those feelings. With FAIRNESS, we strike a balance between our desire to control with what we know to be true. A leader has the ability to positively influence others, encouraging and inspiring effective action. We embrace the quality of LEADERSHIP as influencing others through our "spark" rather than through force. When we cultivate ZEST, we are balanced between action and surrender; it's like building a fire and then allowing it space so it doesn't burn out of control or burn out.
Color	Yellow or gold, seen as a bright and vibrant color that symbolizes confidence, personal power, and vitality. Yellow also represents clarity, intelligence, and a strong sense of self.
Sanskrit	*Manipura,* translating to "city of jewels" or "lustrous gem," as it is in this chakra where our inner "jewels" reside. This is where our power source sits, with the radiation of our benevolent inner light.

Balanced Leadership in the Solar Plexus Chakra

In order to develop and heal ourselves at the third chakra level, we must re-examine the concept of power that involves the domination of one part by another, commonly called power over. Instead, we can develop power as integration, power within, the power of connecting the forces of life.

– Anodea Judith, Ph.D., *Wheels of Life: A User's Guide to the Chakra System*

The Never-Ending (Rat) Race

The top is always in sight but just out of reach. No matter how much you accomplish or get done, it's never enough. The massive gears of Time and To Do are turning, turning, turning. The teeth of the gears are ominously approaching and you find yourself at the intersection of accomplishments and "not enough." If you slow down, even for a second, you will be crushed in the jaws of More. So keep running, keep doing, "Always Be Closing."

Deep breaths.

Sadly, the "More is Better" mantra has been fed to us our entire life. No matter what you have, what you've done or where you've been, there's always another rung on the ladder, a higher mountain to climb, a bigger and better this or that, or a new product you just *have* to have because then and only then have you "made it." Funding for startups is based on how fast investors can make a return and how big of a return they can make. Shareholders of public companies demand higher and higher profit margins, and leadership decisions are too often made in favor of short-term gains, often at the expense of people and the planet.

What we aim for is where we land. Growth without restraint, growth for the sake of exponential growth, is cancer. And it's literally killing us. Since the 1950s and the Industrial Revolution, humans have used up more resources and fuel than in all of human history (over the last 240,000 years).[1] We are currently in the midst of the "6th mass extinction," known as the Holocene Epoch, the first mass extinction to be directly caused by human activity.[2] Many of us have seen the "hockey stick" on the whiteboard, the graphic that illustrates exponential growth and demands we keep up and show up every single day the same way, or better. Yet we cannot grow exponentially. We cannot keep going without rest. We are not machines (and neither is our planet). The highly sought-after and rewarded "hockey stick" trajectory of growth leads to burnout and exhaustion, and assumes we can abuse ourselves, our community, our planet and her precious resources, forever.

There is another way. We all need moments of pause, hibernation, shedding, a time for release and letting go, so that after sufficient rest and recharge, we can sprout anew with fresh ideas and exert action from a place of balance.

Energy flows where our attention goes. And attention naturally goes toward optimizing for the goals and objectives we (or our companies, societies, communities) have set for ourselves. So the question is, can we get off the hedonic treadmill of "more" and the focus of financial gain and align with solutions rather than self-fulfilling or company-aggrandizement goals?

Being Enough

"Oh, isn't that nice, good for you," your friend says after hearing your good news. You can feel the knife slicing the small smidgeon of truth from her words, exposing her jealousy and contempt.

It's the boss that feels threatened by you and even though your success contributes to hers, she goes out of her way to make you look bad, or worse, she withholds precious advice and mentoring because deep down she's afraid you'll outshine her. It's the friend who doesn't yet have a (baby, boyfriend, partner, great job) but when you do, somehow you just can't truly celebrate your big exciting news with her. It is no wonder we have a hard time celebrating our own success. Many of us have simply never learned how. Many of us have been taught that we are all separate, and that if something good happens for someone else, it has nothing to do with us, or that we need to get that too and if we don't, we are "less."

Some of us even learned that celebrating our success is selfish, or boastful. And while we probably all know someone who *is* selfish and brags about herself, the truth is the majority of us are hiding in the shadows of our inner critics who tell us we're never good enough and keep us from stepping into our dreams to shine.

It is time we changed the story. It's time we enable ourselves and others to shine. The leadership exercises that follow offer some important ways to know what success really means to you, along with ways to celebrate yourself and others.

Take out your Rootsilience Leadership Map and review your results. Do you have strengths in the Solar Plexus Chakra? How do they show up for you?

When we are balanced in this energy center, healthy momentum builds to pursue what we are passionate about. We are motivated to get up and out of bed, and "seize the day." We recognize when we need rest and replenishment and know how to make time to recharge. We know what we're good at, we embrace our power, and we have a healthy sense of self-esteem that enables us to shine, without seeing ourselves as "selfish," "better than," or "above" others. We lead naturally, radiating our inner light, giving us power and support to light up the people and causes we care about.

When we're imbalanced in the Solar Plexus Chakra, we may feel lifeless, or sluggish, lacking the energy to take charge of what we believe in. Or, we may find ourselves constantly "on," always finding something else to prioritize on our to-do list, yet never feeling enough and never taking time to slow down. When out of balance, we may become enamored with our own grandeur or hyper-focused on external metrics of success like salary, promotions, or bonuses that could lead us to make selfish and even unethical decisions. We could even begin to abuse our power by exerting it over others for personal gain, rather than radiating our benevolent light and inspiring others to use their skills for good. If chronically imbalanced in this chakra, we become highly agitated, sometimes even aggressive, and we may become "addicted" to the "high" of constantly being on, making us feel like we always need to be doing, always need to be achieving, and always need to be, have, and do MORE.

When there is ease and uninterrupted flow between the Solar Plexus Chakra and the Heart Chakra above, our inner fire burns generously and bright, fueling expansiveness and love. A balanced sense of power and self-worth allows us to forgive and love, ultimately ourselves. Instead of burning out of control, our fire burns consistently, with healthy doses of rest and recovery. When life throws us a curveball, our inner fire has the capacity to transform challenges into lessons learned, and frees up energy to forgive, let go, and evolve.

Leadership signs of imbalance in the Solar Plexus Chakra:

- Being a "control freak" and micromanaging your team

- Extreme drive to be recognized, receive praise and "win"

- Hypervigilance and focus on minutiae

- Impostor Syndrome (fear of being "found out" that you don't deserve your success)

- Inability to slow down and take real rest and recharge

- Inability to feel "proud" of oneself, feeling that pride is selfish or overly boastful, arrogant

- Lack of self-worth

- Mismanagement of power resulting in self-serving or manipulative behavior

- Need to "be right"

- Rumination, going over something again and again, not being able to let it go

- Taking credit for others' work or success

- Tendency toward perfectionism and the feeling that "nothing can ever be right or good enough"

- Tendency to burn out and/or mismanagement of energy

- Self-serving or unethical motivation

VIA Character Strengths Mapped to the Solar Plexus Chakra and Associated Overuse and Underuse[3]

VIA Character Strength	UNDERUSE	OPTIMAL	OVERUSE
FAIRNESS	Prejudice / Partisanship / Complacency	Adhering to Principles of Justice / Unbiased Decision Making	Detached / Indecisive on Justice Issues / Uncaring
LEADERSHIP	Follower / Compliant / Mousy / Passive	Positively Influencing Others / Organizing Group Activities	Bossy / Controlling / Authoritarian
ZEST	Passive / Sedentary / Tired	Vitality / Vigor / Energy / Enthusiasm for Life	Hyper / Overactive / Annoying

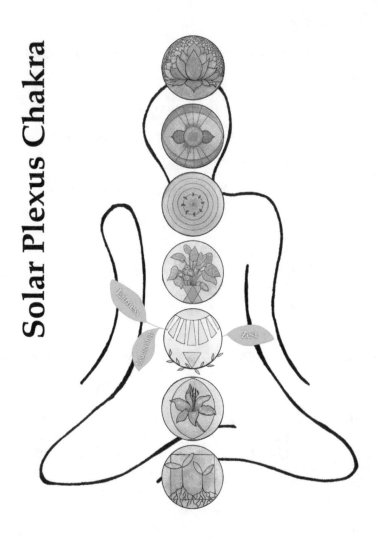

Solar Plexus Chakra

If your Rootsilience Leadership Map indicates that you have a greater strength in the Solar Plexus Chakra, you may have a tendency to overuse that strength. And if your map indicates a lesser strength, you may tend toward underuse. If you have neither a greater nor a lesser strength, it's likely you are in optimal use.

A leader expressing optimal use of FAIRNESS treats all people without bias and prejudice, believing in equal opportunity, with the ability to distinguish our gut feeling of what is truly right or wrong from biasing our decision making.

- A greater strength of Fairness could show up as choosing to ignore or overlook what's right in order to attain a goal, whether it be from pressure to perform or for self-aggrandizement purposes. A leader who overuses this strength could appear detached and uncaring.

- A person with a lesser strength of Fairness could demonstrate prejudice and partisanship, and even favoritism.

A leader expressing an optimal use of LEADERSHIP shows up with an ability to positively influence others, encouraging and inspiring action, and a commitment to maintaining positive relations within a group environment.

- A person with a greater strength of Leadership might show up as controlling and bossy, and they may even have authoritarian behaviors, leading to unsatisfied and unmotivated colleagues and subordinates.

- A person with a lesser strength of Leadership may tend toward passivity and compliance, avoiding conflict and following along with the crowd. They also may not have motivation to stand up and take charge when needed, and when called for.

A leader with optimal use of ZEST has a lot of excitement for life and relishes a variety of activities and interests. They express themselves with a sense of vitality and feel alive, living their lives with adventure and gusto.

- A greater strength of Zest indicates strong willpower, incredible ambition and intense motivation with a tendency toward being hyperactive or overly intense.

- A lesser strength of Zest can show up as sluggishness and lackadaisical behaviors, feeling passive, sedentary, and tired.

If there are any greater or lesser strengths in this chakra, there may also be a tendency toward the physical/emotional imbalances in this chakra or the one above or below it. Your objective is to recognize your unique signs of going out of balance and know how to bring yourself back to center.

Leadership Reflection Exercises to Lead with Balanced Power

The following exercises provide an opportunity for you to reflect on the lessons the Solar Plexus Chakra has for us. Take some time to go through these at your own pace, and remember to connect with our online community to share your questions, comments, and "Aha" moments.

Exercise One:

Rootsilience Solar Plexus Chakra Image Meditation and Reflection

Take at least two minutes to gaze at this image while breathing deeply. Then ask yourself:

- How can you experience power without burnout?

- What is blocking you from embracing your personal power and shining brightly with confidence?

Take some time to write down these responses. Now reflect on what you've written, and read it over a few times.

Exercise Two:

Energy Mapping

Recognizing what gives and takes our energy is a powerful practice that enables us to keep our fire burning healthy and strong. Sometimes we overextend ourselves because we haven't put a boundary in place that we now realize we need. Maybe we weren't clear on what we were willing to give and what we're available for, and now we have a chance to set reasonable expectations. Sometimes the things we love, like intense exercise, can even be depleting if we're exhausted and burned out. The key question is, how can we bring more balance into our lives? How can we bring more ease?

Take out a piece of paper and make two columns:

What lights a fire within you?	**What drains your energy?**

Set a timer for 7 minutes and write continuously about what excites you on one side and on the other side, what drains you. Bullet points, doodles, full sentences, just keep writing until the timer is up. Just let your pen flow on the page without pausing and without censoring or editing what you write.

Ready? GO!

Reflection:

Now, take a few deep breaths and review what you've written.

1. How can you create structures to do more of what excites you and less of what drains you?

2. What boundaries do you need to put in place for your time and energy? With whom?

3. What are you available for? What are you NOT available for? What are you able to give? What is too much?

4. What are you saying YES to? What are you saying NO to?

See if you can make at least one commitment to yourself for a change (boundary, addition of self-care).

Optional: Let us know what that commitment is and gain support from the Rootsilience online community.

Exercise Three:

Decisional Balance Tool

When we think about making changes, we often do what we think we "should" do, avoid doing things we don't feel like doing, or just feel confused or overwhelmed and give up thinking about it at all. Thoughtfully considering all our options from a holistic perspective is an aspect of being a Rootsilient leader. The decisional balance tool helps us think through the pros and cons of both changing and not making a change so we make sure we have fully considered all possibilities. This can also be a tool to help you make decisions about the things you've realized you may need to change in the previous Energy Mapping Exercise.

Directions:

Take out a piece of paper and create the following chart. Write the Number 1 thing that "drains" your energy at the top.

1. Ask yourself: What would be a benefit to staying exactly the same? List all of those in that upper left-hand box.

2. Then, ask: What are your concerns about staying the same? List as many of those as possible in the upper right-hand box.

3. Ask yourself: What would it feel like to say, "No, I do not want to make that change"? And what concerns might you have about making that change? Please list as many of those as possible in the lower left-hand box.

4. And then, how might you benefit from making a change? That goes into the lower right-hand box.

1 Thing that drains my energy: _____

Response to Stay the Same	Response to Make a Change
1. What are the benefits of staying the same? (List as many as possible.)	2. What are your concerns about staying the same? (List as many as possible.)
3. What are your concerns about making a change? (List as many as possible.)	4. What are the benefits of making a change? (List as many as possible.)

Notice what it's like to reflect on what you've written, and consider using the tools in the Throat Chakra chapter to voice your desired change.

Exercise Four:

The Importance of Downtime and Rest – Your Rest Report Card

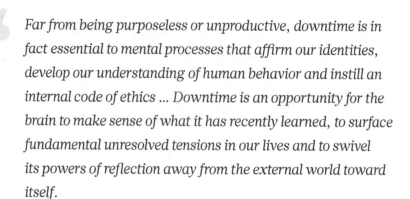

Far from being purposeless or unproductive, downtime is in fact essential to mental processes that affirm our identities, develop our understanding of human behavior and instill an internal code of ethics ... Downtime is an opportunity for the brain to make sense of what it has recently learned, to surface fundamental unresolved tensions in our lives and to swivel its powers of reflection away from the external world toward itself.

– Ferris Jabr, *"Why Your Brain Needs More Downtime"*[4]

We often associate rest or downtime with sleep. While important, it is not the only way we give our brains and body rest and recharge. Please look at the following types of rest and ask yourself if you're getting enough rest. For each of the below, ask yourself how often you do it, and give it a score from 1 to 10*. Remember, these scores aren't another way to judge yourself or "beat yourself up" (a sign of imbalance with the Solar Plexus Chakra), but it's a way for you to be honest with yourself about what you truly need. *On the score: 1 is almost never, 10 is frequently.

Type of Rest	My Honest Score (1–10) *On the score: 1 is almost never, 10 is frequently	What can I do to get more of this type of rest?
Deep restful sleep		
Time away from "doing"		
Permission to not be helpful		
Doing something "unproductive" that is joyful		
Connection to art, music or nature		
Time in solitude to recharge		
Breaks from responsibility		
Stillness or silence		

Exercise Five:

Validating Yourself

One of the ways to go beyond seeking external recognition and praise is to feel validated from within. This is also directly tied to rest, as sometimes we can't rest until we feel we have done or are "enough." There's a tendency to get stuck in always being "better" and creating never-ending to-do lists that reinforce the feeling of never doing enough. Maybe we find ourselves accumulating a litany of certifications because having all those credentials will make you feel "good enough," or maybe it's chasing promotions, salary, the size of your house, the type of car, etc.

To compound the feelings of "not enough," when we do have a win (whether big or small), we fear that sharing our successes could offend someone in our circle or our partner, or we worry that we'll come across as being too boastful. Maybe you've even felt a tinge of jealousy when your colleague shares about getting her dream job and you're still feeling lost and unsure of your direction. When we can fully feel and celebrate our success, it lights us up from within so we don't rely on receiving praise or seeking external validation. Here's how:

Part 1: What I'm Proud Of

Directions:

1. Get out your journal and make a list of twenty things you're proud of. Be specific. It's 20 for a reason, because maybe you can easily get to 5 or 10, but 20 makes you dig deep.

2. Now, go back and look at your list. How does it make you feel? What does pride feel like in your body? Note that.

3. Notice what nags at you, what feelings or sensations or thoughts maybe keep you from feeling truly proud of what's on this list.

4. Take a moment to ask yourself if it's okay to celebrate you. Tell any

parts of you that disagree that they can join you in this practice and that they will benefit. You're there to help.

5. Take a deep breath in and allow yourself to fill up with those joyful feelings of pride. Exhale and release whatever is keeping you from truly celebrating. Inhale, feel light streaming in, feel pride, expansion, joyfulness. Exhale and release fear of being "too big" or "too much."

6. Keep going until you feel and embody this pride, at least 5 minutes.

7. Thank yourself for being willing to feel proud. When you do this for yourself, it has a vibratory effect on the collective.

Part 2: Reprogram and Remove the Collective Barriers to Pride

Directions:

Invite a friend to share her success with you. As you listen, breathe it in as if it's true for you too (even if it isn't). As she shares, imagine that she is starting to glow. Invite her to tell you more, about how she felt, who was there, what it was like, about how amazing it all was. See or imagine or feel her lighting up as she speaks. With each inhale, sip in and expand this light. You are sipping it into a place within you that is infinite, so you're not taking her light but rather expanding it, through you, into the fabric of our collective being. Each time you exhale, expand that light all around. Notice how you feel doing this. What does your friend feel like being supported in this way? As you exhale, release any tension or blocks and notice how you allow your friend the space to celebrate her joy. In this way, we can truly be proud of ourselves and each other, overcoming the barriers to feeling our own beautiful and benevolent light.

How the Solar Plexus Functions in the Body

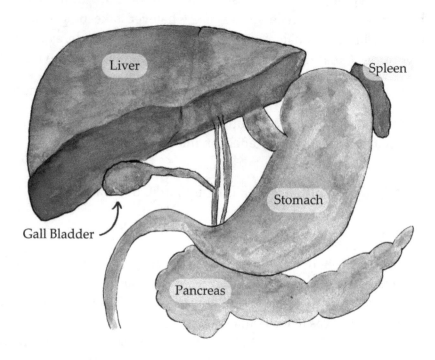

Manipura, translating to "city of jewels" or "lustrous gem" is where our power center sits, emanating the radiation of our benevolent light. The Solar Plexus Chakra extends from just below the sternum down to the navel, in the gut area, and it presides over our bodies' ability to create and store energy. This is where food is broken down so it can be utilized by the body for nourishment.

The body parts that correspond to this chakra are the pancreas, the liver, the gallbladder, the spleen, organizing the digestive system. These organs play a critical role in digesting our food, starting with the production of amylase, a component that breaks down our food from the moment we take a bite and begin chewing. Food is then brought down through the esophagus into the small intestine, where it's digested, and the nutrients are carried through our entire body.[5] Your liver produces bile, which is a yellow-colored substance that helps you absorb fat. Your gallbladder stores the bile. Your pancreas helps to break it all down and assimilates your sugar through enzymes and insulin. Then your stomach and your small intestine transfer all those nutrients from your digested food into the bloodstream, where you get nourished.

You may have heard the saying, "All disease starts in the gut." The Greek physician Hippocrates coined that term 2,000 years ago and that wisdom has withstood the test of time. Modern scientists are learning that dysfunction or "dysbiosis" of the gut microbiome can lead to debilitating diseases such as Alzheimer's, Parkinson's, and also depression and anxiety.[6]

Excess weight or dramatic weight loss can also be a Solar Plexus imbalance because the body is not properly metabolizing food into energy. Someone with an imbalance in this chakra may find their stomach feels very hard, or they may have a large pot belly, or a hollowed-out diaphragm.

Physical signs associated with an imbalance in the Solar Plexus Chakra may include:

- Lack of energy and fatigue

- Muscle tension, particularly in the abdominal area and around the diaphragm

- Poor digestion and metabolism

- Poor assimilation of nutrients (i.e., chronic constipation or diarrhea)

- Poor posture, leading to slouching or hunching over

- Problems with the liver or gallbladder, such as liver congestion or gallbladder dysfunction

- Skin disorders, such as acne, rashes, or eczema

The element associated with the Solar Plexus is fire. It is our digestive fire that metabolizes food into fuel, and our inner fire that lights us up to pursue what we believe in. In this chakra, we work to cultivate our digestive and energetic fire, but in a way that keeps us healthy, motivated and balanced, without burning the house down or burning out.

The fuel that gets us through the day is called glucose. All fruits, vegetables, grains and beans are broken down into glucose and other sugars. We're wired to love sugar and to love sweetness because our bodies understand that sweetness equals energy. Babies often prefer sweeter formulas and tastes. If they're offered a choice between something sweet and something that's more savory, they'll choose sweetness.

Some foods can trigger problems in the gut. Processed foods such as white flour, baked goods, and snacks made from processed white flour, for example, can wreak havoc on our digestive system. Too much sugar can cause inflammation in the body and cause something called "leaky gut," which is what happens when the intestinal lining that covers the surface area of the stomach starts to break down and become porous.

The gut is also known as the "second brain," and 95% of serotonin – the happiness hormone – is secreted in the gut,[7] so when we eat nourishing foods that maintain healthy gut flora, we feel that joy in our bellies. When the gut works properly, a tight barrier prevents food, bacteria, and pathogens from getting into our bloodstream. When we have an unhealthy gut, with cracks in it or even holes, partially digested food, toxins, and unhealthy bacteria can penetrate into the bloodstream, and that can cause inflammation.

We all have, to some extent, leaky gut. Some may even have a genetic predisposition. One of Samantha's children has celiac disease and when doctors investigated, they found that all of her villi – tiny projections on the inner surface of the small intestine which help in absorbing the digested food – were completely flattened because the gluten that she was consuming had destroyed her gut.

The Standard American Diet, the "SAD" diet – which is indeed quite sad! – is low in nutrients and fiber and high in sugar and processed foods.[8] It can also cause gastrointestinal conditions such as bloating and cramping, leaky gut, and other digestive disorders such as irritable bowel syndrome. Other factors, including stress and drugs, or just simply modern life, can also create this type of gut inflammation. People with liver disease are advised to eat a diet that is varied, eliminating ultra-processed industrialized food, sugar-sweetened beverages, and high-fat food.[9]

Healing Foods for the Solar Plexus Chakra to Support a Healthy Gut

Many foods can support our gut and digestive system and soothe the fire in the belly. Foods that support a balanced Solar Plexus Chakra are carbohydrates and proteins such as nuts and beans.

An important part of digestion is keeping everything moving, and this can be accomplished by including sources of soluble and insoluble fiber in your diet. Soluble fiber is found in foods like nuts, seeds, beans, and some fruits and vegetables. Insoluble fiber is found in foods like whole grains and vegetables. The recommendation for fiber intake is 30 grams per day,[10] but most people eat about half of that amount.[11]

Beans such as lentils, black beans, adzuki, and soybeans contain dietary fiber that can support digestion and slow down sugar release to avoid spikes in your blood. These spikes can cause inflammation, which is the cause of many chronic diseases. Nuts such as almonds, Brazil nuts, cashew nuts, macadamia, pecans, and walnuts are also helpful in easing digestion. Flax seeds, chia, and fibers like beet fiber, oat fiber and psyllium can also be healing for the gut.

Slow-burning, gluten-free carbohydrates like amaranth and buckwheat, quinoa, millet, sorghum, teff, and brown rice offer long-lasting, long-burning fuel that will get you through the day. Starchy vegetables like potatoes, acorn squash, summer squash, butternut squash, sweet potato, and yams are great for digestion. Yellow foods such as yellow peppers and pineapple are great sources of energy that burn slowly and fuel your body.

Another important food to assist with gut healing is bone broth. It's warm and nurturing, easy to digest, and it provides minerals that are supportive for gut healing, joint healing, and connective tissue healing. An amino acid found in bone broth can help to seal a leaky gut or increased intestinal permeability.[12] However, you want to make sure that you find organic bone broth made from meat products that are pasture-raised.

Probiotics are live microorganisms that have beneficial effects on the microbiome, which is the collection of all microbes, such as bacteria, fungi, viruses, and their genes, that naturally live on our bodies and inside us.[13] Probiotics promote digestion, enhance nutrient absorption, and help maintain a robust immune system. When you consume probiotics, you're adding more of these beneficial microbes to your gut. It's a bit like inviting new friendly neighbors to live in your gut to help with things like digestion and immunity. Fermented foods are rich in these beneficial probiotics, and they support a healthy gut microbiome and can help heal the gut lining. Consuming fermented foods can also improve digestive health by reducing bloating, gas, and constipation. They are often more easily digested and may enhance the bioavailability of certain nutrients.[14] Examples of these foods include yogurt, sauerkraut, kimchi, kefir, and miso.

Prebiotic foods help the friendly microbes in your gut (your microbiome) stay healthy and happy. These are foods that take care of the friendly microbes already living in your gut. When you eat prebiotic-rich foods, you're giving your existing gut microbes a delicious meal. This helps them grow and thrive, so they can continue doing their good work in your gut. Prebiotics are usually types of fiber found in certain foods, like fruits, vegetables, and whole grains. When you eat these foods, your body can't digest the fiber itself, but it travels to your gut where the friendly microbes love to eat it. When the microbes munch on these prebiotics, they grow stronger and can do a better job of keeping your gut and body healthy. So, prebiotics are like the fertilizer for the good microbes in your gut, helping them grow and keep your gut healthy.

Try out some of these foods to support your Solar Plexus, bringing this powerful energy center into balance.

- Acorn squash
- Asparagus
- Bananas
- Brown rice
- Burdock root
- Butternut squash
- Chicory root
- Dandelion leaves & roots
- Garbanzo beans
- Garlic
- Ginger
- Jerusalem artichoke (also known as sunchoke, sunroot, earth apple)
- Jicama root
- Kefir
- Kimchi
- Konjac root
- Leeks
- Lemon
- Lentils
- Millet
- Onions
- Pineapple
- Plantains
- Psyllium husk powder
- Quinoa
- Sauerkraut
- Summer squash
- Yakon root
- Yellow summer squash
- Yellow bell peppers

Reflection:

1. Notice how foods impact your energy.

2. What foods energize you? What foods deplete you?

3. What foods do you crave when you're low energy or stressed?

4. What foods do you desire when you are rested?

Herbs for the Solar Plexus Chakra

To stay balanced in this chakra, you can experiment with these herbs and spices to support digestive health.

{For any of these suggestions, please check with your doctor or healthcare practitioner to see if there are any contraindications for your health and any conditions you may have.}

CINNAMON *(Cinnamomum verum)*

Cinnamon has been used for centuries in Chinese medicine and has been shown to lower blood glucose and insulin signaling.[15]

DANDELION *(Taraxacum officinale)*

Helps with digestion, helping to keep things moving, and nutrient absorption. It has been used for heartburn and other digestive ailments.[16] The whole plant, especially the root, is beneficial to the liver, with powerful detoxification properties.[17] The leaf is also a diuretic which is helpful for lowering blood pressure. Using the root of dandelion can help avoid the diuretic effect of the leaves.

FENNEL *(Foeniculum vulgare)*

Fennel is a time-honored "after dinner" herb to prevent gas, bloating, and painful cramping in the bowels. It is a powerful colon cleanser. If you've eaten a heavy meal and are feeling bloated in the tummy, chew a tsp of fennel seeds or brew a tea with it.[18]

PAPRIKA or CAYENNE PEPPER *(Capsicum annuum)*

Ranging in spice levels, these culinary peppers are warming and stimulating, supporting digestion and boosting saliva.[19]

TURMERIC *(Curcuma longa)*

Turmeric has an anti-inflammatory effect via the same mechanism as ibuprofen and acetaminophen (paracetamol). This relative of ginger root also relaxes the muscles in the digestive system, promotes healthy gut flora, and fights infection while supporting better liver function.[20] When combined with a small amount of spicy black pepper, it becomes more bioavailable, helping the body absorb it more effectively.

Try out some of the recipes that follow to support your Solar Plexus Chakra, bringing this powerful energy center into balance.

Solar Plexus Chakra Recipes

PSYLLIUM HUSK FLATBREAD

Serves Four

Ingredients:

2 cloves garlic

2 tsp fresh rosemary

4 ounces almonds

8 ounces peeled pumpkin or pumpkin purée

1 tsp baking powder

1 tsp psyllium husk powder

¼ tsp Himalayan salt

2 eggs

1 ½ Tbsp extra virgin olive oil + another 1 ounce for coating top of bread

2 ½ ounces feta cheese (optional)

Preparation:

1. Preheat oven to 350°F. Place garlic and rosemary into a blender and chop for 3 seconds; scrape down and repeat. Scrape out and set aside.

2. Mix almonds for 10 seconds in a blender.

3. Add pumpkin, baking powder, psyllium husk powder and salt. Chop in the blender for 15 seconds.

4. Add eggs and oil, blend for another 20 seconds.

5. Scrape out all ingredients into a square pan lined with parchment paper.

6. Sprinkle with the rosemary and garlic, and add feta (optional).

7. Drizzle with remaining oil.

8. Bake for 30 minutes until dry when pricked.

WARMING LENTIL SOUP

Serves Six

Ingredients:

1 Tbsp olive oil

¼ cup chopped onion

4 cloves garlic, chopped

1 large carrot, chopped

1 large stalk celery, chopped

2 Tbsp tomato paste

⅛ tsp crushed red pepper flakes, or more to taste

⅛ tsp cayenne pepper, or more to taste

Salt and ground black pepper to taste

6 cups chicken (or vegetable) stock

1½ cups dry lentils (rinse before cooking)

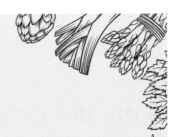

Preparation:

1. Heat olive oil in a large saucepan over medium heat; cook and stir onion and garlic until onion is translucent, about 5 minutes.

2. Stir in carrot and celery; cook, stirring often, until vegetables are tender, about 8 more minutes.

3. Stir in tomato paste, crushed red pepper, cayenne pepper, salt, and black pepper; mix in chicken stock and lentils.

4. Bring soup to a boil and reduce heat to low; simmer until lentils are soft, about 20-30 minutes, until lentils are tender.

FIRE HOT PICKLE JUICE COLESLAW

Serves Four

Ingredients:

4 cups shredded cabbage (green or a mix of green and purple)

1 carrot, grated

½ cup mayonnaise

2 Tbsp pickle juice

1 Tbsp Dijon mustard

1 Tbsp apple cider vinegar

Salt and pepper to taste

Optional: ¼ cup chopped pickles (for extra crunch)

Preparation:

1. In a large mixing bowl, combine the shredded cabbage and grated carrot.

2. In a separate smaller bowl, whisk together the mayonnaise, pickle juice, Dijon mustard, apple cider vinegar, salt, and pepper until well combined.

3. Pour the dressing over the cabbage and carrot mixture and toss until all the ingredients are evenly coated.

4. If desired, add chopped pickles for extra crunch and mix well.

5. Taste and adjust the seasoning, adding more salt, pepper, or pickle juice according to your preference.

6. Cover the coleslaw and refrigerate for at least 30 minutes to allow the flavors to meld together.

7. Serve chilled and enjoy as a refreshing side dish.

Mind-Body Integration to Rest and Recharge

The mind-body integration practice for the Solar Plexus Chakra embodies the qualities of Fairness, Leadership, and Zest. Supporting practices are available in our online resources (www.rootsilience.com/courses/beyond-the-book) and were filmed by an active volcano with steaming geysers and fumaroles. In this practice, we balance our fire. This practice is designed to build some heat (stoke the fire), give it space (expand and twist), and then cool it down (yoga *nidrā*).

Embodying Zest

Activating Our Fire: Release the arms down the body, and slowly start swinging them from side to side, letting them gently hit your lower back. Feeling this gentle awakening with your arms, let them be loose, and your head can move along with your body as you swing. Your arms side to side. If you need to bring a little bend into your knees, that can be nice for the low back.

Now bring in some sound. We'll be using "HA" on the exhale to stoke the fire within. Ha, ha, ha, ha, ha, ha as you swing your arms side to side. Notice how you need to engage your belly muscles to make that sound. Now start to slow down the swinging of your arms from side to side. And then slowly, just bringing your hands to your thighs, take a deep breath, sending your breath into your belly, into your low back, into this whole area of your torso around the rib cage.

Embodying Leadership

We can incorporate several twists to open space around the ribcage and allow the spine to lengthen. Oftentimes our inner fire can be restricted. The twists bring a cleansing and clearing action to release excess energy and enable us to recharge and lead effectively.

Stand with your feet together at the front of your mat and INHALE, lift both arms up to the sky, expanding the area of your belly as you lengthen up, and EXHALE, fold forward, bringing your hands to the floor, on a block, or onto your shins. Knees can be slightly bent here if needed. INHALE, lift the right arm up as you gently bend the left knee a bit more than the right, and feel into a gentle standing twist. You can look up at the extended arm or down at the ground, depending on how your neck is feeling. INHALE and expand your breath into the right side of your body, lengthening from tailbone to crown, and EXHALE, extend through the arm. INHALE, press into the feet to get long in the spine and around the right side of the belly, EXHALE, gently pull the belly button toward the spine. Take three more breaths here and switch sides.

Embodying Fairness

It's easy to be fair when our fire is balanced and we're not reacting out of ego or anger. In order to cultivate Fairness, we use the following practices to cool our fire.

Cooling the fire: This is a powerful practice that involves laying your belly on a rolled-up blanket (or with a blanket over a block, as shown). This is a soothing practice where we slowly drape our belly over the block and use our weight to gently apply pressure and expand breath into our internal organs. We can use the support of our forearms to keep us in a safe position and control how much weight we place on the belly.

*This position is not recommended for anyone who is pregnant, menstruating, or experiencing pain in the belly.

In the middle of your yoga mat, place a soft block on the lowest height with your blanket over the block as shown (or you can use a firm pillow or blanket over a thick book). You're going to slowly lie your belly on the block; the top of the block (or upper edge of the pillow or blanket over the book) should be just below the rib cage. The target area is the belly, so be sure not to place the block too low toward your pelvis. The position is shown here.

Gently lower yourself down, using your forearms to take more of the weight as your belly muscles settle around the block and blanket; may feel a bit uncomfortable as you're compressing the inner organs, but there should be no shooting or electric pains.

If you feel OK, make whatever small adjustments to settle in and start to slow down your breath; See if it feels okay to walk your forearms forward, or not. Trust your gut. Consider lowering the head toward the floor, but it's all about respecting what's going on in your body.

Once you get settled in and find a place where you can be fidget-free for a few breaths, bring your awareness to your belly. You may even feel your heartbeat in your belly.

With each EXHALE, slow it down, breathe a little softer, soften the muscles around your belly and allow the body to gently drape over the block and blanket.

Consider the quality of FAIRNESS here, and create space in the belly to attune to those gut feelings. We can have balance in this leadership quality, so our desire to control doesn't override allowing what we know to be true. Take three to five slow breaths here, or as long as you feel comfortable.

To come out of the pose, very slowly bring your forearms under your shoulders if you walked them forward. Press into your forearms and gently lift the belly up and back, moving your block and blanket set-up over to the side, and come into a child's (*balasana*) pose, knees wide and big toes touching. You can support your head on a block or with your hands if it's more restful. Stay for a few easy breaths here.

Yoga nidrā: The practice of *yoga nidrā* invites us into deep, restorative rest. This practice guides you to shift your attention around your body, using a visualization of feeling your own inner sun and light all through your cells. You can download a guided practice of *yoga nidrā* at <u>www.rootsilience.com/courses/beyond-the-book</u>. The practice was filmed in the active volcanic complex of Furnas, on the island of São Miguel, Azores. Surrounded by bubbling geysers where you can feel the heat of the steam rising, there couldn't be a better place to explore the fire element and lessons of the Solar Plexus Chakra to bring us into balance.

Rootsilience Leadership Map Reflection

Review your Rootsilience Leadership Map results.

1. Do you have greater strengths in the Solar Plexus? What about lesser strengths?

2. Do you tend toward over or underuse in any of your greater or lesser character strengths?

3. Do you have physical, emotional, mental challenges in this chakra?

4. What connections can you make between the physical signs of "dis-

ease" (lack of ease), and how that connects to your emotions? To your state of mind? To your behavior?

5. What are the first signs you are out of balance?

6. What can you do to bring yourself back into ease and flow?

   • Character strengths I'm working to optimize include: _____

   • The practices, tools and foods that bring me back into balance are: _____

7. Reminders to myself to be a Rootsilient Leader: _____

See the Appendix for further readings on the Solar Plexus Chakra.

Chapter Seven

The Sacral Chakra

Leading with Creative Flow
and Cultivating Healthy Partnerships

I was at the top of my career, just promoted to Senior Vice President and on my way to becoming a partner at my management consulting firm. I was going to early morning and late-night networking events, and during the day, I was cranking out deliverables or on back-to-back conference calls. I ate lunch in front of my computer, the crumbs of last week's takeout lodged deep within the recesses of my keyboard. My chronic urinary tract infections (UTIs) started around this time and when I went to my OBGYN, I was prescribed antibiotics. Oftentimes the strong antibiotics would kill all my "good bacteria" too, and almost every time I took antibiotics, I landed an even more uncomfortable yeast infection. Then the urinary tract infections started coming more frequently. My doctor prescribed me antibiotics over the phone, her attendants knew me by name.

Then one day, my annual pap smear turned out "abnormal." I had severe cervical dysplasia, also known as pre-cancer, and my doctor strongly advised that an operation was required immediately; otherwise, I could lose my uterus entirely. I went through the procedure and on follow-up pap smears, I was A-OK. Life continued, UTIs, yeast infections and all, and a few years later, the same thing happened: another abnormal pap smear. Again, my cervix was cut and pre-cancerous cells removed. Follow-up visits turned out fine. But I wondered, why was this happening?

It wasn't until I left my high-intensity job and started my business in the Azores that the UTIs subsided and I got to the root cause. Around this time, I deepened my studies of the chakras and dove into books from Louise Hay, Caroline Myss, and Anodea Judith that spoke about the link between physical disease and lifestyle. I was shocked that many of the texts directly link reproductive issues to a lack of honoring our cycles. I was disappointed that no one in my medical community had even mentioned these concepts, nor asked me about my high-intensity lifestyle that was clearly linked to my health issues. Over time I learned to listen to my body and to my unique indicators of when I needed rest. And I'm pleased to say I no longer have chronic UTIs and my annual exams have been clear for years.

~ Rimi's Sacral Chakra story

● **Sacral** **Appreciation of Beauty ✦ Creativity ✦ Curiosity ✦ Teamwork**

Traditionally, the six lotus petals symbolize the qualities to be overcome for purity: anger, hatred, jealousy, cruelty, desire, and pride. The petals are also associated with femininity.

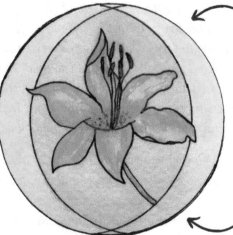

Six petals and stamen, for masculine energy, representing union and partnership

Crescent moons, for feminine energy, representing water, emotion, and creativity

Flower for beauty, movement, form

Overview of the Sacral Chakra

Rootsilience Symbolism of the Sacral Chakra	Our Rootsilience Sacral Chakra image is a blossoming flower, dancing in the glory of creative possibility, safely held in the container of the two crescent moons. The flower at the center symbolizes the cycles of birth, death, rebirth and transformation, *Shakti* and power of all life and creative energy. The six petals represent the vices we must overcome in order to master our creative force: anger, hatred, jealousy, cruelty, desire, and pride. This image offers us an invitation to find balance and partnership, express our beauty and find our flow in the dance of life.
Key Themes	The Sacral Chakra is known as our creative force and is associated with harnessing our sexual or creative energy. This chakra invites us to find our flow, like water, letting emotions flow rather than damming them. Emotion is "energy in motion" and is a portal to our creative potential.
Key Leadership Challenges	• Difficulty being creative or finding creative solutions • Overly dependent or lost in "groupthink" • Tendency to burn bridges with collaborations or partnerships gone wrong
Key Physical Signs of Imbalance	• Bladder or urinary challenges • Chronic back, hip or pelvic pain or tightness • Reproductive challenges

Key Emotional and Behavioral Signs of Imbalance	• Difficulty feeling joy and sensuality • Emotional instability • Lack of creativity
Location	The location of this chakra is found about two inches below the navel, in the pelvic bowl near the sacrum of the spine.
Chakra's Body Functions	The Sacral Chakra's body functions are found in the reproductive organs, hips, bladder, kidney and lower back.
Element	The element associated with the Sacral Chakra is water, and we find freedom and flow in movement that frees our hips, and understanding emotion as energy in motion.

VIA Character Strengths	The strength of APPRECIATION OF BEAUTY offers the ability to see beauty in things that others may overlook. We appreciate beauty in all aspects of life; from art to nature, relationships, work experiences, and in our own and others' talents and skills. When we embrace CREATIVITY, we uncover new ways of doing things or introduce novel ideas to the world. The distinguishing factor of a creative person is their ability to approach problems with the intention of coming up with a new solution. Often creative people inspire others to join in on their ideas, and help them to be productive problem-solvers or think "outside the box." CURIOSITY is often associated with the desire to learn and become knowledgeable or educated about a topic or idea. Approaching life with Curiosity means you are willing to try new things, discover alternative experiences, and see all of life as a learning experience. A person with TEAMWORK as a strength prioritizes the team experience, not just in work relationships, but also with their family or a group of friends. They are committed to the success of the group rather than personal gain.
Color	Orange, a warm and vibrant color that symbolizes creativity, passion, sensuality, and vitality. The color orange signifies emotional well-being, pleasure, joy, and the ability to experience and express one's emotions and desires. Orange also represents the creative life force energy that flows through this chakra, inspiring artistic expression and the exploration of one's passions.

Sanskrit	*Svadhisthana*, meaning "where your being is established," or "dwelling in the seat of the self." *Svadhisthana* is closely linked to creativity, sensuality, emotions, and the expression of one's desires. It is considered the center of our emotional and sexual energy, as well as our capacity for pleasure and enjoyment in life.

Balanced Leadership in the Sacral Chakra

 A tree's most important means of staying connected to other trees is a "wood wide web" of soil fungi that connects vegetation in an intimate network that allows the sharing of an enormous amount of information and goods. The reason trees share food and communicate is that they need each other. It takes a forest to create a microclimate suitable for tree growth and sustenance. So it's not surprising that isolated trees have far shorter lives than those living connected together in forests.

– Peter Wohlleben, *Hidden Life of Trees*

Balancing Masculine and Feminine Energy

In the same ancient texts that gave rise to yoga, meditation and the chakras, it is said that the Universe was created through the union of masculine and feminine energy. *Shakti*, the primordial creative force, the "Divine Feminine," is often depicted as a wild and powerful goddess, with an infinite ability to manifest and create. *Shiva* is absolute consciousness, the "Divine Masculine," often depicted as a *Lord Shiva*, or Source, and is the expansiveness of the Universe and all that is. In the union of *Shakti* and *Shiva*, ideas are manifested into reality, potential is manifested into being, and consciousness is given form.

We each hold masculine and feminine energies within us, and finding balance in the Sacral Chakra is about harmonizing these aspects of ourselves. Feminine and masculine energies are not about gender, but rather about the active or outward energy (masculine) vs. the inward and reflective energy (feminine). We can see some examples of masculine and feminine as follows:

- Night (feminine) and day (masculine)

- Yin (feminine) and yang (masculine)

- Left (feminine) and right (masculine)

- Parasympathetic nervous system; rest and digest (feminine) and sympathetic nervous system; fight or flight (masculine)

- Receiving (feminine) and giving (masculine)

- Surrender (feminine) and force (masculine)

- Inaction/stillness (feminine) and action (masculine)

- Reflective (feminine) and assertive (masculine)

- Brainstorming/preparation (feminine) and performance/action (masculine)

- Cooperation (feminine) and competition (masculine)

Traditionally, society has rewarded, focused on, and prioritized the masculine aspects of our being, and our leaders are taught to be assertive, action-oriented, competitive and focused on material success. However, real success and conscious leadership come when we find balance in our leadership and behavior. We need to stop and slow down to allow the ideas to settle and take shape before we jump into action. We need to listen before we speak. We need to collaborate, not dominate.

If you are someone in a high-paced, deadline-oriented job with a lot of structure and pressure, an exercise routine that includes high-intensity workouts, weight training and a highly restrictive diet that includes intermittent fasting, you are pushing yourself to the extreme in all areas, with an excessive or dominant masculine energy. As Rimi shared in her Sacral Chakra story, her push, push, push and go, go, go in all areas of life led to chronic UTIs and bladder infections, a physical symptom of an imbalance in this chakra. Rimi's journey to finding balance included blocking off time in her calendar with no agenda, time to just be. Rimi switched out a few of her usual HIIT workouts for Yin Yoga and self-massage, restorative practices that were nourishing to the nervous system and balancing for the fight or flight response.

If, on the other hand, you are in a field where there is little structure, you have few to no routines, wake up when you feel like it, eat at odd times of the day, and get easily swept away from your projects by personal drama (in your life or in others), finding yourself unable to finish what you start, you may lack structure and grounding to bring forth your ideas and creations. Striking a balance within our own masculine and feminine energies is about finding enough structure, form, and stability to let the creative waves flow.

Samantha, in raising six children in her blended family, shares that her parenting style is akin to a riverbed, balancing structure with the flow of flexibility. The water in the riverbed moves along, sometimes dammed up with boulders when things are challenging, and at other times flows freely, with easeful and pleasurable experiences. While she can't be in the river with her children all the time, Samantha ensures safe guardrails by creating easy-to-recognize and clear edges of the riverbed so there is space and flow for the kids, but with enough structure and boundaries to keep them safe. This balance between flow and form enabled her to find balance in her personal and professional life. You'll have a chance to reflect on your masculine and feminine energy balance in your life in the leadership exercises a bit later in this chapter.

Honoring Our Cyclical Nature

We are part of and inherently connected to nature and it's time we recognized that we are cyclical beings. There are times when you have loads of energy, like the budding flowers of Spring ready to blossom into their full Summer glory. There are times when you need to slow down and go inward to get still and recharge, like the cool Autumn winds that help trees shed their leaves in preparation for winter hibernation. There are times we are on our "A game" when ideas and presentations flow with ease, and there are times we feel stuck, need to sleep in and allow ourselves to take a break and rest.

For those who have a monthly menstrual cycle, our periods (and the ease or pain that accompanies them) are clear and honest indicators of how aligned or not we are with our natural cycles. Consider the following general overview of the menstrual cycle and note that we've included additional books and resources in the Appendix should you wish to dive deeper. Note that the length of days in a cycle can vary by individual and the below is based on an average 28-day cycle.

- Menstruation | Days 1–5 is your menstrual cycle (count "Day 1" as the first day of full menstrual flow). Consider this time as your "Inner Winter." This is a time to recharge, replenish, and listen to our intuition. We may have premonitory dreams this time of our cycle or receive important messages from the depths of our being (so stay away from binge-watching TV and eating or drinking junk food around this time). It's also a time when you're likely to feel foggy, unable to make big decisions, and the worst possible time to have an important presentation, meeting or networking event. Consider that some of our ancestors bled together in a "Red Tent"[1] where they joined in laughter, tears and storytelling, and were given three days break from all their duties AND all their meals were made for them! (Let's bring this tradition back, please!)

- Follicular Phase | Days 6–12, where your follicle-stimulating hormone (FSH), estrogen, and testosterone start to rise as your body prepares to release a mature egg into your uterus. Consider this phase as your "Inner Spring," where suddenly you come out of the cave of menstruation and feel the desire to get out and about, budding like the start of Spring. This is a great time to get all the things off your to-do list that you don't normally feel like doing. This is also a great time to attend networking events, be more social, or tackle big projects.

- Ovulation | Days 13–15, where your estrogen and testosterone are at their peak levels and one of your ovaries releases a mature egg into your fallopian tubes. This is your "Inner Summer," and it is only during this phase that you could get pregnant (when sperm could inseminate the released egg). This is where your creativity and fertility are at their peak, and along with the higher estrogen levels, you may experience a sense of both looking and feeling your best. This is also a time for clarity – not only in your skin, but about important situations or decisions, so it could be a great time to make big decisions and hold important meetings, talks or presentations.

- Luteal Phase | Days 16–28, where progesterone is produced and then drops if the egg is not fertilized. If you did not conceive during this cycle (i.e., your egg was not inseminated), your estrogen, progesterone, and testosterone levels drop, and you can think of this time as "Inner Autumn," a time to shed what is not essential and let go. This is an important time to honor our boundaries so we can best prepare for the rest and hibernation in the oncoming menstrual phase. The luteal phase, when we're not distracted by the non-essential, is a great time for creative pursuits like brainstorming, writing, and deep reflection. There can be an immense surge in your power and creativity if you're able to clear away the distracting and non-essential around this time. If you did not conceive this cycle, then you will return to Inner Winter and the cycle starts again.

- For those in perimenopause or menopause and those who do not have a regular monthly cycle, remember that even if you are not bleeding, you still have cycles, and we have included a leadership exercise in this chapter (Exercise Five: Cycle Tracking) for you to determine how to recognize your Inner Winter, Spring, Summer, and Autumn.

Healthy Partnerships

Remember when Tom Cruise (playing Jerry) professes his love for Rene Zellweger (playing Dorothy) in the movie *Jerry Maguire* and says, "You complete me"? It's time we ditch the fairytale we've been fed in countless classics like *Cinderella, Snow White, The Little Mermaid* and others, where we are inherently incomplete or broken, and need our romantic partners to "complete us" or that they need us to complete (or take care of) them.

One plus one can equal a lot more than two if each part is whole to begin with. There is a big difference between two partners being complementary, like the balance of masculine and feminine we spoke about earlier, and dependence. Being whole is about recognizing our strengths and gifts, and also acknowledging our vulnerabilities and lesser strengths. When we cultivate partnerships (whether romantic or in business) that balance and support us, we can truly create magic. You'll have a chance to see how you can do this in the leadership exercises that follow.

Healthy partnerships also include our relationship with ourselves, and it's important we strike a balance between being disciplined and giving ourselves permission to experience joy, freedom and pleasure. While having an admirable goal to eat well and be healthy can mean having a disciplined approach to cutting out snacks and unhealthy habits, sometimes we can push "too hard," and discipline turns into denying ourselves joy and pleasure. Cultivating a healthy partnership with yourself can be a lifelong journey, and one that harnesses the infinite creative potential that exists within you. Notice how your external partnerships evolve when you improve your partnership with yourself.

Sex and Self-Care

One important example of creative union is the creation of life and having sex. Whether you are engaging in sex to create life and start or expand your family, or for joy, freedom, and self-expression, it's important to recognize the creative and sacred potential that exists in sex.

Sex (including self-pleasure) can be a profoundly sacred creative practice to foster a more intimate relationship with yourself and/or your partner. Yet there is not a single woman we know that has not experienced some form of sexual trauma (anything that was too fast, too soon, or too much). Couple the awkward experiences many of us have had with the many taboos around sex and misguided messaging from porn and stereotypes around "sex appeal," and women today walk the razor's edge of being beautiful and sexy but not too much, lest you be labeled provocative or worse, a "slut." Reclaiming our innate right to pleasure is part of healing a centuries-old wound around women and sexuality. Further reading is suggested in the Appendix, and for the purposes of this chapter, we can inquire how sex plays a role in your creative expression, what you give yourself permission for, and how you can honor your intuitive yes and no.

Take out your Rootsilience Leadership Map and review your results. Do you have strengths in the Sacral Chakra? How do they show up for you?

When we are balanced in the Sacral Chakra, we are at ease with our emotions, never completely swept away by them, but also not blocking or damming them up, able to express what we feel in a healthy and constructive way. We are disciplined with ourselves in how we eat, exercise, and manage our time, and yet we also give ourselves permission to enjoy what brings us pleasure and joy. We have a clear sense of self and are able to enter into relationships with others (romantic, friends, family, professional) without co-dependency or attachment. We also know how to let go of relationships amicably. When balanced in the Sacral Chakra, we are in tune with our inner child-like wonder, remembering to see and experience things in new and creative ways.

When we are out of balance in the Sacral Chakra, we can become overly identified or consumed by our emotions, forgetting that emotions are a state of being and not who we are (notice the difference between, "I am angry" and "I *feel* angry"). On the other hand, we could be numbing ourselves from feeling or not allowing ourselves to fully experience an emotion. While controlling or not allowing emotions could be a survival mechanism, in the long run, we detach and cut ourselves off from our creative force. We may be overly rigid with ourselves, denying an emotion, or harshly judging it as a part of ourselves we don't accept. We may not allow ourselves to enjoy the simple pleasures that bring us into balance with our sensuality, or we might be extreme with our exercise, diet or hard-working routines. We may have trouble thinking outside of the box or get overly attached to an outcome or situation. We could find ourselves in toxic relationships where we see another (partner, friend, family member) as "completing us," creating unhealthy dependencies and a lack of boundaries, ultimately negating our essential wholeness within. We may also have a hard time letting go of relationships and could even have a tendency to burn bridges with past partners, lovers, or friends out of anger, resentment, jealousy, or pain.

When there is ease and uninterrupted flow between the Sacral Chakra and the Solar Plexus Chakra above, our creative force fuels our passion for what we seek to create. The flow of our creations – be they human beings, projects, novel ideas, businesses, art, or writing – has the fire to transform and bring our essential being into the world to shine. When we find flow, ease, and balance in our Sacral Chakra, we can direct the power of our emotions and the important messages they bring toward that which we seek to manifest.

Leadership signs of imbalance in the Sacral Chakra:

- "Bad endings" with ex-colleagues, partners, past lovers or friends

- Difficulty thinking outside the box, unimaginative

- Hasty decision-making, based in anger or greed, spur-of-the-moment, short-term thinking

- Individualistic, "going it alone" or "I can do it myself"

- Lost in groupthink or attached to what others think

- Overly attached to motivations of money, pleasure, and selfishness

- Stuck in autopilot, unable to go with the flow

VIA Character Strengths Mapped to the Sacral Chakra and Associated Overuse and Underuse[2]

VIA Character Strength	UNDERUSE	OPTIMAL	OVERUSE
APPRECIATION OF BEAUTY AND EXCELLENCE	Oblivious / Stuck in a Rut / Mindlessness	Awe and Wonder for Beauty / Admiration for Skill and Moral Greatness	Snobbery / Perfectionistic / Intolerant / Unrelenting Standards
CURIOSITY	Bored / Uninterested, Apathetic / Self-Involved	Interest / Novelty-Seeking / Exploration / Openness to Experience	Nosy / Intrusive / Self-Serving
CREATIVITY	Conforming / Plain / Dull / Unimaginative	Original / Adaptive / Ingenuity-Seeking and Doing Things in Different Ways	Eccentric / Odd / Scattered
TEAMWORK	Self-Serving / Individualistic, Going It Alone	Citizenship / Social Responsibility / Loyalty / Contributing to a Group Effort	Dependent / Lost in Groupthink / Blind Obedience / Loss of Individuality

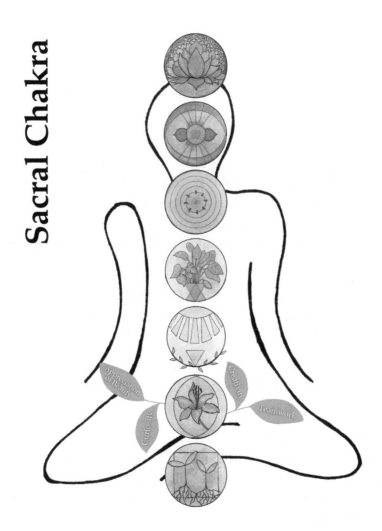

Sacral Chakra

If your Rootsilience Leadership Map indicates that you have a greater strength in the Sacral Chakra, you may have a tendency to overuse that strength. And if your map indicates a lesser strength, you may tend toward underuse. If you have neither a greater nor a lesser strength, it's likely you are in optimal use.

A leader with an optimal use of APPRECIATION OF BEAUTY AND EXCELLENCE has the ability to see beauty in things that others may overlook. They can appreciate the beauty in all aspects of life, from art to nature, relationships, work experiences, and their own or others' talents and skills.

- A greater strength of Appreciation of Beauty could lead to snobbery, an insistence on perfection, and/or an intolerance of others who don't have this kind of aesthetic sensibility.

- A lesser strength of Appreciation of Beauty could lead to mindlessness or overlooking something that is exquisite because it seems mundane or everyday, such as a relationship or a place that you're familiar with.

When we embrace CREATIVITY, we uncover new ways of doing things or introduce novel ideas to the world. The distinguishing factor of a creative person is their ability to approach problems with the intention of coming up with a new solution. A leader with an optimal use of creativity can inspire others to join in on their ideas and help them to be productive problem-solvers.

- A leader with a greater strength of Creativity could be a bit eccentric and possibly even overwhelming, offering too many ideas and solutions, creating confusion in their wake.

- A lesser strength of Creativity could show up as conformity, preventing you from shining your light brightly, leading you to not share ideas for fear of seeming "too much" or "too out there."

CURIOSITY is often associated with the desire to learn and become knowledgeable or educated about a topic or idea. A leader showing optimal use of Curiosity approaches life with eagerness by trying new things, discovering alternative experiences, and seeing all of life as a learning experience.

- A leader with a greater strength of Curiosity can tend toward being nosy, getting in people's business, or appearing to ask too many questions wanting to know colleagues' secrets or problems.

- A person with a lesser strength of Curiosity can have an air of insouciance or disinterest, and even boredom, blocking them from a deeper understanding.

A leader using TEAMWORK optimally as a strength prioritizes the team experience, not just in work relationships, but also with their family or a group of friends. They are committed to the good of the group rather than personal gain.

- A leader with a greater strength of Teamwork can depend too much on the group to make projects flow to the detriment of individual contributions.

- A person with a lesser strength of Teamwork can be perceived as individualistic and bossy, focused on their own personal gain rather than the group's overall success.

Remember that if there are any greater or lesser strengths in the Sacral Chakra, there may also be a tendency toward the physical/emotional imbalances in this chakra or the one above or below it. Your objective is to recognize your unique signs of going out of balance, and know how to bring yourself back to center.

Leadership Reflection Exercises to Lead with Creative Flow and Cultivate Healthy Partnerships

Exercise One:

Rootsilience Sacral Chakra Image Meditation and Reflection

Take at least two minutes to gaze at this image while breathing deeply. Then ask yourself:

1. How do you embrace your creative energy and allow it to flow freely?

2. In what ways do you honor your emotions with ease?

Take some time to write down these responses. Now reflect on what you've written, and read it over a few times.

Exercise Two:

Recognize and Balance Your Masculine and Feminine Energies

Take out a blank sheet of paper, turn it so it's landscape (wider than it is long), and draw a horizontal line; on the right side, write the word "masculine," and on the left, write the word "feminine." We use the words "masculine" and "feminine" not as measures of gender expression, but rather, as we discussed earlier in this chapter, we're exploring the balance between outward versus inward energy. You can even use the words "outward" and "inward," in place of "masculine" and "feminine" should you choose.

Now, under the line you've just laid out, list out the different aspects of yourself in a typical week. Consider your work life, your personal life, how you spend your free time, your activities with friends, and how you eat, and place them in along the line, from "masculine" to "feminine." Most things aren't squarely masculine or feminine, so you could list them somewhere along in the middle and refer to earlier in the chapter with examples given. The objective is to see where you fall on the overall spectrum to recognize if and where you could bring balance. Below are some prompts:

- Work Life: What kinds of things in your work life are highly structured? What about time for brainstorming and creativity or idea generation? Time doodling or creative thinking processes vs. "plow ahead and get it done"?

- Personal Life: Do you fill up your free time with activities? Is there unstructured downtime for rest? What kind of hobbies are you pursuing?

- Relationships and Friends: How are you spending time with those you love? Does it bring you joy? Does it feel forced? Is there play in your relationships and space for fun and joy?

- Exercise and Movement: What is your typical exercise routine? What kind of movement or activities do you participate in?

- Diet: Are you eating the same foods more or less? Are you rigid about what you eat? Are you eating at regular times or is it variable?

Look at your overall list and notice if there are any trends, or where you find yourself overall on the scale. How can you balance the scale?

Exercise Three:

Collaboration Roadmap (for use in any current or potential collaboration)

Use the following table to set yourself up for successful collaborations. This could be a business collaboration, as in hiring marketing support, a contractor or consultant for your business, or in collaborating to co-create something like a book, retreat, course or other.

Current or Potential Collaborator:	
Purpose of Collaboration:	
How does this collaboration align with my values?	
What is the ideal outcome of collaboration?	
How does this collaboration potentially not align or conflict with my values?	
How can I address the potential for conflict?	
What strengths does this collaborator bring to the table?	

How does this collaboration support my greater strengths and enable me to shine?	
How does this collaboration solidify or support my lesser strengths? How do I enable them to shine?	
What are milestones or metrics of a successful collaboration?	
What are signs or red flags of a potential problem, or how will I know to reevaluate the collaboration?	
What key parameters of the collaboration need to be documented?	

Exercise Four:

Fertile Soil Exercise

Get outside or somewhere you can get your hand in some dark, rich, wormy (yes, please!) dirt. Consider the fact that a single handful of soil is home to more living organisms than there are people on Earth. In fact, there are more living organisms within the soil itself than above its surface.[3]

Take a few moments and hold a handful of this fertile soil. Consider using it to plant a seed or return it to the Earth, then wash your hands and get out your journal:

- How can you be "fertile soil" in your family, relationships, and community so that you are a catalyst for growth and regeneration for everything and everyone around you?

- Reflect on the qualities that make you fertile soil in your family, relationships, and community. How have you cultivated these qualities over time, and what impact have they had on those around you?

- Imagine that you are a gardener tending to a plot of fertile soil. What kinds of seeds would you plant to foster growth and regeneration in your family, relationships, and community?

- Think about a time when you struggled to be fertile soil in your relationships or community. What barriers did you encounter, and how did you overcome them?

- Reflect on a time when you felt like you were not being fertile soil in your family, relationships, or community. What were the underlying factors that led to this, and what did you learn from the experience?

- Think about the role of communication in being fertile soil in your family, relationships, and community. How do you communicate effectively with others, and what strategies do you use to navigate conflicts and build healthy relationships?

Exercise Five:

Cycle Tracking

As Rimi healed from her go-go-go lifestyle and got to the root cause of her UTIs, she started to chart her cycles (moods, energy levels, as well as menstruation), and she recognized exactly where and when she needed deep rest. With cycle tracking, Rimi could see a direct correlation between when she didn't honor rest time and when she got another UTI (luckily less frequently). Samantha noticed that while she no longer menstruated post-menopause, she still had a cycle, and there were times of the month she needed more rest and others when she felt clearer and more energized. Samantha created a Menopause Moon Cycle Calendar to track her emotions and physical symptoms during the month and noticed that a pattern of energetic ebbs and flows continued, even after menopause. Other resources for cycle tracking are included in the Appendix.

Key questions here are:

- When is your Inner Winter? A time for deep rest and restoration.

- When is your Inner Spring? A time for blossoming ideas, and energy rising.

- When is your Inner Summer? A time for shining and sharing your gifts.

- When is your Inner Autumn? A time for shedding, releasing, and letting go.

How the Sacral Chakra Functions in the Body

The Sacral Chakra, also known as *Svadhisthana* in Sanskrit, "dwelling in the seat of the self," is considered the center of our emotional and sexual energy, as well as our capacity for pleasure and enjoyment in life. Located in the lower abdomen, about two inches below the navel, it is linked to the kidneys, bladder, and reproductive organs in the pelvic region.

Our Internal Waste and Water System

The kidneys and bladder are essential organs in the human body responsible for filtering waste products and excess fluids from the blood, maintaining fluid and electrolyte balance, and producing hormones that regulate blood pressure and red blood cell production. The kidneys are two bean-shaped organs located on either side of the spine, just above the waist. Each kidney contains millions of tiny filtering units called nephrons, which are responsible for removing waste products and excess fluid from the blood. The kidneys perform several important functions in the body including regulating the balance of water, electrolytes, and acids in the blood, producing hormones that stimulate red blood cell production and regulate blood pressure, and excreting waste products and excess fluids in the form of urine. The kidneys also play a crucial role in maintaining the pH balance of the blood, which is essential for proper cellular function. By filtering waste products and excess fluids from the blood, regulating fluid and electrolyte balance, and producing hormones that help regulate blood pressure and red blood cell production, both the kidney and bladder are critical for overall health and well-being.

Embarking on Creation

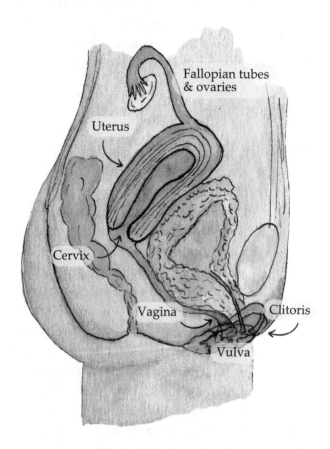

The female reproductive system is a complex system that is responsible for the production and storage of eggs, as well as for nurturing and supporting a growing fetus during pregnancy. The female reproductive organs include the ovaries, fallopian tubes, uterus, cervix, and vagina. Each of these organs plays an essential role in the process of reproduction.

The ovaries are a pair of small, almond-shaped organs located in the pelvis. The ovaries are responsible for producing and releasing eggs, or ova, as well as for producing hormones such as estrogen and progesterone. The ovaries contain thousands of follicles, each of which contains an immature egg. Each month, one of these follicles matures and releases an egg in a process called ovulation.

The fallopian tubes are two narrow tubes that extend from the ovaries to the uterus. The fallopian tubes are the site of fertilization, where the sperm and egg meet and combine to form a zygote. The zygote then travels down the fallopian tube to the uterus, where it implants and develops into a fetus.

The uterus is a muscular, pear-shaped organ located in the pelvis. The uterus is responsible for nurturing and supporting a growing fetus during pregnancy. The uterus is composed of three layers: the endometrium, the myometrium, and the perimetrium. The endometrium is the innermost layer and is shed during menstruation. The myometrium is the middle layer and is responsible for contracting during labor. The perimetrium is the outermost layer and provides support and protection for the uterus.

The cervix is the lower part of the uterus that extends into the vagina. The cervix produces mucus that helps to protect the uterus from infections and to facilitate the passage of sperm through the reproductive tract. The cervix also plays an important role during childbirth, as it must dilate to allow the baby to pass through the birth canal.

The vagina is a muscular canal that extends from the cervix to the external genitalia. The vagina serves as a passageway for menstrual blood, intercourse, and childbirth. The walls of the vagina are composed of layers of muscle, and the lining of the vagina contains many nerve endings that can provide sexual stimulation. Estrogen helps control the pH of vaginal secretions to optimize vaginal flora.[4] Vaginal dysbiosis can result in frequent vaginal bacterial or yeast infections and frequent UTIs.[5]

The vulva is the external portion of the female genitalia. Also known as the pudendum, the vulva includes the clitoris and inner and outer flaps known as the labia majora and labia minora. These flaps protect a woman's sexual organs, urethra, vestibule, and vagina.[6] Estrogen supports elasticity and erogeneity of the vulva to promote pleasure and prevent painful sex.

The clitoris is the most sensitive erogenous zone in a female body, and many people think it's just the "nub" of flesh at the top of the vulva, but it actually has two "legs" (called the crura) that extend well inside a woman's body with a complex network of tissues and nerves.[7] Research is lacking on the exact number of nerve endings in a clitoris, but some estimates put it well over 8,000, about twice as many as the penis.[8]

The Sacral Chakra, Pleasure and Our Emotional Well-Being

The Sacral Chakra is associated with creativity, sensuality, pleasure, and emotional well-being. The Sacral Chakra also regulates and balances sexual energy in the body. It governs our sexuality, sensuality, and creativity, as well as our ability to connect with others and form healthy relationships. The function of the Sacral Chakra is to regulate and balance our emotions, creativity, and sexuality. It governs the way we experience pleasure, joy, and intimacy. This chakra is responsible for our ability to feel connected to others and to enjoy the pleasures of life. It also helps us to express our emotions in a healthy way, and to develop a strong sense of self-worth.

When the Sacral Chakra is balanced and functioning properly, it can help to promote healthy reproductive function. This can include regulating menstrual cycles, supporting healthy fertility, and promoting healthy sexual function. Balanced energy flow through the Sacral Chakra can also help to balance hormones, which are important for reproductive health. Opening up these energies can lead to greater sexual pleasure and joy.[9]

One of the most common symptoms of an imbalanced Sacral Chakra is a lack of pleasure and joy in life. We may feel numb, disconnected, or uninterested in activities that we once enjoyed. We may also experience a lack of motivation or creativity, and may struggle to express ourselves in a meaningful way. Another symptom of an imbalanced Sacral Chakra is difficulty with intimacy and relationships. We may struggle to connect with others on an emotional or physical level, and may find it difficult to form healthy and fulfilling relationships. We may also struggle with our own sexuality and sensuality, and may feel shame or guilt around these aspects of ourselves.[10] Sexual trauma is so prevalent and important in women's health, and it is also incredibly complex and beyond the scope of this book. We provide resources on this topic in the Appendix.

Physical signs associated with an imbalance in the Sacral Chakra may include:

- Kidney or bladder disease or infection

- Lower back pain

- Menstrual problems

- Reproductive and pelvic organ conditions such as endometriosis, ovarian cysts, irregular or extremely heavy/scanty periods

- Urinary tract infections

Healing Foods for the Sacral Chakra to Support Hormone Health

To promote healing and balance of the hormones and flow of the Sacral Chakra, incorporating foods that have an energizing quality can help to stimulate the flow of energy through the chakra, promoting physical and emotional balance. Foods for healing the Sacral Chakra include orange fruits and vegetables. Oranges, mandarins, apricots, and carrots are all rich in carotenoids, which are a type of antioxidant that can help promote healthy cellular function and immune support.[11][12] These foods also contain vitamin C,[13] which is essential for supporting the immune system and promoting healthy hormonal balance.[14] Other orange fruits and vegetables that are beneficial for the Sacral Chakra include pumpkin, sweet potatoes, and butternut squash.

In addition to orange fruits and vegetables, nuts and seeds are also beneficial for the Sacral Chakra. Almonds, cashews, and pumpkin seeds are particularly helpful, as they are high in healthy fats, protein, and minerals such as zinc[15] and magnesium.[16] These minerals are important for supporting reproductive health. Incorporating healthy fats (Omega 3s and Polyunsaturated Fatty Acids or PUFAs) into your diet can also be helpful for promoting a healthy reproductive system.[17] Avocados, olive oil, and fatty fish are all high in these healthy fats, which are important for supporting hormonal balance and overall health. In addition, healthy fats are important for promoting healthy brain function and can help to support emotional balance, joy, and well-being.

Try out some of these foods to support your Sacral Chakra, bringing this energy center into balance.

- Apricots
- Butternut squash
- Cantaloupe
- Carrots
- Nuts and seeds (almonds, chia, flax, pumpkin, sesame, sunflower, walnuts)

- Papaya
- Pumpkin
- Sweet potato
- Yam
- Yellow bell peppers
- Water (hydrate!)

Reflection:

1. What foods create flow in your life?

2. Do you feel creative when you're cooking?

3. What foods do you crave when you're cycling?

4. What foods do you enjoy making with friends?

Herbs for the Sacral Chakra

To stay balanced in the Sacral Chakra, you can experiment with several herbs to support hormonal health.

{For any of these suggestions, please check with your doctor or healthcare practitioner to see if there are any contraindications for your health and any conditions you may have.}

CHASTEBERRY (*Vitex agnus-castus*)

Chasteberry (also known as vitex, chastetree or monk's pepper) has long been used to alleviate symptoms of premenstrual syndrome (breast tenderness, irritability, migraines, and cramps) and improves both estrogen and progesterone levels.[18] This herb is warming and for folks with low or dysregulated prolactin levels. Consult a practitioner for guidance on your particular imbalance and whether this herb is right for you.

GINGER (*Zingiber officinale*)

Ginger has been used for centuries as a natural remedy for menstrual problems and can help promote healthy blood flow and relieve cramping.[19] In addition, ginger has an energizing quality that can help to stimulate the flow of energy through the Sacral Chakra, promoting emotional and physical balance.

SHATAVARI (*Asparagus racemosus*)

Shatavari is an herb that has been used for centuries in Ayurvedic medicine. It is commonly used to support women's reproductive health, as well as to enhance overall vitality and well-being. Shatavari is believed to have a variety of health benefits, including reducing inflammation, improving digestion, boosting immunity, and promoting relaxation. It is also thought to have a positive effect on hormonal balance, particularly in women or people who menstruate, by supporting healthy levels of estrogen and progesterone. Additionally, Shatavari may help to improve lactation in nursing mothers.[20]

Try out some of the recipes that follow to support your Sacral Chakra, bringing this powerful energy center into balance.

Sacral Chakra Recipes

BUTTERNUT SQUASH SWEET MASH

Serves Six

Ingredients:

For the Mash:

4 cups butternut squash

1 medium head cauliflower (chopped)

4 Tbsp butter (divided into two parts; measure solid then melt)

1 tsp cinnamon

¼ tsp sea salt

½ tsp black pepper

For the Topping:

2 cups pecans (divided into 1 ½ cups and ½ cup)

¼ cup monk fruit

1 tsp cinnamon

1/8 tsp sea salt

Preparation:

1. Preheat the oven to 400°F. Line two baking sheets with foil (greased lightly) or parchment paper.

2. In a large bowl, toss together cubed butternut squash, cauliflower, 1 Tbsp of butter, salt, cinnamon, and black pepper.

3. Arrange the vegetables in a single layer on a lined baking sheet. Roast in the oven for about 30–35 minutes, stirring the vegetables periodically, and cook until very soft and golden.

4. For the topping, pulse ½ cup of pecans in the food processor until a powder forms. (Don't overmix.)

5. Chop the remaining 1 ½ cups of pecans. Place both chopped and powdered pecans in a small bowl. Add monk fruit, cinnamon, and salt. Stir in 2 Tbsp of the butter until the mixture is crumbly.

6. When the vegetables are finished roasting, remove from the oven but don't turn it off.

7. Purée the vegetables in the food processor until smooth.

8. Transfer the purée into a ceramic or glass casserole dish.

9. Stir in the remaining 1 Tbsp of butter into the purée.

10. Taste and adjust salt and pepper if desired.

11. Smooth down with spatula.

12. Sprinkle the pecan crumble over the top.

13. Roast the casserole in the oven for about 20 minutes until the top is golden.

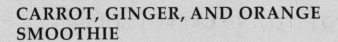

CARROT, GINGER, AND ORANGE SMOOTHIE

Serves One

Ingredients:

2 oranges, peeled and segmented

1 small carrot, peeled and chopped

1-inch piece of fresh ginger, peeled and grated

1 cup coconut water

1 Tbsp honey or sweetener of your choice (optional)

Ice cubes (optional)

Preparation:

1. Place the orange, chopped carrot, grated ginger, coconut water, and honey (if desired) into a blender.

2. Blend all the ingredients until smooth and well combined. If you prefer a colder smoothie, you can add a few ice cubes and blend again.

3. Taste the smoothie and adjust the sweetness or ginger according to your preference by adding more honey or ginger if desired.

4. Pour the smoothie into a glass and serve immediately.

SWEET POTATO AND CARROT SOUP

Serves Four

Ingredients:

2 medium-sized sweet potatoes, peeled and chopped

2 large carrots, peeled and chopped

1 small onion, diced

2 cloves garlic, minced

4 cups vegetable broth

1 cup coconut milk

1 Tbsp olive oil

1 tsp ground cumin

½ tsp ground ginger

Salt and pepper to taste

Fresh cilantro or parsley for garnish (optional)

Preparation:

1. Heat the olive oil in a large pot over medium heat. Add the diced onion and minced garlic, and sauté until the onion becomes translucent.

2. Add the chopped sweet potatoes and carrots to the pot, along with the ground cumin and ground ginger. Stir well to coat the vegetables with the spices.

3. Pour in the vegetable broth, bring to a boil, and then reduce the heat to simmer. Cover the pot and let the vegetables cook until tender, about 15–20 minutes.

4. Once the vegetables are cooked, remove the pot from heat and let it cool slightly.

5. Use an immersion blender or transfer the mixture to a blender to purée the soup until smooth and creamy.

6. Return the pot to low heat and stir in the coconut milk. Season with salt and pepper to taste, and simmer for an additional 5 minutes.

7. Serve the soup hot, garnished with fresh cilantro or parsley if desired.

Mind-Body Integration to Free Your Hips and Invite Flow

The mind-body integration practice for the Sacral Chakra embodies the qualities of Appreciation of Beauty, Curiosity, Creativity, and Teamwork. Supporting practices are available in our online resources (www.rootsilience.com/courses/beyond-the-book) and were filmed near a pond with expansive views to the sea. In this practice, we create space around our pelvis, hips and low back, and create a safe structure to feel the emotions and flow that arise, tapping into our creative potential.

Embodying Appreciation of Beauty

Here we explore Appreciation of Beauty by being present with what is. As we get into this pose, we embrace the beauty that is exploration, the beauty that is finding our way, the beauty that is the feeling of what feels good. And in mermaid pose (variation on *ardha halasana*), we can appreciate the beauty of feeling flow in our hips and pelvis, an area that is often tight or restricted.

Start seated, possibly on top of a folded blanket to elevate the hips so your lumbar spine is long. INHALE, send your breath down into your hips and pelvis, imagine it pooling into this beautiful pond, your entire pelvic bowl, and EXHALE, allow your sit bones to get a little heavier. Take a few more breaths like this here. Now bring your knees up in front of you with your feet on the floor.

Windshield wipers: Gently rock your knees to one side and then to the other with the support of your hands behind you. Move as slowly as you can, like you're underwater. Deep breath in. And deep breath out.

Mermaid pose (ardha halasana variation): Land your windshield wipers with your knees over to the left. Place the left foot so it's touching the right knee and the right leg is bent back at the knee with the right foot by your right hip. Take padding behind the right knee if you need less flexion and/or padding under both hips so your sit bones are lifted off the ground. If bending the knee isn't good for you, you can also extend the right leg straight out.

Your hands can be on either side of your hips or you can also be on your fingertips, and take a breath here with a little wiggle, a gentle shake, and just feel how one sit bone might be a bit more elevated than the other. Likely the left one is more rooted, or closer to the ground. Take one more breath and gently shake, like you're shaking a container of water and getting into every single crevice. Now EXHALE, and let the water settle. Feel or have the intention of lengthening down through your right hip.

Moving into pelvic tilts: INHALE, lengthen, extending the spine, really feeling your tailbone reaching behind you. It's a very subtle movement. EXHALE, the movement comes from your tailbone, bringing your pubic bone closer to your belly button. INHALE, feel for increasing the distance between your belly button and your pubic bone. EXHALE, feel for closing the distance between your belly button and pubic bone. Do that a few more times; you can keep your hands on the floor to support you. See if you're moving in your pelvis and sacrum or if it's coming from the heart space. A tendency if you've done yoga is to move in the heart, and there'll be some movement, of course, but you really want to get movement in the lumbar spine. Do a couple more tilts, really feel every time you exhale, the pubic bone and belly button come closer together, and every time you inhale, they reach further apart. Now take a few breaths in stillness and notice the right and left hips rooting into the Earth. Gently bring your knees back to center and extend both legs long. Notice the right and left sides of the back and hips. Repeat on the other side.

Embodying Creativity

Here we get into some creative movements in our hips. In this way, we allow our creative energies to flow.

Start in downward facing dog (*adho mukha svanasana*), or alternatively, you can be on all fours (tabletop position). With hips high, bend the knees, lift the right leg all the way up behind you, reaching your hands into the ground and keeping the spine long. Bend the back knee, heel toward butt, and take three hip circles in each direction. INHALE and EXHALE, move slowly, and again, you can do this on hands and knees if this is too much. And then switch directions.

Low lunge (anjaneyasana) with hip movements: INHALE, reach the right leg straight back, EXHALE, bend the knee and step (or help with your hands) your right leg forward at the front of your mat for low lunge, left back knee on the floor. (An alternative is from tabletop position, step the right foot forward to the front of your mat.) Hands can be on the floor or up on the front knee. Here we're going to explore a bit of creativity: feel into the watery bowl of your pelvis and as you begin to make circles or figure eight movements (they may be subtle, but there is movement!), feel the moving and swishing, whichever way feels nice. If it's too much to have your hands on the floor, you can have your hands on the knee as well. Take two more breaths, moving slowly or more quickly. It's your creativity. It's your expression, your unique expression of how you feel and also where you're at in your body.

Switch sides or continue to the next part and then switch.

Embodying Curiosity

From low lunge (anjaneyasana): With the left leg forward and right leg back in low lunge, lift the arms up, and let the hips sink down. Protect your low back by pressing into the top of your right foot and back through the left leg into the ground. INHALE, press downward, EXHALE, allow the hips to sink down, feeling the right hip flexor. Get curious about what comes up here. Now INHALE, extend through the arms, and EXHALE, weave the hands in front of the body, crisscrossing across the front of your body. Move your hands like water, be curious and explore. Notice what's happening in the hips, the back, and your breath. A few more breaths here and continue weaving the hands. And slowly come back into downward facing dog or onto all fours if you're taking all fours instead. Switch sides.

Embodying Teamwork

Pigeon pose (kapotasana): From tabletop position, bring your right knee toward the right wrist, ideally to the outside of your right wrist. Now pressing weight into your hands, slide the left leg behind you as far as you can go back while keeping the hips level. You may need a cushion, block, or blanket under the right sit bone or upper thigh. See if you can walk the right foot toward the left hand and be mindful of your knee, hips, and back (the closer the foot is to your hand, or the more parallel your shin to the top of your mat, the more intense a stretch in your hip. For less intensity, the right foot and shin can point toward the groin). An alternative for this pose is to lie on your back and cross the right ankle over the left knee and hug the knees in toward the chest or to your degree of ease.

Here we explore Teamwork, meaning the teamwork between what's happening in the hips. INHALE and lengthen up through your spine, hands on the floor. EXHALE and start to gently press the left hip forward and pull the right hip back. Notice how these work together. INHALE and recruit your stomach muscles. EXHALE and start to walk yourself down onto your forearms, wherever you are. We'll be here for three breaths and really feel into the interplay between the various things that are happening. INHALE, lengthen your breath along your spine, EXHALE, feel for softening and notice the teamwork between breath and awareness, between muscles tensing and holding you, and muscles stretching and softening and releasing. Take three more deep breaths. To come out of the pose, gently lift your torso up, press into your hands and step the right leg back into tabletop or downward facing dog.

Notice the difference between sides and then slowly come into the other side.

A guided practice for finding flow in the Sacral Chakra is located at www.rootsilience.com/courses/beyond-the-book

Dance as Medicine

One of the most nourishing kinds of movement that embodies flow and freedom is dance! Dance like no one is watching and dance in a way that honors how you feel, what you need to nurture, what you need to celebrate and what you need to release. All you need are some tunes that move you and a willingness to move in a way that feels good to you. Samantha is a certified Qoya Inspired Movement teacher. Qoya Inspired Movement is based on a simple idea: through movement, we remember. We remember we are wise, wild, and free. Qoya classes with Samantha are available to our Rootsilience community, so check our online resources at www.rootsilience.com/courses/beyond-the-book for details.

Rootsilience Leadership Map Reflection

Review your Rootsilience Leadership Map results.

1. Do you have greater strengths in the Sacral Chakra? What about lesser strengths?

2. Do you tend toward over or underuse in any of your greater or lesser character strengths?

3. Do you have physical, emotional, or mental challenges in this chakra?

4. What connections can you make between the physical signs of "dis-ease" (lack of ease), and how that connects to your emotions? To your state of mind? To your behavior?

5. What are the first signs you are out of balance?

6. What can you do to bring yourself back into ease and flow?

   • Character strengths I'm working to optimize include: _____

   • The practices, tools, and foods that bring me back into balance are: _____

7. Reminders to myself to be a Rootsilient Leader: _____

See the Appendix for further readings on the Sacral Chakra.

Chapter Eight

The Root Chakra

Leading with Presence and Trust

Every evening on her first visit to the Azores, Samantha made the short walk through the fragrant orange blossoms at Rimi's Quinta (farmhouse) to the vegetable garden to pick organic ingredients to make for dinner. "Ah, this life you've built here, it is so beautiful and inspiring," she shared with Rimi. When Rimi left her corporate world behind, she let go of lofty salary and fancy titles, yet gained financial freedom and a simple, and deeply fulfilling life. "We have enough," Samantha reflected, inspired by what enabled Rimi to make the huge leap to this new way of life. "We have enough and most of us just don't realize it."

As Rimi and Samantha's collaboration and friendship deepened, Rimi shared how overwhelming it was to have her home also be her place of work. "I feel like I can't really be at home knowing that there is always something to do, someone who needs taking care of or a team member that needs managing." Samantha encouraged Rimi to see her combined home and business as "her platform" – it is not only her home but the foundation from which she lives what she teaches. Living in harmony with the land, eating local and in-season foods, honoring the elements and being present with nature is a platform for sharing and inviting guests into a more connected way of life, a way that is grounded in simplicity, sustainability and stewardship.

Samantha's encouragement and perspective enabled Rimi to trust that she and her husband could periodically close their home and business and allow time for rest and recharge. While it was challenging to consider the loss of financial income, Samantha reminded Rimi that "we have enough." Ultimately, the periodic days of closure enabled Rimi and her husband to nourish their nervous systems and strengthen the platform on which her wisdom and teachings are rooted.

Meanwhile, Samantha began manifesting her big dream to heal, as she shared in her Third Eye Chakra story. Moving away from the family home where she had raised a blended family of six children meant recreating a sense of belonging, new friendships, building new community and trusting that the big life changes they were making would support them. Moving from the city life of New York City to the rural life of the Berkshires meant that Samantha could grow her own vegetables and herbs for tinctures, teas, and remedies, live aligned with her vision to support women on their healing journeys, and embody the very lifestyle that inspired her on that first visit to the Azores those many years ago.

~ Samantha + Rimi's Root Chakra story

⬤ Root

Bravery ✦ Humility ✦ Perseverance ✦ Self-Regulation

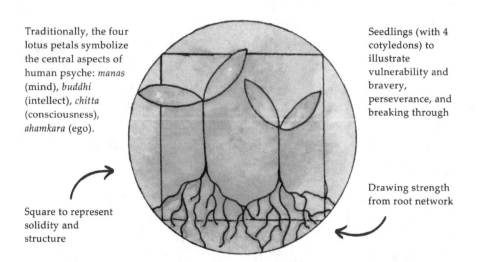

Traditionally, the four lotus petals symbolize the central aspects of human psyche: *manas* (mind), *buddhi* (intellect), *chitta* (consciousness), *ahamkara* (ego).

Square to represent solidity and structure

Seedlings (with 4 cotyledons) to illustrate vulnerability and bravery, perseverance, and breaking through

Drawing strength from root network

Overview of the Root Chakra

Rootsilience Symbolism of the Root Chakra	Our Rootsilience Root Chakra image represents the duality of bravery and vulnerability that is life. Within the square shape of boundaries and a foundation of structure and support, the seedlings spread roots to find stability and nourishment. This image evokes strength and fragility, how brave we are to be in this world and how easily we can be uprooted, moved, and transplanted in another garden or realm. We are not permanent, though we may set down roots; and even when our roots are solid, new germination creates new growth and vibrancy – an expression of perseverance amidst instability.
Key Themes	The Root Chakra is all about form and structure and is the energy center linked to the themes of safety, stability, support, and grounding. When we are rooted, we can grow and thrive. Without roots, we get swept away by whatever is pulling or stretching us beyond our limits.
Key Leadership Challenges	• Decision making from fear or "lack of" mentality, vs. trust and abundance • Inability to set or maintain and meet goals • Poor boundaries and inability to organize a plan to get things done
Key Physical Signs of Imbalance	• Joint Pain • Nervous system issues • Sciatica

Key Emotional and Behavioral Signs of Imbalance	• Difficulty trusting • Fearful • Poor boundaries
Location	The location of this chakra is at the base of the spine between the perineum and the pelvic bone.
Chakra's Body Functions	The Root Chakra's body functions are found in the lower body, including the tailbone, legs and feet.
Element	The element associated with the Root Chakra is Earth. The Earth is our foundation, our ground, and when we can root into the Earth, we are deeply connected to the land and supported.

VIA Character Strengths	When we experience BRAVERY as a character strength, we face our fears, challenges, and difficulties. We stand up for ourselves and others, take risks, and act in spite of the obstacles we may face. A person with the strength of HUMILITY may be competent and accomplished but doesn't brag or seek the spotlight. They like to put other people first and see their own contributions as fitting into the larger picture. A person with the strength of PERSEVERANCE is able to complete what they start, stick to a project and fulfill a goal. Perseverance requires a level of grit and ambition, fueling us to overcome challenges or obstacles that may arise on the journey to our ultimate destination. SELF-REGULATION is the ability to respond from a balanced nervous system, from compassion and trust, vs. from anger or fear. When we are self-regulated, we know how to honor our limits and give ourselves the resources we need to make decisions and take action in a way that is not harmful to ourselves or others.
Color	Red is a vibrant and energizing color that symbolizes vitality, strength, stability, and grounding. The color red signifies a strong connection to the Earth, a sense of stability, and a feeling of being grounded and rooted in one's physical existence. Red also represents the life force energy, courage, and resilience required for survival and self-preservation.

Sanskrit	*Muladhara* translates to "root support" or foundation. Like the nutrient-rich soil that supports the roots of a healthy tree, a healthy Root Chakra supports us in manifesting our dreams. It signifies the importance of establishing a strong and stable foundation for our physical and energetic well-being. It is associated with our connection to the physical world, our sense of stability, and our ability to meet our basic survival needs. It represents the fundamental aspects of our existence, including our sense of safety, security, and rootedness.

Balanced Leadership in the Root Chakra

 F-E-A-R can either mean Forget Everything And Run or Face Everything And Rise, and it's up to you to decide.

– Brandon Beachum, *The Golden Key*

Over the course of this book we have journeyed downward from the Crown Chakra on a path down and in, into ourselves, arriving now at our base and foundation in the Root Chakra. Starting with *thought* in the Crown through the chakra system and now *manifesting* those thoughts, it is here in the Root Chakra that we bring structure to our dreams.

One of the key reasons we chose to go from the top down (as opposed to the more traditional bottom up, as in starting in the Root Chakra and working our way up) is that too often, our motivation to manifest (or bring something into form) arises from fear or a scarcity mentality, or from a reaction to a stressor or whatever is being thrown at us. We buy more stuff because we are convinced that we're not good mothers unless our kids have *this*, or we're not successful unless we have *that*. We take jobs that suck our soul but they pay for the *stuff*, and we convince ourselves we're doing it for our family and (insert your latest fear-based decision-making mental monologue here). Deep breaths – you're not alone.

By focusing on the journey from thought (inspired not by our individual selves but by our connection to Consciousness/Self/Universe) and traveling down the path we've presented in this book, what we manifest stems from trust, connection, and love. It is in knowing we are at peace, in nurturing our roots, and having stable ground and support that we are able to create the world of our dreams.

Manifesting, Money, and Materialism

Being able to manifest from a place of love and trust means knowing we have enough, yet most of us are never taught to know or define exactly how much is enough. Instead, we are fed constant marketing and media messages designed to trigger our fear response with messages like, *"You need to work hard to earn a decent living,"* and *"Keep your nose to the grindstone so you can have enough for retirement," "You've gotta work 60+ hours a week at least to make ends meet,"* or *"How will your kids fare, and watch out, the cost of college is rising fast!"* While it's important to plan for long-term goals such as retirement and saving for our children's education, there is a deep-rooted fear that no matter how much we have, it's never enough, and what we do have may get pulled out from under us at any moment.

Robert Cialdini, a famous psychologist who studied and authored several books on persuasion psychology, lists scarcity as one of the most influential persuasion tools.[1] When you buy an airline ticket and you see in bright red letters, "Only 2 seats left at this price," suddenly there is a belief that there aren't enough seats and you better book fast or else you miss out. Countdown timers for online bookings, giving you "x" minutes to complete important purchases, can feel like someone is breathing down your neck with a stopwatch and you're under the pressure to quickly enter your payment details to make the purchase. You can recognize scarcity tactics in promotions that encourage you to buy something by a certain date, as in an early-bird special, "or else you lose the $250 savings!" triggering your fear of missing out. Turns out scarcity tactics are a highly effective way to persuade consumers to buy.

Really smart people have been hired to master these persuasion techniques, arguably not for our benefit, but solely for increasing profit for whatever company is playing on our fears. How we spend our money is a direct indicator of our values, and with the constant assault of marketing and media messages, we need to be firmly rooted in what's important to us so we don't fall prey to these persuasive sales tactics. We may say that we value something, but do our spending decisions align with those values? Why or why not? How can we put our money into the people and businesses that align with trust and love? The leadership exercises in this chapter will guide you into practical ways to explore this.

Many of the books, courses, and themes around manifesting have to do with abundance, as in financial wealth. While women are still striving for pay equality with their male counterparts, focusing on abundance as material wealth alone misses the mark. When we focus on money as an end in itself, we get swept up in the thinking that we are defined by how much money we have. If instead we focus on money as energy, as a *means to an end* (the "end" being happiness, peace, contentment, or living your purpose), then we move beyond materialism and into manifesting money from where it matters most. Abundance is about more than money; it's about health, happiness, community, connection, and love. Abundance is the fresh air we savor when we walk outside, it's the bouquet of colors in the foods that we cook, it's the joy that we feel when we embrace our loved ones. And when we leave this world and this life, we're not taking our bank accounts with us.

Energy Flows Where Your Attention Goes

You don't need to do any woo-woo magic to manifest. We are constantly manifesting, or putting into form, what we think. Our thoughts create form, and our subconscious mind, as we learned in the Third Eye Chakra chapter, is responsible for 90–95% of our thoughts, constantly manifesting the world around us all the time. We can change the synaptic connections in our brain, rewiring the paths so that we can shift from fear into trust. First, we need to recognize where we're putting our energy, attention, and thoughts. While we're wired to have a negativity bias, one which gave our ancestors an evolutionary gain, it can get us stuck in what's wrong or not working. According to the National Science Foundation, the average person has about 70,000 thoughts per day; of these, about 80% are negative or fear-based, and 95% of them are repetitive.[2]

While we need to acknowledge what's not going right in order to make positive changes, unnecessary focus and obsession on what's going wrong can mean we are manifesting that reality. Energy flows where your attention goes, so be mindful of where you're putting it. Really smart, powerful people like you have a responsibility for how you think as we are co-creating our reality with each thought.

Shifting to an Abundance Mindset

Shifting to an abundance mindset means first recognizing your patterns. As you familiarize yourself with the concepts from Chapter Two and the lessons in the Crown Chakra, you will identify less and less with the voice(s) in your head. You can start to hear them, but not listen to them (i.e., become aware of what they are saying without believing everything they have to say). By first noticing what these voices are saying, you are tapping into deep-rooted belief systems of your subconscious. A daily or even a few times a week automatic writing practice, either first thing in the morning or just before bed, can provide insight into your subconscious. As you observe your thoughts, you will begin to identify the "tracks" of your subconscious (like the tracks of your favorite music album). Then you can begin to ask yourself, "*Is it really so?*" This draws on lessons from Chapter Three and the Third Eye Chakra in asking you to see things as they really are. The voice may be telling you something out of fear, but when you can observe it from a big-picture perspective, you can determine whether it is true and also what you need to support yourself.

Once you've recognized these tracks of your subconscious mind, you can now re-record or generate new tracks for your subconscious. Cultivating a feeling of what you want to experience through visualization, meditation, and focusing on abundance can get you out of the habits you're seeking to break, and the leadership exercises we share a bit later in this chapter offer some practical tools to do this. As we shift into true abundance, we move beyond fear into trust, beyond consumerism into being stewards of our planet; we take responsibility for the world we live in, and manifest the harmonious and beautiful world of our dreams.

Take out your Rootsilience Leadership Map and review your results. Do you have strengths in the Root Chakra? How do they show up for you?

When we are balanced in our Root Chakra, we have a deep sense of belonging, know that we are supported by our community and loved ones, and can make decisions from a place of trust rather than from fear. We firmly believe that no matter what, we will be okay, we will persevere and overcome any obstacle that comes our way. We value the material objects that enable us to thrive, such as our home and our stuff, but we don't allow ourselves to be consumed by or overly attached to our things. We manifest our dreams into reality and set appropriate boundaries to manage our time, energy and availability. We live harmoniously with our planet, recognizing how we can minimize our environmental footprint through our purchasing decisions and behaviors.

When we are imbalanced in our Root Chakra, we feel as if there is no ground beneath us, or that we lack support. We may live in a constant state of fear, always worrying about whether we have enough or are safe. When imbalanced in the Root Chakra, we may give up easily, having trouble manifesting ideas and projects through to their completion. A lack of boundaries and an inability to put structure on our time and availability could mean that we take on too much and have a tendency to miss goals and let others down, furthering our feelings of isolation and lack of belonging. We may erroneously seek belonging by filling up with stuff, making wasteful purchasing decisions with a lack of consideration of our impact on the environment, community and planet.

When there is ease and uninterrupted flow between the Root Chakra and the Sacral Chakra above, there is a strong foundational structure that supports the waves of our creativity. We can surrender to the ebb and flow of life without getting blown away or stretched beyond our limits. We can set down roots and find support in community, friends, partners, and in our relationship with the land that enables us to manifest our creative ideas and inspiration.

Leadership signs of imbalance in the Root Chakra:

- Cowardly, or unwilling to face obstacles or challenges

- Decision-making from fear or "lack of" mentality, vs. trust and abundance

- Difficulty with commitment

- Giving up easily, lack of perseverance

- Hoarding material things, overly attached to stuff

- Inability to set or maintain and meet goals

- Inability to hold down a steady job, home, or provide for basic needs

- Overly rigid boundaries and not allowing anyone in

- Poor boundaries and inability to organize a plan to get things done

- Struggle creating and/or keeping a routine

- Suspicious of others, unable to trust or feel safe and supported

VIA Character Strengths Mapped to the Root Chakra and Associated Overuse and Underuse [3]

VIA Character Strength	UNDERUSE	OPTIMAL	OVERUSE
BRAVERY	Cowardly / Unwilling to Act / Unwilling to Be Vulnerable	Not Shrinking from Threat or Challenge / Facing Fear	Risk Taking / Over-Confidence / Unconcern About Others' Reactions
HUMILITY	Arrogant / Self-Focused	Modesty	Self-Deprecation / Limited Self-Knowledge
PERSEVERANCE	Lazy / Helpless / Giving Up	Persistence / Finishing What One's Started / Overcoming Obstacles	Stubborn / Struggles to Let Go / Fixated
SELF-REGULATION	Self-Indulgent / Emotional Dysregulation / Impulsive / Undisciplined / Unfocused	Self-Control / Disciplined / Managing Impulses / Emotions / Vices	Constricted / Inhibited / Tightly Wound / Obsessive

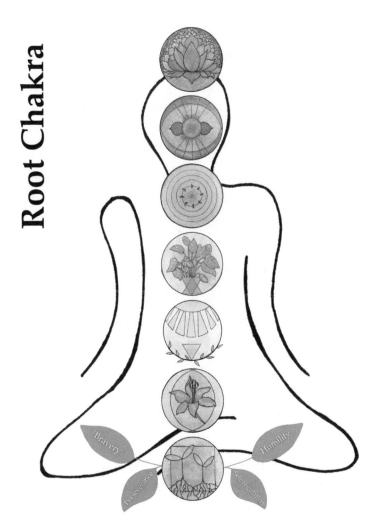

Root Chakra

If your Rootsilience Leadership Map indicates that you have a greater strength in the Root Chakra, you may have a tendency to overuse that strength. And if your map indicates a lesser strength, you may tend toward underuse. If you have neither a greater nor a lesser strength, it's likely you are in optimal use.

A leader with optimal use of BRAVERY is able to face their fears, challenges, and difficulties. They stand up for themselves and others, take risks, and act in spite of the obstacles they may face.

- A greater strength of Bravery might indicate you may take great risks, even at a potential cost to your health and well-being. You may act overconfident, sometimes even foolish, and put yourself and/or others in harm's way.

- A person with a lesser strength of Bravery could be construed as cowardly and unable to act. This person could be afraid to show vulnerability and disinclined to ask for help when needed.

A leader expressing the strength of HUMILITY views themselves as competent and accomplished but doesn't brag or seek the spotlight. They like to put other people first and see their own contributions as fitting into the larger picture.

- A greater strength of Humility could show up as being too self-deprecating, viewing oneself in a limited and unconfident way.

- A person with a lesser strength of Humility can be arrogant, bragging about their talents, self-promoting, and not able to share the spotlight with others.

The strength of PERSEVERANCE, used optimally, allows someone to stick with a project, finishing what they start despite any challenges they might face.

- A greater strength of Perseverance may indicate you may get fixated and stubbornly struggle to let go, even when it's clear the project is not going to materialize.

- A lesser strength of Perseverance could lead to giving up on something, and people with a lesser strength in Perseverance can appear lazy and sometimes helpless.

A leader who effectively utilizes SELF-REGULATION will have the ability to control their reactions to strong emotions when triggered or faced with disappointment. When someone is self-regulated, she knows how to honor her limits and give herself the resources she needs to make decisions and take action.

- A greater strength of Self-Regulation could indicate you may have a tendency to be tightly wound and obsessive, and at times may be inhibited, constricted, and not able to go with the flow.

- A lesser strength of Self-Regulation suggests you may tend toward self-indulgence, acting with impulsivity and a lack of discipline.

Remember that if there are any greater or lesser strengths in this chakra, there may also be a tendency toward the physical/emotional imbalances (expanded upon in the next section) in this chakra or the one above. Your objective is to recognize your unique signs of going out of balance and know how to bring yourself back to center.

Leadership Reflection Exercises to Lead with Presence and Trust

The following exercises provide an opportunity for you to reflect on the lessons the Root Chakra offers. Take some time to go through these at your own pace, and remember to connect with our online community to share your questions, comments, and "Aha" moments.

Exercise One:

Rootsilience Root Chakra Image Meditation and Reflection

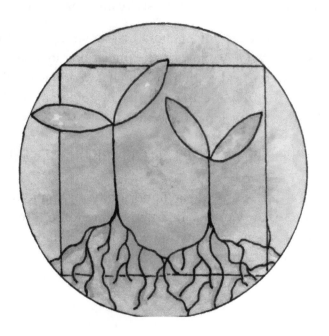

Take at least two minutes to gaze at this image while breathing deeply. Then ask yourself:

1. Do you feel grounded, safe, and secure in your daily life?

2. How can you experience more stability, structure, and belonging in your life?

3. What fears and obstacles do you need to clear in order to expand your Root Chakra and trust yourself and others?

Take some time to write down these responses. Now reflect on what you've written, and read it over a few times.

Exercise Two:

Establishing Healthy Boundaries

Boundaries form the structure upon which you can grow and expand. Without clear and distinct boundaries, we can have a hard time "landing" our big ideas and dreams, or we can get too easily swept up into always supporting (or feeding) others' dreams. Boundaries are about choosing yourself in a way that enables you to live your purpose. Even if your purpose is about supporting and being a foundation for others, boundaries enable you to fill your cup so that you can give and flow freely.

Return to "Exercise Two: Going Beyond Ego and Exploring Values" from the Crown Chakra chapter. When you look at your values and the answers to the above reflection questions, ask yourself:

1. What boundaries do you need to enable you to live aligned with your values?

2. What resources do you need to support living your values?

You can recreate your values table to look like this (an example is included on the next page):

Value / What's Important to Me	How am I living aligned with this Value?	What boundary do I need to put in place / strengthen to live this Value?	What resource do I need to support me in living aligned with this Value?
EXAMPLE			
Accountability	I always do what I say I'm going to do, going above and beyond and I don't let others down.	Boundaries on my time and when I'm available and how I can be reached so I can be accountable but not exhausted and overwhelmed, having to constantly be checking messages.	I need to ask more questions to clearly understand when something is due by rather than setting unnecessary deadlines for myself.
Family	I do everything for my family, they are my pride and joy and it's important for me to create special memories for my family.	While I love my family, I also need time to recharge. I need to set boundaries with my family on my own personal alone time.	I can speak to my partner about coordinating a few times a month so I can have space to do something for myself.

Keep coming back to this table and print it out somewhere you can see it so you can be reminded of ways to set and maintain healthy boundaries along with ways you can feel supported and resourced.

Exercise Three:

Shifting Your Money Mindset

We often don't know what we think about our beliefs around money until we take a closer look at our subconscious beliefs about it. Just like exploring and knowing our values helps us make decisions aligned with them, we can now shift our attention to money and notice what beliefs are limiting or expansive, and how we can shift to an abundance mindset.

Step 1: Take a look at the statements below. These are "money messages" or "money scripts,"[4] – beliefs that we may hold or have been taught around money. Say each one to yourself or out loud two times as you breathe deeply. Make a note of which ones you sense are true for you. Don't jump into judging some of your beliefs as "good" or "bad;" for now, just notice and write down what resonates.

- People only want or love me for my money.
- More money will make things better.
- Money is bad.
- I don't deserve money.
- I deserve to spend money.
- There will never be enough money.
- There will always be enough money.
- Money is unimportant.
- Money is confusing, I don't understand it.
- Money will give my life meaning.
- You don't know the value of money.
- It's not nice (or necessary) to talk about money.
- You must protect your money.
- Live within your means.
- I owe it to the world to give back.

- Time is money.
- Be grateful for what I have.
- Money is filthy.
- I could be earning/charging more.
- Don't speak about money to others.
- They have a lot of money, they are successful.
- It's not okay to spend money on myself.

Step 2: Respond to the following questions in your journal:

1. My views on money are …
2. My family's story about money is …
3. I feel guilty when I spend my money on …
4. I feel good when I spend my money on …
5. If I had more money, I'd spend it on …
6. When I say, "I don't have money for something," what I really mean is …
7. When I really want something that's out of my budget, I handle it by …
8. My budgeting process is …
9. Am I working to live or living to work?
10. How can my money values support living in harmony with the planet?

These questions are pretty profound and once you've had a chance to reflect deeply on your money messages, you can start to identify which patterns are and are not aligned with your values. You can decide what kind of relationship you want to have with money. Additional resources around money mindset are provided in the Appendix.

Exercise Four:
Effective Delegation

Being a successful leader depends on your ability to manage and delegate effectively. At some point, you will simply not be able to do everything by yourself, nor should you have to. This exercise is designed to help you identify what you could delegate and how to manage that delegation effectively.

Think of something you know you shouldn't be doing and could use some help with. A good example is something that takes a lot of your time and energy and either isn't aligned with your values or doesn't bring you joy. It could also be something that follows a set of steps and could be an automated process that someone else could take on for you. If you're not sure about what to delegate, consider going back to "Exercise Three: Balancing Giving and Receiving" in the Heart Chakra chapter, and notice what you feel could be "pruned" from your tree branches, and/or where your roots need more support. Now write out the following:

1. What are you considering delegating?

2. How would delegating this free your time? What could you do with that free time?

3. What is involved to get the delegation set up? (i.e., hiring, training)

4. What resources are you willing to put into the setup? (i.e., time and/ or money)

5. How will you manage this delegation? How often do you need to check in?

6. How will you know that what you delegated is being handled effectively? How can you build trust with whom you delegated to?

7. What will you do if the delegation is not being handled effectively? Is there a time or investment limit?

How the Root Chakra Functions in the Body

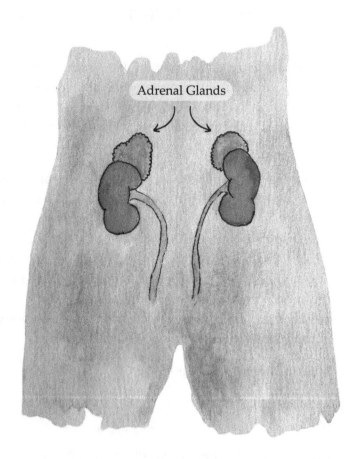

The Root Chakra, also known as the *Muladhara*, translates to "root support" or foundation. It is located at the base of the spine, near the coccyx. It is responsible for grounding us into the physical world, and the energy of this chakra is focused on survival, security, and stability. In the body, the Root Chakra is associated with the adrenal glands, which are located just above the kidneys. The adrenal glands are responsible for the production of adrenaline, cortisol, and other hormones that are essential for our survival.[5] These small, triangular-shaped glands play a vital role in our body's response to stress and help regulate several important bodily functions.

Adrenal Glands in Action

The adrenal glands regulate metabolism, helping us respond to stress and maintain blood pressure.[6] Cortisol, or more specifically, glucocorticoids, plays a crucial role in glucose metabolism.[7] Cortisol helps regulate blood sugar levels, controls insulin release, and promotes the breakdown of fats and proteins to provide energy.[8] [9] When we experience stress, the hypothalamus in the brain sends a signal to the pituitary gland, which then sends a signal to the adrenal glands to release cortisol and adrenaline. These hormones help increase heart rate, respiration, and blood pressure, providing the body with the energy it needs to respond to the stressor.

The adrenal glands also produce aldosterone, a hormone that helps regulate blood pressure.[10] Aldosterone works by promoting the reabsorption of sodium and water in the kidneys, which helps maintain blood volume and blood pressure. The adrenal glands are controlled by a complex system of feedback loops that ensure they produce the right amount of hormones at the right time. The adrenal glands also respond to stress through the sympathetic nervous system, which is part of the autonomic nervous system.[11] When we experience stress, the sympathetic nervous system sends a signal to the adrenal medulla to release adrenaline and noradrenaline, which help prepare the body for a fight/flight/freeze/fawn response.

The Body's Survival Symphony

The fight/flight/freeze/fawn response, also known as the acute stress response, is a complex physiological reaction that occurs in response to a perceived threat or danger. This response is an adaptive survival mechanism that helps animals and humans respond quickly and effectively to dangerous situations. Our pupils dilate, our heart rate increases, our skin can turn pale, all signs that we're ready to fight, run, or freeze in place. These responses are controlled by the sympathetic nervous system, which is responsible for the body's response to stress, helping prepare the body for action. The response is triggered by the amygdala, which is also called "the lizard brain" because it's connected to our primal drives, storing and attaching to deep fearful memories.[12] This is the part of the brain that is responsible for processing emotions and detecting potential threats.

The fight response is the first instinctive response to a perceived threat or danger. It is an aggressive response that is characterized by a surge of energy and adrenaline, and an intense desire to fight or confront the source of the danger. It's triggered in situations when we feel we can defend ourselves or fight our way out of danger.

The flight response, on the other hand, is a defensive response that involves fleeing or running away from the perceived threat or danger. This response is common in situations when we feel we cannot defend ourselves or fight our way out of danger. The flight response is characterized by an increase in heart rate, breathing rate, and adrenaline, which helps us run faster and for longer periods of time.

The freeze response is a physiological reaction to a perceived threat or danger. It is a defensive response that involves becoming completely still and immobile in the hope that the danger will pass. This response is characterized by a decrease in heart rate, breathing rate, and muscle tension, which helps us become less visible to the perceived threat.[13]

The fawn response is a social adaptation that involves appeasing the perceived threat or danger. This response is common in situations where we perceive the danger to be a social threat, such as in cases of bullying or intimidation. This response is characterized by a desire to please or appease the source of the danger, and may present as ingratiating oneself to the perceived threat in order to avoid harm.[14]

Although the fight/flight/freeze/fawn responses are adaptive survival mechanisms, they can also be maladaptive in some situations. For example, in cases of chronic stress, the constant activation of the fight/flight/freeze/fawn responses can lead to a host of physical health problems.[15] Reminders of the trauma causing the response can lead to flashbacks, intrusive thoughts, nightmares, hyperarousal, insomnia, agitation, irritability, impulsivity, anger, numbing, avoidance, withdrawal, confusion, dissociation, and depression.[16]

Nurturing Roots

One of the primary functions of the Root Chakra is to ground us into the physical world. This chakra is associated with the legs, feet, and spine, and its energy helps us connect to the Earth. The legs and feet are essential for our mobility, and they allow us to move around in the physical world. When the Root Chakra is balanced, our legs and feet are strong and healthy, and we feel confident and secure in our physical abilities.

In addition to its physical functions, the Root Chakra also plays a significant role in our emotional and spiritual well-being. This chakra is associated with our sense of belonging, and it helps us connect to our tribe, family, and community. When the Root Chakra is balanced, we feel connected and supported, and we have a sense of purpose and belonging. However, if the Root Chakra is imbalanced, we may feel disconnected and alone, and we may struggle to find our place in the world.

Physical signs associated with an imbalance in the Root Chakra may include:

- Bone injuries

- Constipation

- Feeling ungrounded

- Fight/flight/freeze/fawn responses

- Hemorrhoids

- Joint pain

- Muscle fatigue

- Out-of-balance nervous system, anxiety, stress, racing thoughts, panic

- Sciatica

Healing Foods for the Root Chakra to Support the Nervous System

One way to support the Root Chakra is through a balanced and nourishing diet that includes foods that promote grounding, stability, and physical health. Root vegetables are the most obvious choice when it comes to supporting the Root Chakra. These vegetables are literally rooted in the ground, and their earthy flavor and grounding properties make them a perfect choice for balancing the Root Chakra. Some examples of root vegetables include carrots, beets, turnips, parsnips, and sweet potatoes. These vegetables are rich in fiber, vitamins, and minerals that support overall health, and their grounding properties can help promote a sense of stability and rootedness.

Protein is an essential nutrient that is crucial for building and repairing tissues in the body. Eating protein-rich foods can help promote physical health and provide a sense of grounding and stability. Some examples of protein-rich foods that can support the Root Chakra include meat, fish, poultry, and beans. These foods are rich in amino acids, which are the building blocks of protein and can help promote physical strength and endurance.[17]

Try out some of these foods to support your Root Chakra, bringing this energy center into balance.

- Beans
- Beets
- Carrots
- Casava
- Daikon
- Fennel
- Grass-fed animal protein (beef, buffalo, chicken, lamb, ostrich, pork, turkey, veal, venison)
- Kohlrabi
- Parsnips
- Radish
- Rutabaga
- Sweet potato
- Taro
- Yam

Reflection:

1. What foods ground you?
2. What foods help you feel you're nourishing yourself?
3. What foods create a sense of safety for you?
4. What foods do you enjoy planting and growing?

Herbs for the Root Chakra

Herbs can help support the Root Chakra and promote a sense of grounding and stability.

{For any of these suggestions, please check with your doctor or healthcare practitioner to see if there are any contraindications for your health and any conditions you may have.}

ASHWAGANDHA (*Withania somnifera*)

An adaptogenic herb commonly used to help balance the Root Chakra and the adrenals. It is believed to have calming and grounding properties that can help reduce stress and anxiety.[18] It is also helpful for the slow and steady process of establishing new patterns and routines (especially health-promoting ones). Do not combine Ashwagandha with thyroid medications.

BURDOCK (*Arctium lappa*)

Known as the popular vegetable gobo in Japanese cooking, or a noxious weed that spreads by leaving sneaky Velcro "burrs" in your hair on Autumn hikes, Burdock is the quintessential earthy, nourishing, and grounding medicine and food. The medicine comes from its long stout taproot, buried deep in the earth, and it offers gentle antioxidant and anti-inflammatory support while supplying gut nourishing starches.[19] Simmer it in water to create a broth and add miso paste after removing it from the heat.

HAVAN SAMAGRI

A mixture of various dried herbs, Havan Samagri roots and leaves have been used for centuries for their cleansing, purification, and grounding properties. The medicinal smoke when the herbs are burned has been shown to reduce airborne bacteria by 94%.[20] Many cultures have burned aromatic herbs to cleanse physical and spiritual impurities from the space and bring about a deeper emotional presence. In the Celtic isles, this ancient practice is called "saining," and North American indigenous people call it "smudging."

TULSI (also known as HOLY BASIL) (*Ocimum sanctum Linn.*)

Tulsi can be used to help the body cope with various stressors – like emotional stress, an infection, or other medical conditions.[21]

Try out some of the recipes that follow to support your Root Chakra, bringing this powerful energy center into balance.

Root Chakra Recipes

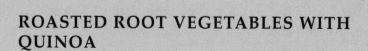

ROASTED ROOT VEGETABLES WITH QUINOA

Serves Four

Ingredients:

2 cups mixed root vegetables (such as carrots, beets, turnips, and sweet potatoes)

2 Tbsp olive oil

1 tsp ground cumin

½ tsp ground coriander

½ tsp smoked paprika

Salt and pepper, to taste

1 cup quinoa

2 cups water or vegetable broth

¼ cup chopped fresh parsley

Preparation:

1. Preheat the oven to 400°F.

2. Peel and chop the root vegetables into bite-sized pieces.

3. In a large bowl, toss the chopped vegetables with olive oil, cumin, coriander, smoked paprika, salt, and pepper.

4. Spread the seasoned vegetables in a single layer on a baking sheet and roast for 25–30 minutes or until tender and golden brown.

5. While the vegetables are roasting, rinse the quinoa and add it to a medium saucepan with water or vegetable broth. Bring to a boil, reduce the heat, cover, and simmer for 15–20 minutes, or until the quinoa is tender and the liquid is absorbed.

6. Fluff the quinoa with a fork and stir in the chopped parsley.

7. Serve the roasted root vegetables on a bed of quinoa and garnish with additional parsley, if desired.

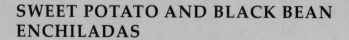

SWEET POTATO AND BLACK BEAN ENCHILADAS

Serves Four

Ingredients:

2 large sweet potatoes, peeled and cubed

1 Tbsp olive oil

1 small onion, diced

1 red bell pepper, diced

2 cloves garlic, minced

1 tsp ground cumin

1 tsp smoked paprika

¼ tsp cayenne pepper (optional)

Salt and pepper, to taste

1 can black beans, drained and rinsed

½ cup chopped fresh cilantro, divided

1 cup enchilada sauce

8 corn tortillas

1 cup shredded cheddar cheese

Preparation:

1. Preheat the oven to 375°F.

2. Place the cubed sweet potatoes in a large pot of boiling water and cook for 10–12 minutes or until tender. Drain and set aside.

3. In a large skillet, heat the olive oil over medium heat.

4. Add the onion and red bell pepper and cook for 5–7 minutes or until softened.

5. Add the garlic, cumin, smoked paprika, cayenne pepper (if using), salt, and pepper to the skillet and cook for an additional minute.

6. Add the black beans and half of the chopped cilantro to the skillet and stir to combine.

7. Spread ¼ cup of the enchilada sauce in the bottom of a 9x13 inch baking dish.

8. Place a tortilla on a flat surface and spoon ¼ cup of the sweet potato mixture and ¼ cup of the black bean mixture down the center of the tortilla.

9. Roll the tortilla up and place it seam-side down in the baking dish. Repeat with the remaining tortillas and filling.

10. Pour the remaining enchilada sauce over the top of the rolled tortillas.

11. Sprinkle the shredded cheddar cheese over the top.

12. Bake for 20–25 minutes or until the cheese is melted and bubbly.

13. Garnish with the remaining chopped cilantro and serve hot.

ROOT VEGETABLE AND LENTIL STEW

Serves Four

Ingredients:

1 cup dried green or brown lentils, rinsed and drained

4 cups vegetable broth or water

2 Tbsp olive oil

1 onion, chopped

2 cloves garlic, minced

2 carrots, peeled and diced

2 parsnips, peeled and diced

2 sweet potatoes, peeled and diced

2 medium-sized beets, peeled and diced

1 turnip, peeled and diced

1 tsp ground cumin

1 tsp ground coriander

½ tsp smoked paprika

Salt and black pepper to taste

Fresh parsley or cilantro for garnish

Preparation:

1. In a large pot, combine the lentils and vegetable broth (or water). Bring to a boil, then reduce the heat to a simmer. Cook for about 20–25 minutes, or until the lentils are tender but not mushy. Drain any excess liquid and set the cooked lentils aside.

2. In the same pot, heat the olive oil over medium heat. Add the chopped onion and garlic, and sauté until they become translucent and fragrant, about 2–3 minutes.

3. Add the diced carrots, parsnips, sweet potatoes, beets, and turnip to the pot. Stir to combine with the sautéed onions and garlic.

4. Sprinkle the ground cumin, ground coriander, smoked paprika, salt, and black pepper over the vegetables. Stir well to coat the vegetables with the spices.

5. Pour in enough water or vegetable broth to cover the vegetables. Bring the mixture to a boil, then reduce the heat to a simmer. Cover and cook for about 20–25 minutes, or until the root vegetables are tender.

6. Once the root vegetables are cooked, add the cooked lentils to the pot. Stir everything together and allow it to heat through for a few more minutes.

7. Taste the stew and adjust the seasoning if needed. Garnish with fresh parsley or cilantro before serving.

Mind-Body Integration to Balance the Nervous System

The mind-body integration practice for the Root Chakra embodies the qualities of Bravery, Humility, Perseverance, and Self-Regulation. Supporting practices are available in our online resources (www. rootsilience.com/courses/beyond-the-book) and were filmed on black basalt rock where lava cooled from an ancient volcanic eruption. In this practice, we balance our nervous system with focus on strengthening our parasympathetic or "rest/digest/heal" response. This practice is designed to calm the nervous system, ground into your legs and feet, and feel a strong connection or rootedness with yourself and the Earth.

Embodying Bravery

Spooning the feet: This can be done in a chair or on the ground, and you will need a stainless-steel spoon. Start by breathing into your feet, and see what it's like to bring your attention there. Without judgment, just noticing. Now, bring your left ankle over your right thigh and knee. You can do this seated as shown or in a chair if more accessible. We're going to spoon our feet (*and yes, you'll wash the spoon after, no worries!*). This is a really powerful grounding practice. The metal from the spoon will draw out negative ions from your feet.[21] We are conductors, our whole bodies are energetic conductors and it's important to ground our energy just like we need to ground electricity (*otherwise, boom! explosion!*).

Take your spoon to the sole of your foot (*no socks, please*) and start to make some figure eights, i.e., design little figure eights on each of your toes as you take a couple of breaths in and out of the nose here. INHALE, direct your breath downward, EXHALE, enjoy this mini-foot rub.

We embody Bravery here by grounding our energy system. When we clear the energy from our day-to-day life, often stored in our feet and blocked from grounding by the "rubber coffins" of our shoes (literally blocking us from grounding our energy), we can come back to balance, safety, and trust. It's from here that we can be brave, stepping out of our comfort zone and even doing crazy things like drawing designs on our feet with a spoon! Now switch sides and place your feet on the ground again, and notice what it's like to breathe into your feet now.

Embodying Self-Regulation

Two ways we can access the autonomic nervous system are via breath and touch, signaling to our body that we are safe. Through slowing our breath and using supportive touch, we can slow down our heart rate, and circulate our blood around the belly[23] to digest and rest and restore. We embody Self-Regulation in this chapter with a powerful self-massage combining both of these elements.

You can download a guided practice at www.rootsilience.com/courses/beyond-the-book.

Embodying Perseverance

Straddle pose (upavistha konasana): Bring your legs out in front and separate them as wide as you can sit comfortably. You may need to place small cushions or a rolled-up towel under each knee to keep the lumbar spine long, and/or elevate your sit bones on a blanket or block. Take your hands underneath your sit bones and lift the flesh of each buttock out to the side so you can feel your sit bones on the ground, and that gives a little space to your low back. Now walk your hands in front of you until you feel a stretch in your legs and/or back. Take a pause at this first "edge" and breathe. Set your timer for three to seven minutes (at first, start with three, then build up over time).

This planet gives us everything. INHALE and take a moment to receive and feel your breath down into your legs and into the Earth, and EXHALE, feel yourself rooting down deeper into the ground. INHALE, send awareness down into the legs, feeling your roots nourished, EXHALE, soften the muscles around the bones so there's no tension in the legs; you are fully supported by the ground. You may naturally find there's some space here to walk the hands a bit further forward, extend through the heels or point your toes to the sky, but remember, we're not trying or forcing our reach here. We're allowing and surrendering. So, allow for space, allow deep breath.

Here we explore the quality of Perseverance. As you stay in the pose, there may be some discomfort in the backs of the legs, or there may be some tingling or sensation in the back. If anything is shooting or electric, please come back to a safe edge. See if you can be present with what is, as we start to become more familiar with the sensations in our body without judging or reacting to them. We retrain the parts of our brain that are responsible for emotion and memory.

Now pick a place where you feel some intensity. And if there are a lot of places, just pick one. INHALE and send your breath to that area; you can imagine it or feel it or simply intend your breath to go there. Send this beautiful energy that you're receiving in your roots, this beautiful Mother Earth energy to this place. Now noticing this area of focus, how are the sensations in this area? Does it change with breath? Take three more breaths here. INHALE, drawing your breath down the nose into the throat, chest, belly, and legs. EXHALE, allowing the Earth to hold you, getting heavier and rooting down. Deep breath in, EXHALE, feeling those roots, really supporting, really nourishing you. One more breath, deep INHALE, and EXHALE.

When your timer goes off, SLOWLY start to come out of the straddle. Press your hands into the floor, start to lift your torso, walk your hands in toward your hips. And then take a moment here, feel your spine long. Now slowly bring your hands under your knees and lift your legs up and slowly straighten them in front of you, taking some time to be still, feeling the effects of this pose.

Embodying Humility

Forward fold (uttanasana): With your legs in front of you, slowly start to hinge forward at the hips, allowing the spine to round over the legs. Find that first edge or the first place you feel some intensity (and that may be sitting upright!). Remember you can have your hips elevated here if your low back is rounding, and you can have a rolled-up towel or pillow under the knees to ease the tension in the hamstrings. If you have any herniated disk issues, keep a generous bend in the knees and fold forward a little bit so there's no compression or tension along the spine. Let your arms be relaxed on the ground (or supported by cushions) and flip the palms up.

INHALE, send your breath into your palms. And EXHALE, imagine roots from the backs of your hands and elbows drawing down to the Earth. Here we explore Humility. Being humble and honoring ourselves, honoring this connection that we have, honoring this planet, Humility in recognizing that we don't have to be all things to all people and we don't have to do it all. As you continue with your breath, you may find there's some more space, the connective tissue starts to soften with time with gentle compression. So, if that's the case, allow yourself to fold down further, or simply deepen your breath. Notice if you can enter into conversation with the sensations in your body, rather than judging or even exiling certain sensations or ignoring them. Again, if you feel any burning or shooting or electric pain, definitely back off. But if there's a pulling in the low back or tension in the backs of the knees, or a feeling of really being stretched in a way that's okay, be aware of the sensations in a way that allows you to be equanimous without judgment, without reaction. And send your breath to the tight spots. Allow that conversation to be more compassionate by sending more breaths there. Allow yourself to embody Humility by being with what is, gently reaching toward and bowing down to ourselves and to the planet that gives us everything.

Rootsilience Leadership Map Reflection

1. Do you have greater strengths in the Root Chakra? What about lesser strengths?

2. Do you tend toward over or underuse in any of your greater or lesser character strengths?

3. Do you have physical, emotional, or mental challenges in this chakra?

4. What connections can you make between the physical signs of "dis-ease" (lack of ease), and how that connects to your emotions? To your state of mind? To your behavior?

5. What are the first signs you are out of balance?

6. What can you do to bring yourself back into ease and flow?

   • Character strengths I'm working to optimize include: _____

   • The practices, tools, and foods that bring me back into balance are: _____

7. Reminders to myself to be a Rootsilient Leader: _____

See the Appendix for further readings on the Root Chakra.

Chapter Nine

Integration

Beyond Resilience to Rootsilience

On Roots and Resilience

Trees are not silent sentinels in the forest,
we just can't hear their communication,
and don't understand their language.
If we could learn to listen, we might absorb
strength from their interdependence,
their interconnected web in the soil,
tangled up in mycorrhiza,
water and minerals coursing from fungus to roots,
sugars from leaves to fungi,
roots below mirroring branches above,
always ready in their capacity to change,
to adapt, to learn from experience,
to share wisdom and strength
in a mutualistic relationship.
Be like the tree in the forest,
neither silent nor alone,
and not only resilient,
but swaying with the stresses,
and standing in the calm,
connecting your whole self
and your relationship with others,
to your own interdependent web.
Let your interconnected roots
provide your true strength,
from canopy to leaf, branch to trunk, root to rhizome.

– Scott Edward Anderson

The landscape of health and well-being can be overwhelming, and we are deluged with books, articles, and fads on what to eat or not eat, what special breathing technique can get us on a rocket ship to "nirvana" or what hot new product we need to reach everlasting happiness. Life is a journey that is constantly swaying our pendulum of balance from one end of the spectrum to the other. Rootsilience is what centers us, again and again. The guidance and wisdom in this book provide you a way to decipher the messages of your behavior, body, and mind, and in a way that asks you to continually come back to yourself, your whole self.

Women leaders have been trained to put aside our own needs to address everyone and everything else first. Resilience teaches us to bounce back, but how can we be expected to bounce back to our status quo after a difficult or traumatic experience without roots to ground us? How can we bounce back if we're not rooted and connected to our whole selves to begin with?

Beyond Resilience to Rootsilience means that you recognize your first signs of dis-ease, whether they be in your behavior, physical, emotional, or mental health, and avoid getting stretched beyond your limits in the first place. Rootsilience provides us with new metrics of success that incorporate our overall health and well-being, downtime, sleep, and the importance of joy and happiness.

A Rootsilient World

It's time we evolved beyond the false notion that success comes through the toil of pushing a boulder up the mountain, again and again. Imagine what the world would be like if we all learned to be Rootsilient leaders. What if our leaders made decisions for the greater good and from a place of trust? What if we all felt safe, had enough, and realized our interconnectedness to each other and the web of life? What if we learned to recognize our bodies' signs of dis-ease, the whispers of fatigue, chronic headaches or stomach upsets, and learned how to listen and adapt before those whispers turned into screeching alarms and disease? What if we worked in collaboration with our medical providers to treat not only the symptom but also the cause? What if we built businesses that solve real problems, and we measure our success by the positive impact we make on our planet, community and people? What if?

Imagine a world where the smart, powerful, and incredible women we know:

- ...are balanced in the Crown Chakra and have clarity and meaning in our lives. We are not attached to a particular outcome, praise, or result. We are grateful for the abundance in our lives, not yearning for material things or "more." We have a strong sense of purpose and a connection to that which is greater than us.

- ...are balanced in the Third Eye Chakra and can discern between reality and illusion. We see where we are going, trust and cultivate our intuition, and are balanced in our moods and how we see the world. We have a vision or "North Star" for what guides us so we're able to stay focused on our intention. We are equanimous, observing a situation before automatically reacting, and have an ability to "see" the big picture.

- ...are balanced in the Throat Chakra and can speak authentically and with confidence. Our voice carries a resonance and depth that is heard and felt because we are deeply connected to our truth. We listen and hear clearly and are able to give space to others and to ourselves. We can be comfortable in the pauses, in the spaces between words and conversations, mindfully bringing ourselves back to breath and back to truth.

- ...are balanced in the Heart Chakra, giving generously without expectation, and without overextending or compromising ourselves. We receive openly from others as well as ourselves. We live in joy, full of gratitude for what we receive and all that we offer to the world. We embrace love and cultivate caring relationships without fear of rejection or dismissal. We forgive what we're ready to, healing and returning to wholeness in ourselves and in our heart.

- …are balanced in the Solar Plexus Chakra with a healthy momentum to pursue what we are passionate about. We have the motivation to get up, get out of bed, and seize the day. We recognize when we need rest and replenishment and know how to make time to recharge. We know what we're good at, we embrace our power, and we have a healthy sense of self-esteem that enables us to shine, without seeing ourselves as selfish, better than, or above others. We lead naturally, radiating our inner light, giving us power and support to light up the people and causes we care about.

- …are balanced in the Sacral Chakra, at ease with our emotions, never completely swept away by them, but also not blocking or damming them up, able to express what we feel in a healthy and constructive way. We are disciplined with ourselves in how we eat, exercise, and manage our time, and yet we also give ourselves permission to enjoy what brings us pleasure and joy. We have a clear sense of self and are able to enter into relationships with others (romantic, friends, family, professional) without co-dependency or attachment. We also know how to let go of relationships amicably. When balanced in the Sacral Chakra, we are in tune with our inner child-like wonder, remembering to see and experience things in new and creative ways.

- …are balanced in the Root Chakra, with a deep sense of belonging, know that we are supported by our community and loved ones, and can make decisions from a place of trust rather than from fear. We firmly believe that no matter what, we will be okay, we will persevere and overcome any obstacle that comes our way. We value the material objects that enable us to thrive such as our home and our stuff, but we don't allow ourselves to be consumed by or overly attached to our things. We have the ability to manifest our dreams into reality and set appropriate boundaries to manage our time, energy, and availability. We live harmoniously with our planet, recognizing how we can minimize our environmental footprint through our purchasing decisions and behaviors.

Notice how you feel reading this. Does it light you up? Is there also some skepticism or doubt as well? Ideals and theories don't mean much if they aren't integrated into our day-to-day lives. Knowledge without embodiment is just an idea, and as we've explored the path from thought to form, from the Crown Chakra down to the Root, you know just how important this journey is.

Here are several examples of women who have worked with the Beyond Resilience to Rootsilience framework to bring balance and integration of overall health and well-being into their lives. We can't wait to hear your stories! Please share them in our private Rootsilience community, which you can find in our compendium of online resources at www.rootsilience.com/courses/beyond-the-book.

A Few Inspirational Stories

Carol is a dedicated activist and CEO of a non-profit dedicated to enabling women to succeed in rural and low-income communities. Carol is incredibly disciplined and dedicated to her work. She never misses a deadline and is the "go-to" for getting things done. She knows that her work directly impacts the hundreds of women counting on her and is deeply connected to her purpose. Carol follows a strict diet and regularly fasts as she finds it easy to skip breakfast, "one less thing to do in the mornings," and a few times a year does a longer 14–21-day fast, giving her a sense of "reset," helping her to focus on her health and well-being. Carol, however, suffered from endometriosis and severe monthly menstrual pains.

When Carol participated in our Rootsilience program, she realized that she was constantly over-giving to others, that she had a hard time giving herself permission to enjoy life and lacked boundaries to make time for her personal space and self-care. Carol's Rootsilience Leadership Map showed two of her five VIA greater strengths in the Heart Chakra and lesser strengths in the Sacral Chakra and Root Chakra. Through the leadership exercises and self-inquiry practices in this book, Carol realized that her zealous fasting was actually an avoidance of truly nurturing herself. As she dedicated herself to savoring and enjoying her meals with no tech to distract her while she ate, she found that her endometriosis pains subsided, along with reduced severity in her menstrual cramps. Carol used the exercises in this book to determine where she was overextending herself and draining her energy and created boundaries that enabled her to honor her value of doing mission-driven work while staying centered. Carol shared, *"The biggest takeaway from Rootsilience is that I have to love and nurture myself in order to live the life that I want, which is filled with meaning and purpose."*

Amanda is a senior manager at a Fortune 500 technology firm who is well respected by her colleagues for her dedication and perseverance. Amanda suffers from debilitating migraines and often feels that she cannot speak up in meetings or in the male-dominated workplace. One of her greater strengths, Judgment, is in the Third Eye Chakra, and Amanda realized through her work with the Rootsilience framework that she often overused this strength and would find herself stuck in a repetitive pattern of thinking, usually judging that her colleagues thought little of her and that whatever she had to say at meetings was a "silly question."

Amanda also has lesser strengths in the Crown Chakra and Throat Chakra, and by working to recognize her thoughts and beginning to not identify solely with them, Amanda reflected, *"It taught me a lot about where I put too much energy toward what's not good for me. I never realized that I could choose not to listen to my thoughts or that they were wrong. This revelation has been life-changing for me."* The combination of finding balance in the Crown Chakra, recognizing her thought patterns, and the Throat Chakra exercises around speaking truth enabled Amanda to find confidence and clarity in her life.

Sarah is a social worker and single mother of two teenage girls. She is always on the run with a busy work schedule and has limited time to prepare meals and shop for groceries. She is addicted to sugar and feels she needs the extra boost it provides in order to manage her rushed lifestyle. Her Rootsilience Leadership Map showed a greater strength in the Solar Plexus Chakra with Zest. It provides her with the "get up and go" energy that she needs to deal with her complex schedule, but she often finds herself overusing this strength as she ruminates about her responsibilities when she's trying to relax. She also suffers from feeling there's never enough time to do all that she needs to do. When she's stressed, she reaches for heavy carbs – a large bowl of pasta or ice cream – and tea with several spoonfuls of sugar. Recognizing this pattern through the Rootsilience exercises, Sarah says, "*I stopped ignoring what my body is telling me, both when something is right and when something is wrong. With the Rootsilience framework, I was able to notice the effects of carbs and sugar on my body and how I turned to them when I felt triggered.*" Sarah was able to use her strength of Zest without burning out, understanding when she needs to rest rather than reach for a bowl of ice cream.

Integration Exercises

Take out your journal and use the following prompts for reflection:

1. What does being a Rootsilient leader mean to you?

2. What are your first signs of imbalance, whether at the behavioral, physical or emotional level?

3. What has been your go-to (behavior shift, movement practice, food)?

4. What is working? What isn't working? And how can you adapt?

You started this book by completing your Rootsilience Leadership Map, which helped you identify the connections between your behavior, physical symptoms and emotions. Throughout each chapter, as you moved through the chakra system from the top down, you have been guided to reflect on leadership exercises, food, and movement to support your overall health and well-being. Take a moment to review what balance looks like in each of the chakras we've journeyed through and expand your idea of what is possible. If you've been implementing some of the leadership, movement, and food wisdom provided in this book, consider re-taking your Rootsilience Leadership Map and notice the following:

- What has changed?

- What has stayed the same?

- How can this be a frequent lens you can use to return to yourself, your roots, and to what supports you?

Overall, creating balance in the seven chakras can be a powerful tool for women leaders to support their physical, emotional, and spiritual well-being. By engaging in the practices we've offered in this book to promote balance and alignment in each chakra, you, as a Rootsilient leader, can cultivate a greater sense of inner strength, resilience, and connection to the world around us and lead with greater clarity, confidence, and purpose.

You dear Reader, are a Rootsilient leader. You can continue to cultivate a greater sense of inner strength and connection to the world around you, leading with greater clarity, confidence, and purpose. By continuing to engage in the practices we've offered in this book, you promote balance and alignment in each of your chakras, as well as within your whole self. May the commitment you've made to yourself and your well-being be amplified into your family, friends, network, community and teams.

Let us rise, Beyond Resilience to Rootsilience!

Gratitude

From Rimi and Samantha:

On our journey to write this book, each step brought us exactly where we were meant to be. We faced the shadows, obstacles, and experiences that we needed to have in order to live and breathe our book and unleash our authentic and unbound selves. We are deeply grateful for the journey that brought us here, along with the incredible people on our path who made this book possible.

For the Journey

Having led successful online courses teaching this framework, we received powerful feedback on how this work was transformational and potent, sparking us to pursue writing a book to codify and share our wisdom.

We thought all we needed to do was get the transcripts of our workshops cleaned up, write the intro and ending and *voila*: We have our book!

It seemed simple enough and with the confidence (and naivete) of first-time authors, we started 2022 with a perfect plan to write our book. We committed to writing our book in four and a half months, two weeks per chapter to write the chapters of our book. What could go wrong?

As we dove into writing the Crown Chakra chapter, which in part focuses on brain health, Samantha emerged from a bout of COVID-induced brain fog and shared: *"It felt like a damp wool blanket was covering my head and I couldn't see or breathe. I needed to stop and slow down, and allow my brain to rest and restore."*

As we began the chapter on the Third Eye Chakra (a month later, already "behind schedule"), Samantha had an insightful vision for her future: *"I began to see a new path for my healing. I realized I needed to leave NYC and move into nature."* This move was a pivotal change to align Samantha with her life purpose and journey, but meant more delays in the writing of the book.

Starting to write the Throat Chakra chapter, Rimi was intent on plowing full force ahead and feeling frustrated, panicked, annoyed even, by what seemed like Samantha's inability to keep up with the deadlines we had set. Rimi shared, *"I felt deeply conflicted about how to have this uncomfortable conversation with Samantha. While I wanted to be considerate about her healing journey and massive life transition, I couldn't help but feel like we were never going to get the book done."*

Now over a month and half "behind" on the book, embarking on the writing of the Heart Chakra chapter, Samantha had a concerning heart scan which showed plaque on her arteries. *"I sat with the symbolism of plaque as an indicator of healing; the plaque on my heart representing the scarring over wounded tissue to enable healing, realizing we can't heal without scars."*

Approaching the summer, Rimi had planned to take the month off in a silent retreat to take the reins and get the damn book done! However, upon her arrival, her diary entry reads, *"I arrive broken, heavy with tears I've been unable to shed, a heart that is beyond exhausted after this marathon of giving and holding space for all. I arrive well overdue for true solitude. For time to BE, without pressure, without countless To Dos."*

Faced with burnout, ironically the sign of imbalance in the very chapter we were working on (Solar Plexus Chakra), Rimi embodied the key balancing tools of rest and recharge and did not write a single word of the book. That month off, while initially hard to accept, led us to finally recognize what we had been failing to see: we had boxed ourselves into a self-imposed, rigorous and unrealistic process and timeline that was inhibiting us from writing our book. We found ourselves in the depths of "should" and "ought to," spiraling down into a black hole of all the reasons great authors give up on their books.

Not surprisingly, we were ready to write the Sacral Chakra chapter with themes exploring collaboration and partnership, and in sharing our observations around the book writing process thus far, agreed that there had to be another way. And so, as we entered the final Root Chakra chapter of writing our book, we began the process of unbinding, trusting, finding community and home. And as we explored these themes, we found our magical partners at The Unbound Press.

For the People on Our Path

We are forever thankful for finding Nicola Humber, the founder of The Unbound Press, for her unbound dedication to beaming powerful messages from women authors out into the world. Her encouragement and support were the key that unlocked our ability to finish this book. We are grateful for Jesse Lynn Smart, our editor who meticulously reviewed our manuscript drafts, offering gentle suggestions and redirections. Lynda Mangoro brilliantly captured our vision for the book design, and did it with grace and humor.

We have abundant gratitude for Maeve Mangine (www.maeveelise.com) for her beautiful illustrations throughout this book. It was early on in our writing process that we realized that while the Sanskrit chakra symbols hold a sacredness and purity of the ancient tradition, we needed to create new ones to translate them to our audience of women leaders. Maeve artfully infused our chakra images with a deep understanding from her own Ayurvedic and yoga training.

We are particularly grateful to Alexandra Adler for leading us through powerful reflections to explore our core values and then helped us translate those values into our visual identity, supported by the design work of Hannah Jurist-Schoen.

We asked three colleagues to read the manuscript for medical accuracy, and we are especially grateful to Katherine Elmer (M.S., NB-HWC and Lecturer at the University of Vermont in Clinical Herbalism and Whole Foods Nutrition), Chelsea Shea, Certified Nurse Midwife, and Catherine Willows, RN, BA, FMC-HC, NBC-HWC, for their thorough review and resource suggestions.

In a conversation with Jack Ricchiuto, he cleverly observed: "You can't change consciousness without changing language," and that insight led us to embrace our newly invented word, "Rootsilience." Despite our challenge coaching people to pronounce the word (it rhymes with "resilience"), we're so grateful that Jack guided us to devise a new vocabulary to create a new path for leadership.

A heartfelt tribute goes out to the incredible women who have embarked on the transformative journey of our Rootsilience programs. Their courage, vulnerability, and willingness to open their hearts and minds have reshaped the landscape of our understanding of women and leadership. Through their shared stories and shared growth, they have not only enriched their own lives but also inspired a profound shift in the way we perceive strength, resilience, and courage. Their voices have expressed wisdom that will forever remain a part of the fabric of our program. With immeasurable gratitude, we honor each of them for their tenacity, vulnerability, and the indelible mark they've left on us.

Gratitude from Samantha:

In my early 50s, after a long and successful career in philanthropic advising, prompted by significant health challenges, I decided to take an enormous leap of faith to go back to school to become a Functional Medicine Health Coach at the Functional Medicine Coaching Academy (FMCA). It was daunting to start over again with books and aggressive deadlines and exams, but it was the best decision of my life.

Since then, I've become a National Board Certified Health and Wellness Coach (NBC-HWC), ReCODE 2.0 certified (to prevent and reverse Alzheimer's Disease), certified as a Qoya Inspired Movement teacher, and received my SHE RECOVERS Coach Designation. My passion is motivating and empowering change by providing practical tools to help women leaders cultivate purpose and vision while connecting to their whole selves and to that which restores balance by focusing on mind-body lifestyle practices– such as food and nutrition, joyful movement, restorative sleep, and stress relief.

It's been an incredibly rewarding journey, and I have many people to thank who have supported me along the way.

My Functional Medicine Coaching Academy cohort of colleagues, notably Autumn Brown Ellis, Nicole Gleason, Amy Clakley-Hadden, Missy Haynes, Stephani Sheehy, Nancy Stocks, and Erin Monahan Stauffer lifted me up when I was burned out from my studies and are always on the other end of a text with answers to questions and support. Gratitude abounds for the team at Apollo Health who work so hard to bring awareness to Alzheimer's Disease prevention – Christine Coward, Valerie Driscoll, Julie Gregory, Lance Kelly, and the entire ReCODE medical and coaching team that I'm fortunate to collaborate with. To Rochelle Schieck, founder of Qoya Inspired Movement, and my Qoya dance sisters, Jessi Fiske, Katie Kempthorne, Alison Love, Jenna Klink, Alex Mosness, and Krissy Shields, I love you so, and may we always remember that we are wise, wild, and free. And, to Dawn Nichols and Taryn Strong, co-founders of SHE RECOVERS, I'm so thankful that you created a place where I found community as I navigated my own recovery journey and now uplift others in their quest for freedom.

To my husband, Scott Edward Anderson, you have been a rock and anchor, and your presence has been an inspirational light behind the creation of this book. Your unwavering support and abundant love have illuminated every step. Your thoughtful insights and inquiries have not only shaped the words on these pages but have also enriched our writing experience in ways beyond measure. As a published author, your own artistic path has mirrored both the triumphs and the challenges that writing entails. When I asked you to write a poem to include in the final Integration chapter, you shared a beautiful piece that came from your heart to mine, and for that I am so grateful. During moments when I found myself facing obstacles, you offered encouragement and precious advice that propelled me forward. Your love, unwavering belief in me, and enduring patience are my everything.

My six children – Jasper, Max, Erica, Elizabeth, Walker, and Sasha - a blended family that I've created with Scott combining three of my own and three of his – continue to be my inspiration and motivation. Their inquisitiveness, unyielding encouragement, and optimism have provided the foundation of my inspiration and determination throughout this transformative writing odyssey. It is my hope that this book will not only ignite the minds of our readers, but also nurture the seeds of forthcoming leadership. For the next generation of leaders, I wish that the wisdom within these pages serves as a reminder to remain grounded, rooted, and attuned to the authentic essence of who we are.

At last, I thank my dear friend, colleague, and co-author Rimi Chakraborty. After our first meeting in 2019, we knew we had to create something together. We didn't know it would turn into Rootsilience, or even this book, but we intuited that we shared a special connection. Our collaboration has been a symphony of shared ideas, mutual understanding, and boundless inspiration. Through countless brainstorming sessions, late-night edits, and moments of writer's block turned triumph, Rimi, your unwavering support and insightful perspective have been the cornerstone of our work together. Our words have danced together on the pages, forming a tapestry of thought and emotion that neither of us could have woven alone. Rimi, our friendship has illuminated this path, making every word written a joy and every challenge conquered with a celebration. With profound appreciation, I look forward to the chapters yet to be written and the stories waiting to be told, side by side.

Gratitude from Rimi:

It is as if every step in my life thus far has uniquely prepared me to share the lessons within these pages. It was in 2015 when I made the critical decision that would alter the course of my life and forever shift my definition of success and well-being. When I left behind a stable job and "successful" career in Boston, MA to co-found Minuvida Lodge and Learning Center along with my husband, in the Azores, we decided to run Minuvida based on "triple bottom line" values that focus on prosperity, people, and the planet. Our place of business is also our home and I developed metrics of success that enabled me to thrive personally and professionally. It was from the Minuvida Yoga Studio I started teaching regular classes, bringing together guests and local residents in a shared community of movement, breathing and exploration. It was in hosting nearly fifty international yoga and leadership retreats that I met world-class facilitators and teachers, and experienced firsthand the transformative power of intentional retreats. There have been many supporting friends, teachers and mentors and I'd like to take a moment to thank them here.

To Ana Forrest – thank you for introducing me to the concept that "emotional gunk" gets stuck in the body. Your Foundational Teacher Training set me on the path to teach and forever connected me to my Wiser Self and how to weave Spirit and Ceremony into my teachings.

To Mandy Brinkley – my teacher, mentor and friend. You weren't afraid to tell me just how badly I needed Yin and introduced me to techniques, concepts and ideas that are now foundational to my practice and teachings. Your dedication is a fountain of inspiration, support and guidance. And you were the catalyst for Samantha and I to meet!

To Marilynn Mendell – thank you for encouraging me to embrace the "bigness" of who I am and telling me what I needed to hear when I needed to hear it. Your mentoring enabled major positive shifts along my path.

To my dedicated local yoga students including: Filipa Castro, Joana Borges Coutinho, Paula Furtado, Plamena Gogovska, Berta Custodio Grave, Bettina Reifferscheid, Seth Reino, thank you for your dedication to the practice and to your own evolution. Your willingness to show up and experiment with me in the many practices that led to those within this book have amplified these teachings.

To my friends and fellow coaches who have inspired me along my path:

Gena Pinheiro, my "soul sister" (although I know I'm not your only!), I love how we've signed up for the "same life curriculum" and that we've been able to share and support each other so deeply in our journeys.

Juliet Hahn, thank you for enabling me to tell my story! I am convinced it was fate (and God) that brought us together. You held space for me in the most profound and meaningful way, supporting me to share many of the gems that have come through in this book.

Erin Riley, thank you for your guidance and support in coaching me to bring to fruition many of the great ideas that shaped this book.

To my husband, João Ferreira: With each step of this incredible journey, you've been my anchor and my wind, propelling me forward with your love and encouragement. You've been our "unofficial editor", our "unofficial graphic designer", my "unofficial coach and consultant (insultant)" and played more roles in supporting me and this book than I can list here. You offered and held space for me in times of challenge, and have helped me celebrate the big and small moments along the way. Your belief in me is one of my greatest treasures, and I offer my deepest gratitude.

To my "guides and spirit team": Thank you for always supporting me to be the most effective channel for this wisdom and teaching to flow through me. May I always be of service, for the highest good.

To my family: writing this book and having the courage to share my stories has deepened my gratitude for your love, support, and understanding. I am deeply grateful for all the experiences that have shaped me into who I am today, and for our continued connection, powerful relationship, and shared healing journeys.

To my remarkable co-author, mentor and dear friend Samantha Anderson: in the journey of this collaboration, your role and support have been nothing short of transformative. From weekly check-in calls with oracle cards and our innumerable collaboration "retreats" both online and in person between New York and the Azores, when we come together, magic just happens. Your ability to feel wisdom and trust knowledge in your body is an inspiration. I am grateful our paths came together for not only friendship but also for co-creating this work and amplifying the embodied wisdom and shared values we live by.

Next Steps On Your Rootsilient Path

Dear Reader,

We trust this journey has been a meaningful one, and we want to stay in touch! Here are some additional ways you can stay connected and bring Rootsilience to your community.

- Please continue to work on the lessons of this book by accessing the free supplemental book resources and our online community at https://www.rootsilience.com/courses/beyond-the-book and use the hashtag #IAmRootsilient when posting on social media about what you're learning.

- Receive a free gift when you review Beyond Resilience to Rootsilience on Amazon, Goodreads or wherever you purchase your books. Just send a link to your published review to info@rootsilience.com and allow 5-7 business days to receive your free gift.

- Start a book club with your community! Experience the power of being led through the exercises, movement and experimenting with the recipes in a cohort of leaders along this journey with you.

- Sign up for our mailing list on our website and follow us on our social links below to receive tips and ways to implement the practices, and to be the first to know about upcoming courses, workshops, and retreats.

Rootsilience on Social Media

🌐 info@rootsilience.com | www.rootsilience.com

📷 Rootsilience on Instagram: https://www.instagram.com/rootsilience/

f Rootsilience on Facebook: https://www.facebook.com/rootsilience/

in Rootsilience on LinkedIn: www.linkedin.com/company/rootsilience/

Appendix

Resources for Your Rootsilient Path
Rootsilience Leadership Map

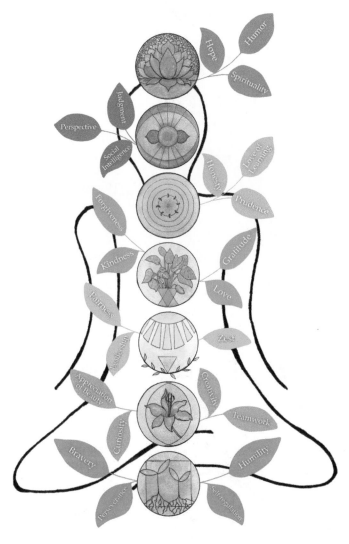

This image maps the VIA Character Strengths to the chakras, and the VIA Character Strengths are used with permission by the VIA Institute on Character.

Key Physical Signs of Imbalance

Crown
Addictions
Seasonal Affective Disorder
Sleep Disorders and Insomnia

Third Eye
Alzheimer's Disease and Dementia
Migraines
Vision impairment

Throat
Neck, jaw pain and difficulty
    hearing
Thyroid imbalance or disease
Sinus infections

Heart
Breast cancer
Heart disease
Lung or respiratory disease

Solar Plexus
Diabetes
Gastrointestinal issues
Heartburn

Sacral
Bladder or urinary challenges
Chronic back, hip or pelvic pain or
    tightness
Reproductive challenges

Root
Joint Pain
Nervous system issues
Sciatica

Key Emotional and Behavioral Signs of Imbalance

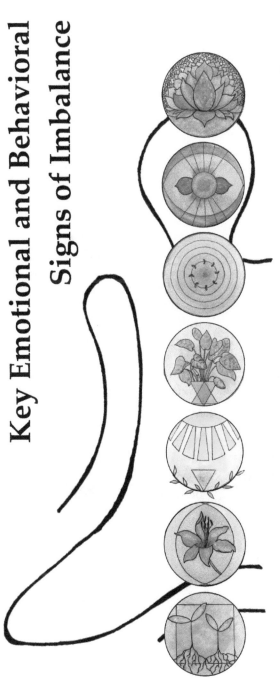

Crown
Alienated
Depressed
Lack of Purpose

Third Eye
Anxiety
Difficulty concentrating
Paranoia

Throat
Dishonesty
Inability to express
Overly talkative

Heart
Stuck in grief or sadness
Unable to forgive
Vindictive

Solar Plexus
Burned out
Lack of self-worth
Low self-esteem
Obsessiveness

Sacral
Difficulty feeling joy and sensuality
Emotional instability
Lack of creativity

Root
Difficulty trusting
Fearful
Poor boundaries

VIA Character Strengths and their Underuse/Optimal/ Overuse Mapped to the Seven Chakras

Chakra	Character Strength	Underuse	Optimal	Overuse
CROWN	Spirituality	Lack of Purpose	Connected to Meaning	Preachy / Holier Than Thou
	Homor	Overly Serious, Stilted	Playfulness / Lighthearted	Tasteless, Socially Inappropriate
	Hope	Negative, Pessimistic	Expecting the Best in the Future	Head in the Clouds / Unrealistic
THIRD EYE	Perspective	Shallow, Superficial	Wisdom / Taking Big Picture View	Overbearing / Arrogant
	Social Intelligence	Socially Naive, Emotionally Insensitive	Aware of Motives and Feelings of Self and Others	Overly Analytical / Overly Sensitive
	Judgment	Illogical, Close Minded	Critical Thinking on All Sides	Narrow Minded / Cynical / Rigid / Indecisive

THROAT 	Honesty	Inauthentic / Lacking Integrity	True to Oneself / Authenticity	Self-Righteous / Rude
	Prudence	Reckless / Thrill Seeking	Careful / Cautious	Rigid / Passive / Prudish
	Love of Learning	Smug / Uninterested	Mastering New Skills	Know It All / Elitist
HEART	Love	Afraid to Care / Isolating	Genuine Warmth / Close Relationships	Sugary Sweet / Emotional Overkill
	Gratitude	Entitled / Unappreciative / Self-Absorbed	Thankful for Good / Feeling Blessed	Contrived / Ingratiation / Profuse
	Forgiveness	Vengeful / Merciless / Easily Triggered	Mercy / Accepting Shortcomings / Letting Go of Hurt	Permissive / Doormat / Too Soft
	Kindness	Indifferent / Selfish / Uncaring to Self / Mean-Spirited	Nurturance / Compassion / Doing for Others	Intrusive / Overly Focused on Others

SOLAR	Zest	Passive / Sedentary / Tired	Vitality / Vigor / Energy / Enthusiasm for Life	Hyper / Overactive / Annoying
	Leadership	Follower / Compliant / Mousy / Passive	Positively Influencing Others / Organizing Group Activities	Bossy/ Controlling / Authoritarian
	Fairness	Prejudice / Partisanship / Complacency	Not Allowing Feelings to Bias Decisions / Adhering to Principles of Justice	Detached / Indecisive on Justice Issues / Uncaring

SACRAL 	Creativity	Conforming / Plain / Dull / Unimaginative	Original / Adaptive / Seeing Things in New and Different Ways	Eccentric / Odd / Scattered
	Teamwork	Self-Serving / Individualistic / Going at It Alone	Social Responsibility / Citizenship / Loyalty / Group Effort	Dependent / Lost in Groupthink / Blind Obedience
	Curiosity	Bored / Uninterested / Apathetic / Self-Involved	Interest / Novelty-Seeking / Exploration / Openness to Experience	Nosy / Intrusive / Self-Serving
	Appreciation of Beauty	Oblivious / Stuck in Autopilot / Mindlessness	Awe and Wonder for Beauty / Admiration for Skill and Moral Greatness	Snobbery / Perfectionist / Intolerant / Unrelenting Standards

ROOT				
	Bravery	Cowardly / Unable to Act / Unwilling to Be Vulnerable	Not Shrinking from Threat or Challenge / Facing Fears	Reckless Risk-Taking / Overconfident / Unconcerned of Others' Reactions
	Self-Regulation	Self-Indulgent / Emotional Dysregulation / Impulsive / Undisciplined / Unfocused	Self-Control / Disciplined / Healthy Management of Emotions and Impulses	Constricted / Inhibited / Tightly Wound / Obsessive
	Perseverance	Lazy / Helpless / Giving Up	Persistence / Finishing What One Starts / Overcoming Obstacles	Stubborn / Struggles to Let Go / Fixated
	Humility	Arrogant / Self-Focused	Modesty	Self-Deprecation / Limited Self Knowledge

Beyond the Book

To view the resources that we've shared in this book, please visit our website: https://www.rootsilience.com/courses/beyond-the-book

Click on "Register Now."

After entering your email, you will be directed to the page to access the materials, and you will also receive an email with your log-in information and instructions on how to access the materials.

We've curated a selection of resources for your continued learning and exploration of the topics covered in this book. Below is a compilation aimed at aiding your deeper exploration and self-education on the subjects we've discussed.

About the Chakras

Dale, Cyndi. *Llewellyn's Complete Book of Chakras: Your Definitive Source of Energy Center Knowledge for Health, Happiness, and Spiritual Evolution.* Llewellyn Worldwide, Ltd, 2016.

Hoopen, Peter Ten, and Alfons Trompenaars. *The Enlightened Leader: An Introduction to the Chakras of Leadership.* Jossey-Bass, 2009.

Jago, Erica, and Kamp Der. *Angelus: Experiential Chakra Workbook for Practitioners and Teachers.* Erica Jago and Roos van Der Kamp, 2019.

Judith, Anodea, and Lion Goodman. *Creating on Purpose: The Spiritual Technology of Manifesting through the Chakras.* Sounds True, 2012.

Judith, Anodea. *Eastern Body, Western Mind.* Potter/TenSpeed/Harmony, 2011.

Judith, Anodea. *Wheels of Life: A User's Guide to the Chakra System.* Llewellyn Publications, 2021.

Perrakis, Athena. *The Ultimate Guide to Chakras: The Beginner's Guide to Balancing, Healing, and Unblocking Your Chakras for Health and Positive Energy*. Fair Winds Press, an Imprint of The Quarto Group, 2018.

About the Chakras and Food

Dale, Cyndi, and Dana Childs. *Chakras, Food, and You: Tap Your Individual Energy System for Health, Healing, and Harmonious Weight*. St. Martin's Essentials, 2021.

Gagné, Steve. *Food Energetics: The Spiritual, Emotional, and Nutritional Power of What We Eat*. Healing Arts Press, 2008.

Minich, Deanna. *Chakra Foods for Optimum Health: A Guide to the Foods That Can Improve Your Energy, Inspire Creative Changes, Open Your Heart, and Heal Body, Mind, and Spirit*. Mango Publishing Group, 2020.

Minich, Deanna. *Whole Detox: A 21-Day Personalized Program to Break through Barriers in Every Area of Your Life*. HarperOne, 2017.

About the Chakras and Mind-Body Practices

Judith, Anodea. *Chakra Yoga*. Éditions Médicis.

Dale, Cyndi, and Richard Wehrman. *The Subtle Body: An Encyclopedia of Your Energetic Anatomy*. Sounds True, 2009.

Long, Ray, and Chris Macivor. *The Key Muscles of Yoga: Your Guide to Functional Anatomy in Yoga*. Bandha Yoga Publications, 2009.

About Positive Psychology

Niemiec, Ryan M., and Robert E. McGrath. *The Power of Character Strengths: Appreciate and Ignite Your Positive Personality*. VIA Institute on Character, 2019.

Niemiec, Ryan M. *Mindfulness and Character Strengths: A Practical Guide to Flourishing*. Hogrefe Publishing, 2014.

Polly, Shannon, et al. *Character Strengths Matter: How to Live a Full Life.* Positive Psychology News, LLC, 2015.

Tarragona, Margarita. *Positive Identities: Narrative Practices and Positive Psychology.* Positive Acorn: Createspace Independent Publishing Platform, 2013.

About Resilience

Graham, Linda. *Resilience: Powerful Practices for Bouncing Back from Disappointment, Difficulty, and Even Disaster.* New World Library, 2018.

Hanson, Rick, with Forrest Hanson. *Resilient: How to Grow an Unshakable Core of Calm, Strength, and Happiness.* Harmony Books, 2018.

Konnikova, Maria. *"How People Learn to Become Resilient."* The New Yorker, (February 11, 2016).

Zolli, Andrew, and Ann Marie Healy. *Resilience: Why Things Bounce Back.* Simon et Schuster, 2013.

Crown Chakra Resources

Calhoun, Ada. *Why We Can't Sleep: Women's New Midlife Crisis.* Grove Press UK, 2021.

Eknath, Easwaran. *The Bhagavad Gita.* Nilgiri Press, 2019.

Finger, Alan, and Wendy Newton. *Tantra of the Yoga Sutras: Essential Wisdom for Living with Awareness and Grace.* Shambhala, 2018.

Maté, Gabor. *In the Realm of Hungry Ghosts: Close Encounters with Addiction.* Vintage Canada, 2021.

Nichols, Dawn. *She Recovers Everyday: Meditations for Women.* Hazelden Publishing. 2023

Perlmutter, David. *Brain Wash: Detox Your Mind for Clearer Thinking, Deeper Relationships, and Lasting Happiness.* Yellow Kite, 2021.

Roche, Lorin. *The Radiance Sutras: 112 Gateways to The Yoga of Wonder & Delight*. Sounds True, 2014.

Singer, Michael A. *The Untethered Soul: The Journey beyond Yourself*. Noetic Books, Institute of Noetic Sciences, 2013.

Tolle, Eckhart. *The Power of Now: A Guide to Spiritual Enlightenment*. Distributed to the Trade by Publishers Group West, 2004.

Walker, Matthew. *Why We Sleep*. Scribner, 2017

Walsch, Neale Donald, et al. *The Little Soul and the Sun: A Children's Parable*. Hampton Roads, 1998.

Warrington, Ruby. *Sober Curious*. HarperOne, 2019.

Whitaker, Holly Glenn. *Quit like A Woman*. Bloomsbury Publishing PLC, 2020.

Third Eye Chakra Resources

Bredesen, Dale E. *The End of Alzheimer's: The First Program to Prevent and Reverse Cognitive Decline*. Thorndike Press, a Part of Gale, a Cengage Company, 2021.

Bredesen, Dale E. *The End of Alzheimer's Program: The First Protocol to Enhance Cognition and Reverse Decline at Any Age*. Avery, 2022.

Naidoo, Uma. *This Is Your Brain on Food: An Indispensable Guide to the Surprising Foods That Fight Depression, Anxiety, PTSD, OCD, ADHD, and More*. Little, Brown Spark, 2020.

Mosconi, Lisa, *XX Brain: The Groundbreaking Science Empowering Women to Prevent Dementia*. Allen & Unwin, 2021.

Mosconi, Lisa. *Brain Food: The Surprising Science of Eating for Cognitive Power*. Penguin Life, 2019.

Ramsey, Drew. *Eat to Beat Depression and Anxiety: Nourish Your Way to Better Mental Health in Six Weeks*. Harper Wave, an Imprint of HarperCollins Publishers, 2021.

Werner-Gray, Liana. *Anxiety-Free with Food: Natural, Science-Backed Strategies to Relieve Stress and Support Your Mental Health*. Hay House, Inc., 2020.

Throat Chakra Resources

Cain, Susan. *Quiet: The Power of Introverts in a World That Can't Stop Talking*. Broadway Paperbacks, 2013.

Myers, Amy. *The Thyroid Connection: Why You Feel Tired, Brain-Fogged, and Overweight - and How to Get Your Life Back*. Little, Brown Spark, 2021.

Wentz, Izabella. *Hashimoto's Protocol: A 90-Day Plan for REVERSIG Thyroid Symptoms and Getting Your Life Back*. HarperOne, 2017.

Wentz, Izabella. *Hashimoto's Food Pharmacology: Nutrition Protocols and Healing Recipes to Take Charge of Your Thyroid Health*. HarperCollins, 2020.

Markley, Lisa, and Jill Grunewald. *The Essential Thyroid Cookbook: Over 100 Nourishing Recipes for Thriving with Hypothyroidism and Hashimoto's*. Blue Wheel Press, 2017.

Nichols, Wallace J., and Celine Cousteau. *Blue Mind: The Surprising Science That Shows How Being near, in, on, or under Water Can Make You Happier, Healthier, More Connected and Better at What You Do*. Back Bay Books, Little, Brown and Company, 2015.

Romm, Aviva. *The Adrenal Thyroid Revolution*. HarperOne, 2017.

Heart Chakra Resources

Chödrön, Pema. *When Things Fall Apart: Heart Advice for Difficult Times*. Thorsons Classics, 2017.

Fredrickson, Barbara. *Love 2.0: How Our Supreme Emotion Affects Everything We Feel, Think, Do, and Become*. Plume, 2014.

Maté, Gabor, and Daniel Maté. *The Myth of Normal: Trauma, Illness and Healing in a Toxic Culture*. Vintage Canada, 2023.

Menolascino, Mark. *Heart Solution for Women: A Proven Program to Prevent and Reverse Heart Disease*. HarperOne, 2020.

Schwartz, Richard, Ph. D. *No Bad Parts*. Sounds True, 2021.

Steinbaum, Suzanne. *Dr. Suzanne Steinbaum's Heart Book: Every Woman's Guide to a Heart-Healthy Life: Reduce the Effects of Stress, Promote Heart Heath, and Restore the Balance in Your Life*. Avery, 2013.

Van der Kolk Bessel. *The Body Keeps the Score: Brain, Mind and Body in the Healing of Trauma*. Penguin Books, 2015.

Weed, Susun S., et al. *Breast Cancer? Breast Health!: The Wise Woman Way*. Ash Tree Pub., 2020.

Weller, Francis, and Michael Lerner. *The Wild Edge of Sorrow: Rituals of Renewal and the Sacred Work of Grief*. ReadHowYouWant, 2017.

Solution to the Heart Chakra "Nine Dots" Exercise

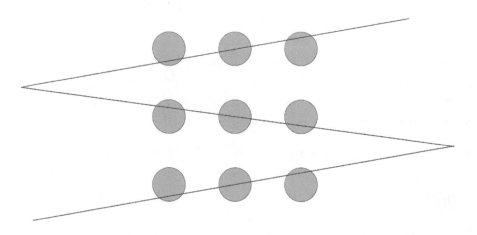

Solar Plexus Resources

Blake, Jenny. *Free Time: Lose the Busywork, Love Your Business*. Swift Press, 2022.

Boushey, Heather. *Finding Time: The Economics of Work-Life Conflict*. Harvard University Press, 2019.

Chemaly, Soraya. *Rage Becomes Her: The Power of Women's Anger*. Atria Books, 2019.

Cole, Will. *The Inflammation Spectrum: Find Your Food Triggers and Reset Your System*. Avery, 2022.

Dalton-Smith, Saundra. *Sacred Rest: Recover Your Life, Renew Your Energy, Restore Your Sanity*. Faith Words, 2019.

Davis, William. *Wheat Belly*. Rodale, 2011.

Hyman, Mark. *The Blood Sugar Solution*. Hodder Headline, 2016.

Nagoski, Emily, and Amelia Nagoski. *Burnout: The Secret to Unlocking the Stress Cycle*. Ballantine Books, 2020.

Rodsky, Eve. *Fair Play: A Game-Changing Solution for When You Have Too Much to Do (and More Life to Live)*. G.P. Putnam's Sons, 2021.

Sacral Chakra Resources

Blankenbaker, Betsy. *Autobiography of an Orgasm*. Betsy Blankenbaker Publisher, 2014.

Bluming, Avrum, and Carol Tavris. *Estrogen Matters: Why Taking Hormones in Menopause Can Improve Women's Well-Being and Lengthen Their Lives-- without Raising the Risk of Breast Cancer*. Little, Brown Spark, 2021.

Caldwell, Christine. *Bodyfulness: Somatic Practices for Presence, Empowerment, and Waking up in This Life*. Shambhala, 2018.

Csikszentmihalyi, Mihaly. *Finding Flow: The Psychology of Engagement with Everyday Life*. Basic Books, 2008.

Estés, Clarissa Pinkola. *Women Who Run with the Wolves: Myths and Stories of the Wild Woman Archetype*. Rider, 2022.

Estés, Clarissa Pinkola. *Joyous Body: Myths and Stories of the Wise Woman Archetype*. Sounds True (Audiobook), 2011.

Emoto, Masaru. *The True Power of Water: Healing and Discovering Ourselves*. Beyond Words Pub., 2005.

Hay, Louise L. *You Can Heal Your Life*. Camden, 2008.

Nelson, Bradley. *The Emotion Code: How to Release Your Trapped Emotions for Abundant Health, Love, and Happiness*. St. Martins Essentials, 2019.

Pope, Alexandra, et al. *Wild Power: Discover the Magic of Your Menstrual Cycle and Awaken the Feminine Path to Power*. Hay House, 2017.

Romm, Aviva.. *Hormone Intelligence: The Complete Guide to Calming Hormone Chaos and Restoring Your Body's Natural Blueprint for Well-Being*. HarperOne, 2022.

Schieck, Rochelle. *Qoya: A Compass for Navigating an Embodied Life That Is Wise, Wild and Free*. Inspire and Move Press, 2016.

Silver, LiYana. *Feminine Genius: The Provocative Path to Waking up and Turning on the Wisdom of Being a Woman*. Sounds True, 2017.

Stover, Sara Avant. *Book of She - Your Heroines Journey into the Heart of Feminine Power*. New World Library, 2015.

Vitti, Alisa. *In the Flo: Unlock Your Hormonal Advantage and Revolutionize Your Life*. HarperOne, 2021.

Root Chakra Resources

Blackie, Sharon. *If Women Rose Rooted a Life-Changing Journey to Authenticity and Belonging*. September Publishing, 2019.

Foor, Daniel. *Ancestral Medicine: Rituals for Personal and Family Healing*. Bear & Company, 2017.

Herman, Judith Lewis. *Trauma and Recovery*. Pandora, 2015.

Levine, Peter A. *Waking the Tiger: Healing Trauma*. Tantor Media, Incorporated, 2016.

Levinson, Kate. *Emotional Currency: A Woman's Guide to Building a Healthy Relationship with Money.* Celestial Arts, 2011.

Lighthorse, Pixie. *Boundaries and Protection: Honoring Self, Honoring Others.* Row House Publishing, 2023.

McMorrow, Erin Yu-Juin. *Grounded: A Fierce, Feminine Guide to Connecting with the Soil and Healing from the Ground Up.* Sounds True, 2021.

Menakem, Resmaa. *My Grandmother's Hands: Racialized Trauma and the Pathway to Mending Our Hearts and Bodies.* Penguin Books.

Piastrelli, Becca. *Root & Ritual: Timeless Ways to Connect to Land, Lineage, Community, and the Self.* Sounds True, 2021.

Twist, L. (2017). *The Soul of Money: Transforming Your Relationship with Money and Life.* W. W. Norton & Company.

Endnotes

Introduction

[1]Kim, Mike. n.d. https://mikekim.com/stay-out-of-the-bubble-biosphere-2-2/

[2]Definition of "Resilience" in Merriam-Webster. 1983. *The Merriam-Webster Dictionary*.

[3]Castrillon, Caroline. 2023. "Why Women Leaders Are Leaving Their Jobs At Record Rates." *Forbes*, May 7, 2023.

[4]"Women in the Workplace 2022." n.d. LeanIn.Org and McKinsey & Company.

[5]Pattani, Aneri. 2021. "Women Now Drink as Much as Men — And Are Prone to Sickness Sooner." KFF Health News. June 10, 2021.

[6]Karaye, Ibraheem M., Nasim Maleki, Norzaihan Hassan, and Ismaeel Yunusa. 2023. "Trends in Alcohol-Related Deaths by Sex in the US, 1999-2020." *JAMA Network Open* 6 (7): e2326346. https://doi.org/10.1001/jamanetworkopen.2023.26346.

[7]Special thanks to Jack Ricchiuto for his contribution in helping us think about using new words to create new awareness and consciousness.

[8]This thesis originates from Dr. Aviva Romm, *Hormone Intelligence: The Complete Guide to Calming Hormone Chaos and Restoring Your Body's Natural Blueprint for Well-Being*. HarperOne, 2021.

Chapter One: Beyond Resilience to Rootsilience

[1]Post, Corinne. 2021. "Research: Adding Women to the C-Suite Changes How Companies Think." Harvard Business Review. September 17, 2021. https://hbr.org/2021/04/research-adding-women-to-the-c-suite-changes-how-companies-think

[2]All in: Female Founders in the US VC Ecosystem | 2021 Pitchbook. pitchbook.com/news/reports/2021-all-in-female-founders-in-the-us-vc-ecosystem.

[3]Berinato, Scott. 2021. "Banks with More Women on Their Boards Commit Less Fraud." Harvard Business Review. April 13, 2021. https://hbr.org/2021/05/banks-with-more-women-on-their-boards-commit-less-fraud?utm_medium=social&utm_source=instagram&utm_campaign=have2haveit

[4]Catalyst. 2023. "Women CEOs of the S&P 500." February 6, 2023. https://www.catalyst.org/research/women-ceos-of-the-sp-500/

[5]Amar, Solomon. 2023. "Why Everyone Wins With More Women In Leadership." Forbes, February 7, 2023. https://www.forbes.com/sites/forbesbusinesscouncil/2023/02/07/why-everyone-wins-with-more-women-in-leadership/?sh=6d0f8e293cdd

[6]U.S. Census Bureau. 2021. "Women Still Have to Work Three Months Longer to Equal What Men Earned in a Year." Census.Gov. October 8, 2021. https://www.census.gov/library/stories/2020/03/equal-pay-day-is-march-31-earliest-since-1996.html

[7]"Black Women's Equal Pay Day — Equal Pay Today." n.d. Equal Pay Today. http://www.equalpaytoday.org/black-womens-equal-pay-day

[8]"Women Still Have to Work Three Months Longer to Equal What Men Earned in a Year." Census.Gov. October 8, 2021. https://www.census.gov/library/stories/2020/03/equal-pay-day-is-march-31-earliest-since-1996.html

[9]DerSarkissian, Carol. 2021. "If COVID-19 Wasn't Bad Enough, It's Also a Sexist Disease." US News & World Report, November 19, 2021. https://health.usnews.com/health-care/for-better/articles/covid-19-impact-on-women

[10]"Women in the Workplace 2022." LeanIn.Org and McKinsey & Company, www.womenintheworkplace.com

[11]"Women's Experiences with Health Care During the COVID-19

Pandemic: Findings from the KFF Women's Health Survey." 2021. KFF Health News April 15, 2021. https://www.kff.org/womens-health-policy/issue-brief/womens-experiences-with-health-care-during-the-covid-19-pandemic-findings-from-the-kff-womens-health-survey/

[12]"Women Have More Active Brains than Men, According to Science." 2020. World Economic Forum. February 6, 2020. https://www.weforum.org/agenda/2017/08/women-have-more-active-brains-than-men-according-to-science/

[13]"Sex Hormones & the Female Brain: A Focus on Mood Disorders." The Institute for Functional Medicine." 2023. https://www.ifm.org/news-insights/sex-hormones-the-female-brain-a-focus-on-mood-disorders/

[14]Nebel, Rebecca A., Neelum T. Aggarwal, Lisa L. Barnes, Aimee Gallagher, Jill M. Goldstein, Kejal Kantarci, Monica P. Mallampalli, et al. 2018. "Understanding the Impact of Sex and Gender in Alzheimer's Disease: A Call to Action." *Alzheimers & Dementia* 14 (9): 1171–83. https://doi.org/10.1016/j.jalz.2018.04.008

[15]Kuehner, Christine. 2017. "Why Is Depression More Common among Women than among Men?" *The Lancet Psychiatry* 4 (2): 146–58. https://doi.org/10.1016/s2215-0366(16)30263-2

[16]Hantsoo, Liisa, and C. Neill Epperson. 2017. "Anxiety Disorders among Women: A Female Lifespan Approach." *Focus* 15 (2): 162–72. https://doi.org/10.1176/appi.focus.20160042

[17]"Women Now Drink as Much as Men — And Are Prone to Sickness Sooner." KFF Health News. June 10, 2021. https://kffhealthnews.org/news/article/women-now-drink-as-much-as-men-and-are-prone-to-sickness-sooner/

[18]Huffington, Arianna. 2022. "Resilience+ Is My Word of the Year." Thrive Global, January 2022. https://thriveglobal.com/stories/arianna-huffington-resilience-plus-word-of-year-2022/

[19]Eisenstein, Charles. *Sacred Economics : Money, Gift, & Society in the Age of Transition*. North Atlantic Books, 2021.

[20]McAlister, Anna R., and T. Bettina Cornwell. *Children's Brand Symbolism Understanding*. Wiley-Blackwell, 2010.

[21]Peterson, Christopher, and Martin E. P. Seligman. 2004. "Character Strengths and Virtues: A Handbook and Classification." *Choice Reviews Online* 42 (01): 42–0624. https://doi.org/10.5860/choice.42-0624

[22]Nummenmaa, Lauri, Enrico Glerean, Riitta Hari, and Jari K. Hietanen. "Bodily Maps of Emotions." *Proceedings of the National Academy of Sciences of the United States of America* 111, no. 2 (December 30, 2013): 646–51. https://doi.org/10.1073/pnas.1321664111.

[23]This image maps the VIA Character Strengths to the chakras, and the VIA Character Strengths are used with permission by the VIA Institute on Character.

Chapter Two: The Crown Chakra – Leading with Purpose and Finding Connection

[1]Easwaran, Eknath. *The Upanishads*. Nilgiri Press, 2007. The Upanishads, the earliest philosophical writings that exist dating back nearly five thousand years from India.

[2]Morgan, Edward. 2018. "Etymology of the Word Alcohol: "Body Eating Spirit." *Prepare for Change* https://prepareforchange.net/2018/04/10/etymology-of-the-word-alcohol-body-eating-spirit

[3]"Alcoholic Beverages Market Size, Share, Trends | Forecast, 2021-2031." n.d. Allied Market Research. https://www.alliedmarketresearch.com/alcoholic-beverages-market

[4]Aicr. "New AICR Breast Cancer Report." *American Institute for Cancer Research*, 20 July 2022, www.aicr.org/news/new-aicr-breast-cancer-report/

[5]"Women Now Drink as Much as Men — And Are Prone to Sickness Sooner." KFF Health News. June 10, 2021. https://kffhealthnews.org/news/article/women-now-drink-as-much-as-men-and-are-prone-to-sickness-sooner/

[6]Pollard, Michael S., Joan S. Tucker, and Harold D. Green. 2020. "Changes in Adult Alcohol Use and Consequences during the COVID-19 Pandemic in the US." *JAMA Network Open* 3 (9): e2022942. https://doi.org/10.1001/jamanetworkopen.2020.2294

[7]Grossman, Elyse R., Sara E. Benjamin-Neelon, and Susan Sonnenschein. 2020. "Alcohol Consumption during the COVID-19 Pandemic: A Cross-Sectional Survey of US Adults." *International Journal of Environmental Research and Public Health* 17 (24): 9189. https://doi.org/10.3390/ijerph17249189

[8]"One Year On: Unhealthy Weight Gains, Increased Drinking Reported by Americans Coping with Pandemic Stress," March 11, 2021. https://www.apa.org/news/press/releases/2021/03/one-year-pandemic-stress

[9]Pollard, Michael S. 2020. "Changes in Adult Alcohol Use and Consequences during the COVID-19 Pandemic in the US." RAND. October 16, 2020. https://www.rand.org/pubs/external_publications/EP68312.html

[10]Rodriguez, Lindsey M., Dana M. Litt, and Sherry H. Stewart. 2020. "Drinking to Cope with the Pandemic: The Unique Associations of COVID-19-Related Perceived Threat and Psychological Distress to Drinking Behaviors in American Men and Women." *Addictive Behaviors* 110 (November): 106532. https://doi.org/10.1016/j.addbeh.2020.106532

[11]Park, Soon Yeob, Mi Kyeong Oh, Bum Soon Lee, Haa Gyoung Kim, Won Joon Lee, Ji Ho Lee, Jae Min Lim, and Jin Young Kim. 2015. "The Effects of Alcohol on Quality of Sleep." *Korean Journal of Family Medicine* 36 (6): 294. https://doi.org/10.4082/kjfm.2015.36.6.294

[12]Pacheco, Danielle, "Alcohol and Sleep." *Sleep Foundation.* https://www.sleepfoundation.org/nutrition/alcohol-and-sleep

[13]This table is an adaptation of Niemiec, Ryan M. 2019. "Finding the Golden Mean: The Overuse, Underuse, and Optimal Use of Character Strengths." *Counselling Psychology Quarterly* 32 (3–4): 453–71. https://doi.org/10.1080/09515070.2019.1617674

[14]Arendt, Josephine. 2022. "Physiology of the Pineal Gland and Melatonin." Endotext - NCBI Bookshelf. October 30, 2022. https://www.ncbi.nlm.nih.gov/books/NBK550972/

[15]Ibid.

[16]Cleveland Clinic Medical. June 9, 2023. "Sleep Disorders: Conditions That Prevent You from Getting Restful Sleep." Cleveland Clinic. https://my.clevelandclinic.org/health/articles/11429-common-sleep-disorders

[17]"Insomnia | Office on Women's Health." n.d. https://www.womenshealth.gov/a-z-topics/insomnia

[18]Neuroscience News. 2022. "Living in Areas with More Greenery May Boost Cognitive Function." *Neuroscience News*, April 2022. https://neurosciencenews.com/green-space-cognition-20493/

[19]Eads, Audrey. Feb 16, 2023. "What Is Shift Work? (Definition, Types and Jobs)" Indeed.Com www.indeed.com/career-advice/finding-a-job/what-is-shift-work

[20]"Waking Just One Hour Earlier Cuts Depression Risk by Double Digits, Study Finds." 2021. ScienceDaily. May 21, 2021. https://www.sciencedaily.com/releases/2021/05/210528114107.htm

[21]Glick, Sandra Barth, and Kay F. Macleod. 2010. "Autophagy: Cellular and Molecular Mechanisms." *The Journal of Pathology* 221 (1): 3–12. https://doi.org/10.1002/path.2697

[22]Lorca, Cristina, María Mulet, Catalina Arévalo-Caro, Marco a. Piña Sánchez, Ainhoa Perez, María Perrino, Anna Bach-Faig, et al. 2022. "Plant-Derived Nootropics and Human Cognition: A Systematic Review." *Critical Reviews in Food Science and Nutrition*, January, 1–25. https://doi.org/10.1080/10408398.2021.2021137

[23]Costantini, Erica, Srinivas Jarlapoodi, Federica Serra, Lisa Aielli, Haroon Khan, Tarun Belwal, Katia Falasca, and Marcella Reale. 2023. "Neuroprotective Potential of Bacopa Monnieri: Modulation of Inflammatory Signals." *Cns & Neurological Disorders-Drug Targets* 22 (3): 441–51. https://doi.org/10.2174/1871527321666220111124047

[24]Chandrika, U.G., and Prasad Kumarab Pa. 2015. "Gotu Kola (Centella Asiatica)." *Advances in Food and Nutrition Research*, 125–57. https://doi. org/10.1016/bs.afnr.2015.08.001

[25]Koulivand, Peir Hossein, Maryam Khaleghi Ghadiri, and Ali Gorji. 2013. "Lavender and the Nervous System." *Evidence-Based Complementary and Alternative Medicine* 2013 (January): 1–10. https://doi. org/10.1155/2013/681304

[26]Ghazizadeh, Javid, Saeed Sadigh-Eteghad, Wolfgang Marx, Ali Fakhari, Sanaz Hamedeyazdan, Mohammadali Torbati, Somaiyeh Taheri-Tarighi, Mostafa Araj-Khodaei, and Mojgan Mirghafourvand. 2021. "The Effects of Lemon Balm (*Melissa Officinalis* L.) on Depression and Anxiety in Clinical Trials: A Systematic Review and Meta-analysis." *Phytotherapy Research* 35 (12): 6690–6705. https://doi.org/10.1002/ptr.7252

[27]Hussain, Shalam Mohamed, Syeda Ayesha Farhana, Mohammed Salem, Alshammari, Sulaiman Mohammed Alnasser, Naif Alenzi, Shamsa Alanazi, and Krishnadas Nandakumar. 2022. "Cognition Enhancing Effect of Rosemary (Rosmarinus Officinalis L.) in Lab Animal Studies: A Systematic Review and Meta-Analysis." *Brazilian Journal of Medical and Biological Research* 55 (January 2022). https://doi. org/10.1590/1414431x2021e11593

[28]Joy. n.d. "Calming Stress Neurovascular Points." https://www. handsonhealthy.com/2016/04/holdingneurovascular-points-found-on. html

[29]Cianchetti, Carlo. 2012. "The Role of the Neurovascular Scalp Structures in Migraine." *Cephalalgia* 32 (10): 778–84. https://doi. org/10.1177/0333102412449930

Chapter Three: The Third Eye – Setting a Clear Vision and Manifesting Your Path

[1]Lumen Learning. n.d. "How We See | Introduction to Psychology." https://courses.lumenlearning.com/waymaker-psychology/chapter/

vision/

[2]Morse, Gardiner. June 2002. "Hidden Minds." *Harvard Business Review*. https://hbr.org/2002/06/hidden-minds

[3]Lipton, Bruce H. *The Biology of Belief: Unleashing the Power of Consciousness, Matter & Miracles*. Hay House, Inc., 2016.

[4]Ranganathan, Vinoth K., Vlodek Siemionow, Jing Z. Liu, Vinod Sahgal, and Guang H. Yue. 2004. "From Mental Power to Muscle Power— Gaining Strength by Using the Mind." *Neuropsychologia* 42 (7): 944–56. https://doi.org/10.1016/j.neuropsychologia.2003.11.018

[5]Armstrong, Kim. 2019. "Interoception: How We Understand Our Body's Inner Sensations." Association for Psychological Science - APS. September 25, 2019. https://www.psychologicalscience.org/observer/interoception-how-we-understand-our-bodys-inner-sensations

[6]Cota/L, Jessica Hill. "What Is Interoception?" *Harkla*, September 2021. https://harkla.co/blogs/special-needs/interoception

[7]This table is an adaptation of Niemiec, Ryan M. 2019. "Finding the Golden Mean: The Overuse, Underuse, and Optimal Use of Character Strengths." *Counselling Psychology Quarterly* 32 (3–4): 453–71. https://doi.org/10.1080/09515070.2019.1617674

[8]This exercise is based on concepts from Neuro Linguistic Programming (NLP) and the work of Richard Brandler.

[9]Some correlate the Pineal Gland in the Third Eye, but we have chosen to situate that gland in the Crown Chakra. These two chakras work in union together, and the body functions are interconnected.

[10]"Your Complex Brain." n.d. https://www.brainfacts.org/core-concepts/your-complex-brain

[11]The WHAM Report. (2022, October 31). *Brain Health - The WHAM Report* https://thewhamreport.org/report/brain/

[12]Mosconi, Lisa. *XX Brain: The Groundbreaking Approach for Women to Prevent Dementia and Alzheimer's Disease and Improve Brain Health*. Allen

& Unwin, 2020.

[13]Ibid, pg. 8

[14]Alzheimer's Disease and Dementia."Women and Alzheimers". n.d. https://www.alz.org/alzheimers-dementia/what-is-alzheimers/women-and-alzheimer-s

[15]Mosconi, pg. 10.

[16]World Health Organization: WHO. 2022. "Mental Disorders.". https://www.who.int/news-room/fact-sheets/detail/mental-disorders

[17]"Any Anxiety Disorder." n.d. National Institute of Mental Health (NIMH). https://www.nimh.nih.gov/health/statistics/any-anxiety-disorder.

[18]Bredesen, Dale E. *The End of Alzheimer's Program: The First Protocol to Enhance Cognition and Reverse Decline at Any Age.* Avery, 2022.

[19]Ko, Y., Kim, S., Lee, S., & Jang, C. (2020). Flavonoids as therapeutic candidates for emotional disorders such as anxiety and depression. *Archives of Pharmacal Research,* 43(11), 1128–1143. https://doi.org/10.1007/s12272-020-01292-5

[20]News-Medical.net. (2021, July 29). *Foods high in flavonoids may lower risk of cognitive decline.* https://www.news-medical.net/news/20210728/Foods-high-in-flavonoids-may-lower-risk-of-cognitive-decline.aspx

[21]Medina, J. H., Viola, H., Wolfman, C., Marder, M., Wasowski, C., Calvo, D. J., & Paladini, A. C. (1998). Neuroactive flavonoids: new ligands for the Benzodiazepine receptors. *Phytomedicine,* 5(3), 235–243. https://doi.org/10.1016/s0944-7113(98)80034-2

[22]Toups, Kat, Ann Hathaway, Deborah R. Gordon, Chung H, Cyrus A. Raji, Alan Boyd, Benjamin D. Hill, et al. 2022. "Precision Medicine Approach to Alzheimer's Disease: Successful Pilot Project." *Journal of Alzheimer's Disease* 88 (4): 1411–21. https://doi.org/10.3233/jad-215707

[23]Kent, Katherine, Maziar Yousefi, Vinicius Do Rosario, Zoe Fitzgerald, Samantha J. Broyd, Denis Visentin, Steven Roodenrys, Karen Walton,

and Karen E Charlton. 2022. "Anthocyanin Intake Is Associated with Improved Memory in Older Adults with Mild Cognitive Impairment." *Nutrition Research* 104 (August 2022): 36–43. https://doi.org/10.1016/j.nutres.2022.04.003

[24]Sokolov, A. N., Pavlova, M., Klosterhalfen, S., & Enck, P. (2013). "Chocolate and the brain: Neurobiological impact of cocoa flavanols on cognition and behavior." *Neuroscience & Biobehavioral Reviews*, 37(10), 2445–2453. https://doi.org/10.1016/j.neubiorev.2013.06.013

[25]Rasaei, N., Asbaghi, O., Samadi, M., Setayesh, L., Bagheri, R., Gholami, F., Soveid, N., Casazza, K., Wong, A., Suzuki, K., & Mirzaei, K. (2021). "Effect of Green tea supplementation on Antioxidant Status in Adults: A Systematic Review and Meta-Analysis of Randomized Clinical Trials."*Antioxidants,* 10(11), 1731. https://doi.org/10.3390/antiox10111731

[26]Katz, D. L., Doughty, K. N., & Ali, A. (2011). "Cocoa and chocolate in human health and disease." *Antioxidants & Redox Signaling,* 15(10), 2779–2811. https://doi.org/10.1089/ars.2010.3697

[27]Talebi, Marjan, Selen İlgün, Vida Ebrahimi, Mohsen Talebi, Tahereh Farkhondeh, Hadi Ebrahimi, and Saeed Samarghandian. 2021. "Zingiber Officinale Ameliorates Alzheimer's Disease and Cognitive Impairments: Lessons from Preclinical Studies." *Biomedicine & Pharmacotherapy* 133 (January): 111088. https://doi.org/10.1016/j.biopha.2020.111088

[28]Field, B. H., & Vadnal, R. (1998). "Ginkgo bilobaand Memory: An Overview." *Nutritional Neuroscience,* 1(4), 255–267. https://doi.org/10.1080/1028415x.1998.11747236

[29]Pengelly, A. W., James Snow, Simon Mills, Andrew Scholey, Keith Wesnes, and Leah Reeves Butler. 2012. "Short-Term Study on the Effects of Rosemary on Cognitive Function in an Elderly Population." *Journal of Medicinal Food* 15 (1): 10–17. https://doi.org/10.1089/jmf.2011.0005

[30]Lee, Y., Jung, J., Jang, S., Kim, J., Ali, Z., Khan, I. A., & Oh, S. (2013). "Anti-Inflammatory and Neuroprotective Effects of Constituents

Isolated from Rhodiola rosea." *Evidence-based Complementary and Alternative Medicine*, 2013, 1–9. https://doi.org/10.1155/2013/514049

[31]Stojcheva, E. I., & Quintela, J. C. (2022). "The Effectiveness of Rhodiola rosea L. Preparations in Alleviating Various Aspects of Life-Stress Symptoms and Stress-Induced Conditions—Encouraging Clinical Evidence." *Molecules*, 27(12), 3902. https://doi.org/10.3390/molecules27123902

[32]"Neuroscience For Kids - Stroop Effect," n.d. http://faculty.washington.edu/chudler/words.html

Chapter Four: The Throat Chakra – Leading with Truth and Expressing your Authentic Voice Fearlessly

[1]Ruiz, Miguel. *The Four Agreements: A Practical Guide to Personal Freedom.* Amber-Allen Publishing, 2017.

[2]"The Influence of Information Overload and Problematic Internet Use on Adults Wellbeing -ORCA." n.d. https://orca.cardiff.ac.uk/id/eprint/121873/

[3]Wikipedia contributors. 2023. "Default Mode Network." Wikipedia. https://en.wikipedia.org/wiki/Default_mode_network

[4]Jabr, Ferris. 2013. "Why Your Brain Needs More Downtime." Scientific American. October 15, 2013. https://www.scientificamerican.com/article/mental-downtime/

[5]This table is an adaptation of Niemiec, Ryan M. 2019. "Finding the Golden Mean: The Overuse, Underuse, and Optimal Use of Character Strengths." *Counselling Psychology Quarterly* 32 (3–4): 453–71. https://doi.org/10.1080/09515070.2019.1617674

[6]This exercise is adapted from a practice experienced in a Food & Spirit workshop with Dr. Deanna Minich.

[7]Shahid, M. A. (2023, June 5). *Physiology, thyroid hormone*. StatPearls - NCBI Bookshelf. https://www.ncbi.nlm.nih.gov/books/NBK500006/

[8]"Thyroid Patient Information | American Thyroid Association." American Thyroid Association, January 23, 2023. https://www.thyroid. org/thyroid-information/

[9]Romm, Aviva. "Overlooked & Ignored: Why Women Don't Get a Thyroid Diagnosis." https://avivaromm.com/hypothyroidism-feminist-issue/

[10]"The Untapped Potential of the Thyroid Axis." *The Lancet Diabetes and Endocrinology*. November, 2013 DOI: https://doi.org/10.1016/S2213-8587(13)70166-9

[11]Kalra, S., Unnikrishnan, A. G., & Sahay, R. (2014). "The hypoglycemic side of hypothyroidism." *Indian Journal of Endocrinology and Metabolism*, 18(1), 1. https://doi.org/10.4103/2230-8210.126517

[12]"Hypothyroidism (underactive thyroid) - Symptoms and Causes" - Mayo Clinic. December 10, 2022. https://www.mayoclinic.org/diseases-conditions/hypothyroidism/symptoms-causes/syc-20350284

[13]"Hyperthyroidism - Symptoms and Causes" - Mayo Clinic," November 30, 2022. https://www.mayoclinic.org/diseases-conditions/hyperthyroidism/symptoms-causes/syc-20373659

[14]Benvenga S., and Guarneri, F. "Molecular Mimicry and Autoimmune Thyroid Disease." *Reviews in Endocrine & Metabolic Disorders*, U.S. National Library of Medicine, pubmed.ncbi.nlm.nih.gov/27307072/

[15]De Punder, Karin, and Leo Pruimboom. "The Dietary Intake of Wheat and Other Cereal Grains and Their Role in Inflammation." *Nutrients* 5, no. 3 (March 12, 2013): 771–87. https://doi.org/10.3390/nu5030771

[16]Matheson, Christine. "Pelvic Health & Jaw Tension- How Their Connection Will Make Your Jaw Drop." *Dr. Christine Matheson, ND*, February 23, 2021. https://www.christinemathesonnd.com/blog/pelvic-health-jaw-tension-connection

[17]"Pelvic Floor Muscle Activation during Singing: A Pilot Study." *Journal of the Association of Chartered Physiotherapists in Women's Health* 110 (2012): 27–32. https://thepogp.co.uk/_userfiles/pages/files/bedekar.pdf

[18]Forsberg, Michele, and Michele Forsberg. "The Mysterious Connection between Your Pelvis and Jaw." *Align PT*, April 24, 2023. https://www.alignpt.com/mysterious-connection-pelvis-jaw/

[19]Gamage, G. C. V., Lim, Y. Y., & Choo, W. S. (2021). "Anthocyanins From Clitoria ternatea Flower: Biosynthesis, Extraction, Stability, Antioxidant Activity, and Applications." *Frontiers in Plant Science, 12.* https://doi.org/10.3389/fpls.2021.792303

[20]Beheshti-Rouy, M. (2015, June 1). "The antibacterial effect of sage extract (Salvia officinalis) mouthwash against Streptococcus mutans in dental plaque: a randomized clinical trial." PubMed Central (PMC). https://www.ncbi.nlm.nih.gov/pmc/articles/PMC4676988/

[21]Nunez, K. (2020, September 23). "What you need to know about the medicinal benefits of the toothache plant." Healthline. https://www.healthline.com/health/toothache-plant

[22]Elufioye, T. O., Habtemariam, S., & Adejare, A. (2020). "Chemistry and Pharmacology of Alkylamides from Natural Origin." *Revista Brasileira De Farmacognosia, 30*(5), 622–640. https://doi.org/10.1007/s43450-020-00095-5

[23]Sharma, Rahul and Neelakantan Arumugam. "N-Alkylamides of Spilanthes (Syn: Acmella): Structure, Purification, Characterization, Biological Activities and Applications – A Review." *Future Foods,* Elsevier, 3 Mar. 2021.www.sciencedirect.com/science/article/pii/S2666833521000125.

[24]Ibid.

Chapter Five: The Heart Chakra – Leading a Life You Love and Nurturing Your Whole Self

[1]This table is an adaptation of Niemiec, Ryan M. 2019. "Finding the Golden Mean: The Overuse, Underuse, and Optimal Use of Character Strengths." *Counselling Psychology Quarterly* 32 (3–4): 453–71. https://doi.org/10.1080/09515070.2019.1617674

[2]"What Is So Sacred About The Number 108?," n.d. https://www.himalayanyogainstitute.com/what-is-so-sacred-about-the-number-108/

[3]DailyOM.com. "21 Days of Prayer to Change Your Life," n.d. https://www.dailyom.com/courses/21-days-of-prayer-to-change-your-life/

[4]Judith, Anodea. *Wheels of Life: A User's Guide to the Chakra System.* Llewellyn Worldwide Limited, 1999.

[5]Centers for Disease Control and Prevention. "Congenital Heart Defects- How the heart works." (Nov 19, 2019).

[6]Centers for Disease Control and Prevention. "Women and Heart Disease." Women and Heart Disease | cdc.gov, n.d. https://www.cdc.gov/heartdisease/women.htm

[7]"Women and Heart Disease Facts," http://www.womensheart.org/content/heartdisease/heart_disease_facts.asp

[8]"Breast cancer Statistics | How common is breast cancer?" American Cancer Society. https://www.cancer.org/cancer/types/breast-cancer/about/how-common-is-breast-cancer.html

[9]"Adults Meeting Fruit and Vegetable Intake Recommendations — United States, 2019". https://www.cdc.gov/mmwr/volumes/71/wr/mm7101a1.htm?s_cid=mm7101a1_w

[10]Eurostat. (2022, January 4). "How much fruit and vegetables do you eat daily?" *Eurostat.* https://ec.europa.eu/eurostat/web/products-eurostat-news/-/ddn-20220104-1

[11]Stach, Kamilla, Wojciech Stach, and Katarzyna Augoff. "Vitamin B6 in Health and Disease." *Nutrients* 13, no. 9 (September 17, 2021): 3229. https://doi.org/10.3390/nu13093229

[12]Thorpe, Matthew, MD PhD. "10 Natural Ways to Lower Your Cholesterol Levels." Healthline, July 13, 2023. https://www.healthline.com/nutrition/how-to-lower-cholesterol#consider-plant-sterols

[13]Madormo, Carrie. "7 Foods with Estrogen: How to Balance Your Levels." *Verywell Health*, January 3, 2023. https://www.verywellhealth.com/foods-with-estrogen-to-eat-or-avoid-6831143

[14]Williamson, Laura. "How to Boost Your Mood through Food."American Heart Association News, March 30, 2022. https://www.heart.org/en/news/2022/03/30/how-to-boost-your-mood-through-food

[15]Zhang, Yue, et al. "Does an Apple a Day Keep Away Diseases? Evidence and Mechanism of Action." *Food Science & Nutrition*, U.S. National Library of Medicine, 20 June 2023. www.ncbi.nlm.nih.gov/pmc/articles/PMC10494637/

[16]"6 Benefits of Bitter Melon (Bitter Gourd) and Its Extract, Healthline https://www.healthline.com/nutrition/bitter-melon#TOC_TITLE_HDR_5

[17]Hobbs, Christopher, Ph. D. "Hawthorn: For the Heart," 1998. https://christopherhobbs.com/library/articles-on-herbs-and-health/hawthorn-for-the-heart/

[18]Mendicino, Siobhan. "Motherwort: 5 Benefits, Dosage, & Safety | The Botanical Institute." *The Botanical Institute*, December 27, 2022. https://botanicalinstitute.org/motherwort/

[19]"An Emotional Flower: The Rose." (n.d.) *Pennsylvania Horticultural Society*. https://phsonline.org/for-gardeners/gardeners-blog/an-emotional-flower-the-rose

Chapter Six: The Solar Plexus Chakra – Leading with Balanced Power

[1]Macy, Joanna, and Chris Johnstone. *Active Hope: How to Face the Mess We're in Without Going Crazy.* New World Library, 2012.

[2]World Wildlife Fund. "What Is the Sixth Mass Extinction and What Can We Do about It? | Stories | WWF," n.d. https://www.worldwildlife.org/stories/what-is-the-sixth-mass-extinction-and-what-can-we-do-about-it

[3]This table is an adaptation of Niemiec, Ryan M. 2019. "Finding the Golden Mean: The Overuse, Underuse, and Optimal Use of Character Strengths." *Counselling Psychology Quarterly* 32 (3–4): 453–71. https://doi.org/10.1080/09515070.2019.1617674

[4]Jabr, Ferris. "Why Your Brain Needs More Downtime." Scientific American, October 15, 2013. https://www.scientificamerican.com/article/mental-downtime/

[5]"Your Digestive System & How it Works." (2023). *National Institute of Diabetes and Digestive and Kidney Diseases.* https://www.niddk.nih.gov/health-information/digestive-diseases/digestive-system-how-it-works

[6]Lyon, Louisa. "'All Disease Begins in the Gut': Was Hippocrates Right?" *Brain* 141, no. 3 (February 12, 2018): e20. https://doi.org/10.1093/brain/awy017

[7]Banskota, S., Ghia, J., & Khan, W. I. (2019). "Serotonin in the gut: Blessing or a curse." *Biochimie,* 161, 56–64. https://doi.org/10.1016/j.biochi.2018.06.008

[8]Grotto, D., & Zied, E. (2010). "The standard American diet and its relationship to the health status of Americans." *Nutrition in Clinical Practice,* 25(6), 603–612. https://doi.org/10.1177/0884533610386234

[9]Jamioł-Milc, D., Gudan, A., Kaźmierczak-Siedlecka, K., Hołowko-Ziółek, J., Maciejewska-Markiewicz, D., Janda-Milczarek, K., &

Stachowska, E. (2023). "Nutritional support for liver diseases." *Nutrients*, 15(16), 3640. https://doi.org/10.3390/nu15163640

[10]Smiley, Brett. "How Much Fiber Should I Eat Per Day?" Healthline, May 30, 2023. https://www.healthline.com/health/food-nutrition/how-much-fiber-per-day.

[11]McKeown, N. M., Fahey, G. C., Slavin, J., & Van Der Kamp, J. (2022). "Fibre intake for optimal health: how can healthcare professionals support people to reach dietary recommendations?" *BMJ*, e054370. https://doi.org/10.1136/bmj-2020-054370

[12]Mar-Solís, Laura M, Adolfo Soto-Domínguez, Luis E. Rodríguez-Tovar, Humberto Rodriguez-Rocha, Aracely Garcia-Garcia, V. E. Aguirre-Arzola, Diana Elisa Zamora-Ávila, Aimé Jazmín Garza-Arredondo, and Uziel Castillo-Velázquez. "Analysis of the Anti-Inflammatory Capacity of Bone Broth in a Murine Model of Ulcerative Colitis." *Medicina-Lithuania* 57, no. 11 (October 20, 2021): 1138. https://doi.org/10.3390/medicina57111138.

[13]"Microbiome." *National Institute of Environmental Health Sciences*, U.S. Department of Health and Human Services. www.niehs.nih.gov/health/topics/science/microbiome/index.cfm.

[14]Leeuwendaal, Natasha, Catherine Stanton, Paul W. O'Toole, and Tom Beresford. "Fermented Foods, Health and the Gut Microbiome." *Nutrients* 14, no. 7 (April 6, 2022): 1527. https://doi.org/10.3390/nu14071527

[15]Davis, Paul A., and Wallace Yokoyama. "Cinnamon Intake Lowers Fasting Blood Glucose: Meta-Analysis." *Journal of Medicinal Food* 14, no. 9 (September 1, 2011): 884–89. https://doi.org/10.1089/jmf.2010.0180

[16]Li, Yanni, et al. "The potential of dandelion in the fight against gastrointestinal diseases: A Review." Journal of Ethnopharmacology, vol. 293, 2022, p. 115272. https://doi.org/10.1016/j.jep.2022.115272

[17]Tilgner, Sharol. *Herbal Medicine: From the Heart of the Earth*. Wise Acres, 2020.

[18]Das, Barun, John Rabalais, Philip Kozan, Tina Lu, Nassim Durali, Kevin Okamoto, Matthew D. McGeough, et al. "The Effect of a Fennel Seed Extract on the STAT Signaling and Intestinal Barrier Function." *PLOS ONE* 17, no. 7 (July 8, 2022): e0271045. https://doi.org/10.1371/journal.pone.0271045

[19]Maji, Amal K., and Pratim Banerji. "Phytochemistry and Gastrointestinal Benefits of the Medicinal Spice, Capsicum Annuum L. (Chilli): A Review." *Journal of Complementary and Integrative Medicine* 13, no. 2 (January 1, 2016). https://doi.org/10.1515/jcim-2015-0037

[20]Sharifi-Rad, Javad, Youssef El Rayess, Alain Abi Rizk, Carmen Sadaka, Raviella Zgheib, Wissam Zam, Simona Sestito, et al. "Turmeric and Its Major Compound Curcumin on Health: Bioactive Effects and Safety Profiles for Food, Pharmaceutical, Biotechnological and Medicinal Applications." *Frontiers in Pharmacology* 11 (September 15, 2020). https://doi.org/10.3389/fphar.2020.01021

Chapter Seven: The Sacral Chakra – Leading with Creative Flow and Cultivating Healthy Partnerships

[1]Pearce, Lucy H. "The Red Tent Has a History, but What Is It?" The Happy Womb, February 13, 2015. https://thehappywomb.com/2015/02/13/the-red-tent-has-a-history-but-what-is-it/

[2]This table is an adaptation of Niemiec, Ryan M. 2019. "Finding the Golden Mean: The Overuse, Underuse, and Optimal Use of Character Strengths." *Counselling Psychology Quarterly* 32 (3–4): 453–71. https://doi.org/10.1080/09515070.2019.1617674

[3]"What's in a Handful of Soil?" *Farmer's Weekly*, June 27, 2018. https://www.farmersweekly.co.za/opinion/by-invitation/whats-in-a-handful-of-soil/

[4]Sobel, Jack MD. "Vaginitis in adults: Initial evaluation, *UpToDate*," https://www.uptodate.com/contents/vaginitis-in-adults-initial-evaluation

[5]Lin, Yen-Pin, Wei-Chun Chen, Chao-Min Cheng, and Ching-Ju Shen. "Vaginal PH Value for Clinical Diagnosis and Treatment of Common Vaginitis." *Diagnostics* 11, no. 11 (October 27, 2021): 1996. https://doi.org/10.3390/diagnostics11111996

[6]Cleveland Clinic Medical, *"Female Reproductive System."* https://my.clevelandclinic.org/health/articles/9118-female-reproductive-system

[7]Cleveland Clinic Medical, *"Clitoris."* https://my.clevelandclinic.org/health/body/22823-clitoris

[8]Cassella, Carly. "We May Finally Know How Many Nerve Endings Are in The Human Clitoris : ScienceAlert." ScienceAlert, November 6, 2022. https://www.sciencealert.com/we-may-finally-know-how-many-nerve-endings-are-in-the-human-clitoris

[9]Ogden, Gina. *The Return of Desire: A Guide to Rediscovering Your Sexual Passion.* Shambhala Publications, 2008.

[10]Nagoski, Emily. *Come As You Are: Revised and Updated: The Surprising New Science That Will Transform Your Sex Life.* Simon & Schuster, 2021.

[11]"Antioxidants: Protecting Healthy Cells." *Antioxidants: Protecting Healthy Cells.* www.eatright.org/health/essential-nutrients/vitamins/antioxidants-protecting-healthy-cells

[12]Khalil, Ayman, Diana Tazeddinova, Khaled Aljoumaa, Zhumayeva Araigul Kazhmukhanbetkyzy, Ayan Orazov, and Abduvali Djabarovich Toshev. "Carotenoids: Therapeutic Strategy in the Battle against Viral Emerging Diseases, COVID-19: An Overview." *Journal of Food Science and Nutrition* 26, no. 3 (September 30, 2021): 241–61. https://doi.org/10.3746/pnf.2021.26.3.241

[13]Murray, Alison, Michael Molinek, Sj Baker, F. N. Kojima, Michael F. Smith, Stephen G. Hillier, and Norah Spears. "Role of Ascorbic Acid in Promoting Follicle Integrity and Survival in Intact Mouse Ovarian Follicles in Vitro." *Reproduction*, January 1, 2001, 89–96. https://doi.org/10.1530/rep.0.1210089

[14]Henmi, Hirofumi, Toshiaki Endo, Yoshimitsu Kitajima, Kengo Manase, Hiroshi Hata, and Ryuich Kudo. "Effects of Ascorbic Acid Supplementation on Serum Progesterone Levels in Patients with a Luteal Phase Defect." *Fertility and Sterility Home* 80, no. 2 (August 2003). https://www.fertstert.org/article/S0015-0282(03)00657-5/fulltext

[15]Nasiadek, Marzenna, Joanna Stragierowicz, Michał Klimczak, and Anna Kilanowicz. "The Role of Zinc in Selected Female Reproductive System Disorders." *Nutrients* 12, no. 8 (August 16, 2020): 2464. https://doi.org/10.3390/nu12082464

[16]Porri, Debora, Hans Konrad Biesalski, Antonio Limitone, Laura Bertuzzo, and Hellas Cena. "Effect of Magnesium Supplementation on Women's Health and Well-Being." *NFS Journal* 23 (June 1, 2021): 30–36. https://doi.org/10.1016/j.nfs.2021.03.003

[17]Ma, Xiao, Luming Wu, Yinxue Wang, Shiqiang Han, Marwa M. El-Dalatony, Fan Feng, Zhongbin Tao, Liulin Yu, and Yiqing Wang. "Diet and Human Reproductive System: Insight of Omics Approaches." *Food Science and Nutrition* 10, no. 5 (March 21, 2022): 1368–84. https://doi.org/10.1002/fsn3.2708

[18]Romm, Aviva."Vitex (Chasteberry) and Women's Hormone Balance." https://avivaromm.com/vitex-hormones/

[19]Khayat, Samira, Masoomeh Kheirkhah, Zahra Behboodi Moghadam, Hamed Fanaei, Amir Kasaeian, and Mani Javadimehr. "Effect of Treatment with Ginger on the Severity of Premenstrual Syndrome Symptoms." *ISRN Obstetrics and Gynecology (Print)* 2014 (May 4, 2014): 1–5. https://doi.org/10.1155/2014/792708

[20]Alok, Shashi, Sanjay Jain, Amita Verma, Mayank Kumar, Alok Mahor, and Monika Sabharwal. "Plant Profile, Phytochemistry and Pharmacology of Asparagus Racemosus (Shatavari): A Review." *Asian Pacific Journal of Tropical Disease* 3, no. 3 (April 1, 2013): 242–51. https://doi.org/10.1016/s2222-1808(13)60049-3

Chapter Eight: The Root Chakra – Leading with Presence and Trust

[1]Cialdini, Robert B. *Influence, New and Expanded: The Psychology of Persuasion*. Harper Business, 2021.

[2]Antanaityte, About Neringa. "Mind Matters: How To Effortlessly Have More Positive Thoughts" | TLEX Institute," n.d. https://tlexinstitute. com/how-to-effortlessly-have-more-positive-thoughts

[3]This table is an adaptation of Niemiec, Ryan M. 2019. "Finding the Golden Mean: The Overuse, Underuse, and Optimal Use of Character Strengths." *Counselling Psychology Quarterly* 32 (3–4): 453–71. https://doi. org/10.1080/09515070.2019.1617674

[4]"Your Mental Wealth Advisors - Home," n.d. https://www. yourmentalwealthadvisors.com/

[5]Cleveland Clinic Medical. "*Adrenal Gland.*" https://my.clevelandclinic. org/health/body/23005-adrenal-gland

[6]Johns Hopkins Medicine. "Adrenal Glands," August 8, 2021. https:// www.hopkinsmedicine.org/health/conditions-and-diseases/adrenal-glands

[7]Kuo, Taiyi, Allison McQueen, Tzu-Chieh Chen, and Jen-Chywan Wang. "Regulation of Glucose Homeostasis by Glucocorticoids." *Advances in Experimental Medicine and Biology*, 99–126, 2015. https://pubmed.ncbi. nlm.nih.gov/26215992/

[8]Chourpiliadis C; Aeddula, NR. "Physiology, Glucocorticoids." National Center for Biotechnology Information, U.S. *National Library of Medicine.* https://pubmed.ncbi.nlm.nih.gov/32809732/

[9]Thau, Lauren. "Physiology, Cortisol." StatPearls - NCBI Bookshelf, August 29, 2022. https://www.ncbi.nlm.nih.gov/books/NBK538239/

[10]Cleveland Clinic Medical, "*Aldosterone.*" https://my.clevelandclinic. org/health/articles/24158-aldosterone

[11]"Cleveland Clinic Medical, *"Epinephrine (Adrenaline)."* https://my.clevelandclinic.org/health/articles/22611-epinephrine-adrenaline

[12]Nikolenko, Vladimir N, et al. "Amygdala: Neuroanatomical and Morphophysiological Features in Terms of Neurological and Neurodegenerative Diseases." *Brain Sciences*, U.S. National Library of Medicine, 31 July 2020. www.ncbi.nlm.nih.gov/pmc/articles/PMC7465610/

[13]Kozlowska, Kasia, Peter G. Walker, Loyola McLean, and Pascal Carrive. "Fear and the Defense Cascade." *Harvard Review of Psychiatry* 23, no. 4 (July 1, 2015): 263–87. https://doi.org/10.1097/hrp.0000000000000065

[14]Bailey, Rebecca, Jaycee Dugard, Stefanie F. Smith, and Stephen W. Porges. "Appeasement: Replacing Stockholm Syndrome as a Definition of a Survival Strategy." *European Journal of Psychotraumatology* 14, no. 1 (January 19, 2023). https://doi.org/10.1080/20008066.2022.2161038

[15]Taylor, Martin. "What Does Fight, Flight, Freeze, Fawn Mean?" WebMD, May 19, 2022. https://www.webmd.com/mental-health/what-does-fight-flight-freeze-fawn-mean

[16]Sherin, Jonathan E, and Charles B Nemeroff. "Post-Traumatic Stress Disorder: The Neurobiological Impact of Psychological Trauma." *Dialogues in Clinical Neuroscience*, U.S. National Library of Medicine, 2011. www.ncbi.nlm.nih.gov/pmc/articles/PMC3182008/

[17]The Nutrition Source. "Protein," November 12, 2021. https://www.hsph.harvard.edu/nutritionsource/what-should-you-eat/protein/

[18]Speers, Alex, Kadine A Cabey, Amala Soumyanath, and Kirsten M. Wright. "Effects of Withania Somnifera (Ashwagandha) on Stress and the Stress- Related Neuropsychiatric Disorders Anxiety, Depression, and Insomnia." *Current Neuropharmacology* 19, no. 9 (September 1, 2021): 1468–95. https://doi.org/10.2174/1570159x19666210712151556

[19]De Souza, A. R. C., De Oliveira, T. L., Fontana, P. D., Carneiro, M. C., Corazza, M. L., De Messias-Reason, I. J., & Bavia, L. (2022).

"Phytochemicals and Biological Activities of Burdock (*Arctium lappa L.*) Extracts: A Review." *Chemistry & Biodiversity, 19*(11). https://doi.org/10.1002/cbdv.202200615

[20]Nautiyal, Chandra Shekhar, Puneet Singh Chauhan, and Yeshwant Laxman Nene. "Medicinal Smoke Reduces Airborne Bacteria." *Journal of Ethnopharmacology* 114, no. 3 (December 1, 2007): 446–51. https://doi.org/10.1016/j.jep.2007.08.038

[21]Cohen, M. (2014). "Tulsi - Ocimum sanctum: A herb for all reasons." *Journal of Ayurveda and Integrative Medicine*, 5(4), 251. https://pubmed.ncbi.nlm.nih.gov/25624701/

[22]Walker, Lauren. "4 Simple Ways To Stay Grounded." Yoga Digest," n.d. https://yogadigest.com/4-simple-ways-to-stay-grounded/

[23]Zaccaro, Andrea, Andrea Piarulli, Marco Laurino, Erika Garbella, Danilo Menicucci, Bruno Neri, and Angelo Gemignani. "How Breath-Control Can Change Your Life: A Systematic Review on Psycho-Physiological Correlates of Slow Breathing." *Frontiers in Human Neuroscience* 12 (September 7, 2018). https://doi.org/10.3389/fnhum.2018.00353

Bibliography

Adults Meeting Fruit and Vegetable Intake Recommendations — United States, 2019. https://www.cdc.gov/mmwr/volumes/71/wr/mm7101a1.htm?s_cid=mm7101a1_w

Aicr. "New AICR Breast Cancer Report." American Institute for Cancer Research, 20 July 2022.

All in: Female Founders in the US VC Ecosystem | 2021 Pitchbook.

Allied Market Research. Alcoholic Beverages Market Size, Share, Trends | Forecast, 2021-2031. n.d.

Alok, Shashi, Sanjay Jain, Amita Verma, Mayank Kumar, Alok Mahor, and Monika Sabharwal. "Plant Profile, Phytochemistry and Pharmacology of Asparagus Racemosus (Shatavari): A Review." *Asian Pacific Journal of Tropical Disease* 3, no. 3 (April 1, 2013): 242–51.

Alzheimer's Disease and Dementia."Women and Alzheimers". n.d. https://www.alz.org/alzheimers-dementia/what-is-alzheimers/women-and-alzheimer-s

Amar, Solomon. 2023. "Why Everyone Wins With More Women In Leadership." *Forbes*, February 7, 2023.

Arendt, Josephine. 2022. "Physiology of the Pineal Gland and Melatonin." Endotext - NCBI Bookshelf. October 30, 2022.

Armstrong, Kim. 2019. "Interoception: How We Understand Our Body's Inner Sensations." *Association for Psychological Science* - APS. September 25, 2019.

"An Emotional Flower: The Rose." (n.d.) *Pennsylvania Horticultural Society*. https://phsonline.org/for-gardeners/gardeners-blog/an-emotional-flower-the-rose

"Any Anxiety Disorder." n.d. National Institute of Mental Health (NIMH). https://www.nimh.nih.gov/health/statistics/any-anxiety-disorder

Antanaityte, About Neringa. "Mind Matters: How To Effortlessly Have More Positive Thoughts | TLEX Institute," n.d.

"Antioxidants: Protecting Healthy Cells." Antioxidants: Protecting Healthy Cells.

"6 Benefits of Bitter Melon (Bitter Gourd) and Its Extract." Healthline, February 10, 2023.

Bailey, Rebecca, Jaycee Dugard, Stefanie F. Smith, and Stephen W. Porges. "Appeasement: Replacing Stockholm Syndrome as a Definition of a Survival Strategy." *European Journal of Psychotraumatology* 14, no. 1 (January 19, 2023).

Banskota, S., Ghia, J., & Khan, W. I. (2019). Serotonin in the gut: Blessing or a curse. *Biochimie*, 161, 56–64.

Beachum, Brandon. *The Golden Key: Modern Alchemy to Unlock Infinite Abundance*. Bookbaby, 2021.

Beheshti-Rouy, M. (2015, June 1). *The antibacterial effect of sage extract (Salvia officinalis) mouthwash against Streptococcus mutans in dental plaque: a randomized clinical trial*. PubMed Central (PMC).

Benvenga S; Guarneri, F. "Molecular Mimicry and Autoimmune Thyroid Disease." *Reviews in Endocrine & Metabolic Disorders*, U.S. National Library of Medicine.

Berinato, Scott. 2021. "Banks with More Women on Their Boards Commit Less Fraud." *Harvard Business Review*. April 13, 2021.

"Black Women's Equal Pay Day — Equal Pay Today." n.d. Equal Pay Today.

Breast cancer Statistics | How common is breast cancer? (n.d.). American Cancer Society.

Bredesen, Dale E. *The End of Alzheimer's: The First Program to Prevent and Reverse Cognitive Decline*. Thorndike Press, a Part of Gale, a Cengage

Company, 2021.

Bredesen, Dale E. *The End of Alzheimer's Program: The First Protocol to Enhance Cognition and Reverse Decline at Any Age.* Avery, 2022.

Cassella, Carly. "We May Finally Know How Many Nerve Endings Are in The Human Clitoris : ScienceAlert." ScienceAlert, November 6, 2022.

Castrillon, Caroline. 2023. "Why Women Leaders Are Leaving Their Jobs At Record Rates." *Forbes*, May 7, 2023.

Catalyst. 2023. "Women CEOs of the S&P 500." February 6, 2023.

Centers for Disease Control and Prevention. "Women and Heart Disease." Women and Heart Disease | cdc.gov, n.d.

Chandrika, U.G., and Prasad Kumarab Pa. 2015. "Gotu Kola (Centella Asiatica)." *Advances in Food and Nutrition Research*, 125–57.

Chourpiliadis C; Aeddula, NR. "Physiology, Glucocorticoids." National Center for Biotechnology Information, U.S. National Library of Medicine.

Cialdini, Robert B. *Influence, New and Expanded: The Psychology of Persuasion.* Harper Business, 2021

Cianchetti, Carlo. 2012. "The Role of the Neurovascular Scalp Structures in Migraine." *Cephalalgia* 32 (10): 778–84.

Cleveland Clinic Medical. "Adrenal Gland." Cleveland Clinic, n.d.

Cleveland Clinic Medical. "Epinephrine (Adrenaline)." Cleveland Clinic, n.d.

Cleveland Clinic Medical. "Clitoris." Cleveland Clinic, n.d.

Cleveland Clinic Medical. "Sleep Disorders: Conditions That Prevent You from Getting Restful Sleep.")." Cleveland Clinic, n.d.

Cohen, M. (2014). Tulsi - Ocimum sanctum: A herb for all reasons.

Journal of Ayurveda and Integrative Medicine, 5(4), 251.

Costantini, Erica, Srinivas Jarlapoodi, Federica Serra, Lisa Aielli, Haroon Khan, Tarun Belwal, Katia Falasca, and Marcella Reale. 2023. "Neuroprotective Potential of Bacopa Monnieri: Modulation of Inflammatory Signals." *Cns & Neurological Disorders-Drug Targets* 22 (3): 441–51.

Cota/L, Jessica Hill. 2021. "What Is Interoception?" Harkla, September 2021.

DailyOM.com. "21 Days of Prayer to Change Your Life," n.d.

Das, Barun, John Rabalais, Philip Kozan, Tina Lu, Nassim Durali, Kevin Okamoto, Matthew D. McGeough, et al. "The Effect of a Fennel Seed Extract on the STAT Signaling and Intestinal Barrier Function." PLOS ONE 17, no. 7 (July 8, 2022): e0271045.

Dyer, Wayne. *You'll See It When You Believe It: The Way to Your Personal Transformation.* William Morrow, 2021.

Davis, Paul A., and Wallace Yokoyama. "Cinnamon Intake Lowers Fasting Blood Glucose: Meta-Analysis." *Journal of Medicinal Food* 14, no. 9 (September 1, 2011): 884–89.

De Punder, Karin, and Leo Pruimboom. "The Dietary Intake of Wheat and Other Cereal Grains and Their Role in Inflammation." *Nutrients* 5, no. 3 (March 12, 2013): 771–87.

DerSarkissian, Carol. 2021. "If COVID-19 Wasn't Bad Enough, It's Also a Sexist Disease." *US News & World Report,* November 19, 2021.

De Souza, A. R. C., De Oliveira, T. L., Fontana, P. D., Carneiro, M. C., Corazza, M. L., De Messias-Reason, I. J., & Bavia, L. (2022). Phytochemicals and Biological Activities of Burdock (Arctium lappa L.) Extracts: A Review. *Chemistry & Biodiversity,* 19(11).

Eads, Audrey. Feb 16, 2023.

Easwaran, Eknath. *The Upanishads.* Nilgiri Press, 2007.

Eisenstein, Charles. 2011. *Sacred Economics: Money, Gift, & Society in the Age of Transition*. North Atlantic Books, 2021.

Elufioye, T. O., Habtemariam, S., & Adejare, A. (2020). Chemistry and Pharmacology of Alkylamides from Natural Origin. *Revista Brasileira De Farmacognosia*, 30(5), 622–640.

Eufic. "Fruit and Vegetable Consumption in Europe," n.d. https://www.eufic.org/en/healthy-living/article/fruit-and-vegetable-consumption-in-europe-do-europeans-get-enough

Female Reproductive System in Cleveland Clinic website: https://my.clevelandclinic.org/health/articles/9118-female-reproductive-system

Field, B. H., & Vadnal, R. (1998). Ginkgo bilobaand Memory: An Overview. *Nutritional Neuroscience*, 1(4), 255–267.

Forsberg, Michele, and Michele Forsberg. "The Mysterious Connection between Your Pelvis and Jaw." *Align PT*, April 24, 2023.

Frawley, David. *Tantric Yoga and the Wisdom Goddesses: Spiritual Secrets of Ayurveda*. Lotus Press, 2000.

Gamage, G. C. V., Lim, Y. Y., & Choo, W. S. (2021). Anthocyanins From Clitoria ternatea. Flower: Biosynthesis, Extraction, Stability, Antioxidant Activity, and Applications. *Frontiers in Plant Science, 12*.

Ghazizadeh, Javid, Saeed Sadigh-Eteghad, Wolfgang Marx, Ali Fakhari, Sanaz Hamedeyazdan, Mohammadali Torbati, Somaiyeh Taheri-Tarighi, Mostafa Araj-Khodaei, and Mojgan Mirghafourvand. 2021. "The Effects of Lemon Balm (Melissa Officinalis L.) on Depression and Anxiety in Clinical Trials: A Systematic Review and Meta-analysis." *Phytotherapy Research* 35 (12): 6690–6705.

Glick, Sandra Barth, and Kay F. Macleod. 2010. "Autophagy: Cellular and Molecular Mechanisms." *The Journal of Pathology* 221 (1): 3–12.

Good While It Lasted - I: 6th Mass Extinction Underway, Courtesy Humans," n.d.

Grotto, D., & Zied, E. (2010). The standard American diet and its relationship to the health status of Americans. *Nutrition in Clinical Practice*, 25(6), 603–612.

Grossman, Elyse R., Sara E. Benjamin-Neelon, and Susan Sonnenschein. 2020. "Alcohol Consumption during the COVID-19 Pandemic: A Cross-Sectional Survey of US Adults." *International Journal of Environmental Research and Public Health* 17 (24): 9189.

Hantsoo, Liisa, and C. Neill Epperson. 2017. "Anxiety Disorders among Women: A Female Lifespan Approach." *Focus* 15 (2): 162–72.

Henmi, Hirofumi, Toshiaki Endo, Yoshimitsu Kitajima, Kengo Manase, Hiroshi Hata, and Ryuich Kudo. "Effects of Ascorbic Acid Supplementation on Serum Progesterone Levels in Patients with a Luteal Phase Defect." *Fertility and Sterility Home* 80, no. 2 (August 2003).

Hobbs, Christopher, Ph. D. "Hawthorn: For the Heart," 1998.

Huffington, Arianna. 2022. "Resilience+ Is My Word of the Year." Thrive Global, January.

Hussain, Shalam Mohamed, Syeda Ayesha Farhana, Mohammed Salem Alshammari, Sulaiman Mohammed Alnasser, Naif Alenzi, Shamsa Alanazi, and Krishnadas Nandakumar. 2022. "Cognition Enhancing Effect of Rosemary (Rosmarinus Officinalis L.), Lab Animal Studies: A Systematic Review and Meta-Analysis." *Brazilian Journal of Medical and Biological Research* 55 (January 2022).

"Insomnia | Office on Women's Health." n.d.

Jabr, Ferris. 2013. "Why Your Brain Needs More Downtime." *Scientific American*. October 15, 2013.

Jamioł-Milc, D., Gudan, A., Kaźmierczak-Siedlecka, K., Hołowko-Ziółek, J., Maciejewska-Markiewicz, D., Janda-Milczarek, K., & Stachowska, E. (2023). Nutritional support for liver diseases. *Nutrients*, 15(16), 3640.

Johns Hopkins Medicine. "Adrenal Glands," August 8, 2021.

Joy. n.d. "Calming Stress Neurovascular Points."

Judith, Anodea. *Wheels of Life: A User's Guide to the Chakra System.* Llewellyn Worldwide Limited, 1999.

Kalra, S., Unnikrishnan, A. G., & Sahay, R. (2014). The hypoglycemic side of hypothyroidism. *Indian Journal of Endocrinology and Metabolism,* 18(1), 1.

Karaye, Ibraheem M., Nasim Maleki, Norzaihan Hassan, and Ismaeel Yunusa. 2023. "Trends in Alcohol-Related Deaths by Sex in the US, 1999-2020." *JAMA Network Open* 6 (7): e2326346.

Katz, D. L., Doughty, K. N., & Ali, A. (2011). Cocoa and chocolate in human health and disease. *Antioxidants & Redox Signaling,* 15(10), 2779–2811.

Kent, Katherine, Maziar Yousefi, Vinicius Do Rosario, Zoe Fitzgerald, Samantha J. Broyd, Denis Visentin, Steven Roodenrys, Karen Walton, and Karen E Charlton. 2022. "Anthocyanin Intake Is Associated with Improved Memory in Older Adults with Mild Cognitive Impairment." *Nutrition Research* 104 (August 2022): 36–43.

Khalil, Ayman, Diana Tazeddinova, Khaled Aljoumaa, Zhumayeva Araigul Kazhmukhanbetkyzy, Ayan Orazov, and Abduvali Djabarovich Toshev. "Carotenoids: Therapeutic Strategy in the Battle against Viral Emerging Diseases, COVID-19: An Overview." *Journal of Food Science and Nutrition* 26, no. 3 (September 30, 2021): 241–61.

Khayat, Samira, Masoomeh Kheirkhah, Zahra Behboodi Moghadam, Hamed Fanaei, Amir Kasaeian, and Mani Javadimehr. "Effect of Treatment with Ginger on the Severity of Premenstrual Syndrome Symptoms." *ISRN Obstetrics and Gynecology (Print)* 2014 (May 4, 2014): 1–5.

Kim, Mike. n.d. https://mikekim.com/stay-out-of-the-bubble-biosphere-2-2/

Kimmerer, Robin Wall. *Braiding Sweetgrass,* 2014.

Ko, Y., Kim, S., Lee, S., & Jang, C. (2020). Flavonoids as therapeutic candidates for emotional disorders such as anxiety and depression. *Archives of Pharmacal Research*, 43(11), 1128–1143.

Koulivand, Peir Hossein, Maryam Khaleghi Ghadiri, and Ali Gorji. 2013. "Lavender and the Nervous System." *Evidence-Based Complementary and Alternative Medicine* 2013 (January): 1–10.

Kozlowska, Kasia, Peter G. Walker, Loyola McLean, and Pascal Carrive. "Fear and the Defense Cascade." *Harvard Review of Psychiatry* 23, no. 4 (July 1, 2015): 263–87.

Kuehner, Christine. 2017. "Why Is Depression More Common among Women than among Men?" *The Lancet Psychiatry* 4 (2): 146–58.

Kuo, Taiyi, Allison McQueen, Tzu-Chieh Chen, and Jen-Chywan Wang. "Regulation of Glucose Homeostasis by Glucocorticoids." *Advances in Experimental Medicine and Biology*, 99–126, 2015.

Lee, Y., Jung, J., Jang, S., Kim, J., Ali, Z., Khan, I. A., & Oh, S. (2013). "Anti-Inflammatory and Neuroprotective Effects of Constituents Isolated from Rhodiola rosea." *Evidence-based Complementary and Alternative Medicine*, 2013, 1–9.

Leeuwendaal, Natasha, Catherine Stanton, Paul W. O'Toole, and Tom Beresford. "Fermented Foods, Health and the Gut Microbiome." *Nutrients* 14, no. 7 (April 6, 2022): 1527.

Li, Yanni, et al. "The potential of dandelion in the fight against gastrointestinal diseases: A Review." *Journal of Ethnopharmacology*, vol. 293, 2022, p. 115272.

Lin, Yen-Pin, Wei-Chun Chen, Chao-Min Cheng, and Ching-Ju Shen. "Vaginal PH Value for Clinical Diagnosis and Treatment of Common Vaginitis." *Diagnostics* 11, no. 11 (October 27, 2021): 1996.

Lipton, Bruce H. *The Biology of Belief: Unleashing the Power of Consciousness, Matter & Miracles.* Hay House, Inc., 2016.

Lorca, Cristina, María Mulet, Catalina Arévalo-Caro, Marco a. Piña

Sánchez, Ainhoa Perez, María Perrino, Anna Bach-Faig, et al. 2022. "Plant-Derived Nootropics and Human Cognition: A Systematic Review." Critical Reviews in Food Science and Nutrition, January, 1–25.

Lumen Learning. n.d. "How We See | Introduction to Psychology."

Lyon, Louisa. "'All Disease Begins in the Gut': Was Hippocrates Right?" Brain 141, no. 3 (February 12, 2018): e20.

Ma, Xiao, Luming Wu, Yinxue Wang, Shiqiang Han, Marwa M. El-Dalatony, Fan Feng, Zhongbin Tao, Liulin Yu, and Yiqing Wang. "Diet and Human Reproductive System: Insight of Omics Approaches." Food Science and Nutrition 10, no. 5 (March 21, 2022): 1368–84.

Macy, Joanna, and Chris Johnstone. Active Hope: How to Face the Mess We're in Without Going Crazy. New World Library, 2012.

Madormo, Carrie. "7 Foods with Estrogen: How to Balance Your Levels." Verywell Health, January 3, 2023.

Maji, Amal K., and Pratim Banerji. "Phytochemistry and Gastrointestinal Benefits of the Medicinal Spice, Capsicum Annuum L. (Chilli): A Review." Journal of Complementary and Integrative Medicine 13, no. 2 (January 1, 2016).

Mar-Solís, Laura M, Adolfo Soto-Domínguez, Luis E. Rodríguez-Tovar, Humberto Rodriguez-Rocha, Aracely Garcia-Garcia, V. E. Aguirre-Arzola, Diana Elisa Zamora-Ávila, Aimé Jazmín Garza-Arredondo, and Uziel Castillo-Velázquez. "Analysis of the Anti-Inflammatory Capacity of Bone Broth in a Murine Model of Ulcerative Colitis." Medicina-Lithuania 57, no. 11 (October 20, 2021): 1138.

Matheson, Christine. "Pelvic Health & Jaw Tension- How Their Connection Will Make Your Jaw Drop." February 23, 2021.

Mayo Clinic. "Hypothyroidism (underactive thyroid) - Symptoms and Causes." December 10, 2022.

Mayo Clinic. "Hyperthyroidism - Symptoms and Causes".November 30, 2022.

McAlister, Anna R., and T. Bettina Cornwell. *Children's Brand Symbolism Understanding*. Wiley-Blackwell, 2010.

McKeown, N. M., Fahey, G. C., Slavin, J., & Van Der Kamp, J. (2022). Fibre intake for optimal health: how can healthcare professionals support people to reach dietary recommendations? *BMJ*, e054370.

Medina, J. H., Viola, H., Wolfman, C., Marder, M., Wasowski, C., Calvo, D. J., & Paladini, A. C. (1998). Neuroactive flavonoids: new ligands for the Benzodiazepine receptors. *Phytomedicine*, 5(3), 235–243.

Mendicino, Siobhan. "Motherwort: 5 Benefits, Dosage, & Safety | The Botanical Institute." The Botanical Institute, December 27, 2022.

"Microbiome." National Institute of Environmental Health Sciences, U.S. Department of Health and Human Services.

Morgan, Edward. 2018. "Etymology of the Word Alcohol: "Body Eating Spirit" Prepare for Change.

Morse, Gardiner. June 2002. "Hidden Minds." *Harvard Business Review*.

Mosconi, Lisa. *XX Brain: The Groundbreaking Approach for Women to Prevent Dementia and Alzheimer's Disease and Improve Brain Health*. Allen & Unwin, 2020.

Murray, Alison, Michael Molinek, Sj Baker, F. N. Kojima, Michael F. Smith, Stephen G. Hillier, and Norah Spears. "Role of Ascorbic Acid in Promoting Follicle Integrity and Survival in Intact Mouse Ovarian Follicles in Vitro." *Reproduction*, January 1, 2001, 89–96.

Nagoski, Emily. *Come As You Are: Revised and Updated: The Surprising New Science That Will Transform Your Sex Life*. Simon & Schuster, 2021.

Nasiadek, Marzenna, Joanna Stragierowicz, Michał Klimczak, and Anna Kilanowicz. "The Role of Zinc in Selected Female Reproductive System Disorders." *Nutrients* 12, no. 8 (August 16, 2020): 2464.

Nautiyal, Chandra Shekhar, Puneet Singh Chauhan, and Yeshwant

Laxman Nene. "Medicinal Smoke Reduces Airborne Bacteria." *Journal of Ethnopharmacology* 114, no. 3 (December 1, 2007): 446–51.

Nebel, Rebecca A., Neelum T. Aggarwal, Lisa L. Barnes, Aimee Gallagher, Jill M. Goldstein, Kejal Kantarci, Monica P. Mallampalli, et al. 2018. "Understanding the Impact of Sex and Gender in Alzheimer's Disease: A Call to Action." *Alzheimers & Dementia* 14 (9): 1171–83.

Neuroscience News. 2022. "Living in Areas with More Greenery May Boost Cognitive Function." *Neuroscience News*, April 2022

"Neuroscience For Kids - Stroop Effect," n.d. http://faculty.washington.edu/chudler/words.html

News-Medical.net. (2021, July 29). Foods high in flavonoids may lower risk of cognitive decline.

Niemiec, Ryan M. 2019. "Finding the Golden Mean: The Overuse, Underuse, and Optimal Use of Character Strengths." *Counselling Psychology Quarterly* 32 (3–4): 453–71.

Nikolenko, Vladimir N, et al. "Amygdala: Neuroanatomical and Morphophysiological Features in Terms of Neurological and Neurodegenerative Diseases." *Brain Sciences*, U.S. National Library of Medicine, 31 July 2020.

Nunez, K. (2020, September 23). *What you need to know about the medicinal benefits of the toothache plant.* Healthline. https://www.healthline.com/health/toothache-plant

"One Year on: Unhealthy Weight Gains, Increased Drinking Reported by Americans Coping with Pandemic Stress," March 11, 2021.

Ogden, Gina. *The Return of Desire: A Guide to Rediscovering Your Sexual Passion.* Shambhala Publications, 2008.

Pacheco, Danielle, "Alcohol and Sleep." Sleep Foundation.

Park, Soon Yeob, Mi Kyeong Oh, Bum Soon Lee, Haa Gyoung Kim, Won Joon Lee, Ji Ho Lee, Jae Min Lim, and Jin Young Kim. 2015. "The

Effects of Alcohol on Quality of Sleep." *Korean Journal of Family Medicine* 36 (6): 294.

Pattani, Aneri. 2021. "Women Now Drink as Much as Men — And Are Prone to Sickness Sooner." KFF Health News. June 10, 2021.

Pearce, Lucy H. "The Red Tent Has a History, but What Is It?" The Happy Womb, February 13, 2015.

"Pelvic Floor Muscle Activation during Singing: A Pilot Study." *Journal of the Association of Chartered Physiotherapists in Women's Health* 110 (2012): 27–32.

Pengelly, A. W., James Snow, Simon Mills, Andrew Scholey, Keith Wesnes, and Leah Reeves Butler. 2012. "Short-Term Study on the Effects of Rosemary on Cognitive Function in an Elderly Population." *Journal of Medicinal Food* 15 (1): 10–17.

Peterson, Christopher, and Martin E. P. Seligman. 2004. "Character Strengths and Virtues: A Handbook and Classification." *Choice Reviews Online* 42 (01): 42–0624.

Pollard, Michael S., Joan S. Tucker, and Harold D. Green. 2020. "Changes in Adult Alcohol Use and Consequences during the COVID-19 Pandemic in the US." *JAMA Network Open* 3 (9): e2022942.

Porri, Debora, Hans Konrad Biesalski, Antonio Limitone, Laura Bertuzzo, and Hellas Cena. "Effect of Magnesium Supplementation on Women's Health and Well-Being." *NFS Journal* 23 (June 1, 2021): 30–36.

Post, Corinne. 2021. "Research: Adding Women to the C-Suite Changes How Companies Think." *Harvard Business Review*. September 17, 2021.

Ranganathan, Vinoth K., Vlodek Siemionow, Jing Z. Liu, Vinod Sahgal, and Guang H. Yue. 2004. "From Mental Power to Muscle Power— Gaining Strength by Using the Mind." *Neuropsychologia* 42 (7): 944–56.

Rasaei, N., Asbaghi, O., Samadi, M., Setayesh, L., Bagheri, R., Gholami, F., Soveid, N., Casazza, K., Wong, A., Suzuki, K., & Mirzaei, K. (2021). Effect of Green tea supplementation on Antioxidant Status in Adults: A

Systematic Review and Meta-Analysis of Randomized Clinical Trials. *Antioxidants*, 10(11), 1731.

"Resilience" in Merriam-Webster. 1983. The Merriam-Webster Dictionary.

Rodriguez, Lindsey M., Dana M. Litt, and Sherry H. Stewart. 2020. "Drinking to Cope with the Pandemic: The Unique Associations of COVID-19-Related Perceived Threat and Psychological Distress to Drinking Behaviors in American Men and Women." *Addictive Behaviors* 110 (November): 106532.

Romm, Aviva. "Overlooked & Ignored: Why Women Don't Get a Thyroid Diagnosis." https://avivaromm.com/hypothyroidism-feminist-issue/

Romm, Aviva. *Hormone Intelligence: The Complete Guide to Calming Hormone Chaos and Restoring Your Body's Natural Blueprint for Well-Being.* HarperOne, 2021.

Ruiz, Miguel. *The Four Agreements: A Practical Guide to Personal Freedom.* Amber-Allen Publishing, 2017.

Schwartz, Richard, PhD. *No Bad Parts: How the Internal Family Systems Model Changes Everything.* Sounds True, 2021.

"Sex Hormones & the Female Brain: A Focus on Mood Disorders | The Institute for Functional Medicine." 2023.

Shahid, M. A. (2023, June 5). Physiology, thyroid hormone. StatPearls - NCBI Bookshelf. Stach, Kamilla, Wojciech Stach, and Katarzyna Augoff. "Vitamin B6 in Health and Disease." *Nutrients* 13, no. 9 (September 17, 2021): 3229.

Sharifi-Rad, Javad, Youssef El Rayess, Alain Abi Rizk, Carmen Sadaka, Raviella Zgheib, Wissam Zam, Simona Sestito, et al. "Turmeric and Its Major Compound Curcumin on Health: Bioactive Effects and Safety Profiles for Food, Pharmaceutical, Biotechnological and Medicinal Applications." *Frontiers in Pharmacology* 11 (September 15, 2020).

Sherin, Jonathan E, and Charles B Nemeroff. "Post-Traumatic Stress Disorder: *The Neurobiological Impact of Psychological Trauma.*" *Dialogues in Clinical Neuroscience*, U.S. National Library of Medicine, 2011.

Shetty, Jay. *Think like a Monk: Train Your Mind for Peace and Purpose Every Day.* Simon & Schuster, 2020.

Singer, Michael A. *The Untethered Soul: The Journey beyond Yourself*, 2007.

Smiley, Brett. "How Much Fiber Should I Eat Per Day?" Healthline, May 30, 2023.

Sobel, Jack MD. "Vaginitis in adults: Initial evaluation, UpToDate," n.d.

Sokolov, A. N., Pavlova, M., Klosterhalfen, S., & Enck, P. (2013). Chocolate and the brain: Neurobiological impact of cocoa flavanols on cognition and behavior. *Neuroscience & Biobehavioral Reviews*, 37(10), 2445–2453.

Speers, Alex, Kadine A Cabey, Amala Soumyanath, and Kirsten M. Wright. "Effects of Withania Somnifera (Ashwagandha) on Stress and the Stress- Related Neuropsychiatric Disorders Anxiety, Depression, and Insomnia." *Current Neuropharmacology* 19, no. 9 (September 1, 2021): 1468–95.

Stojcheva, E. I., & Quintela, J. C. (2022). The Effectiveness of Rhodiola rosea L. Preparations in Alleviating Various Aspects of Life-Stress Symptoms and Stress-Induced Conditions—Encouraging Clinical Evidence. *Molecules*, 27(12), 3902.

Talebi, Marjan, Selen İlgün, Vida Ebrahimi, Mohsen Talebi, Tahereh Farkhondeh, Hadi Ebrahimi, and Saeed Samarghandian. 2021. "Zingiber Officinale Ameliorates Alzheimer's Disease and Cognitive Impairments: Lessons from Preclinical Studies." *Biomedicine & Pharmacotherapy* 133 (January): 111088.

Taylor, Martin. "What Does Fight, Flight, Freeze, Fawn Mean?" WebMD, May 19, 2022.

Thau, Lauren. "Physiology, Cortisol." StatPearls - NCBI Bookshelf, August 29, 2022.

The WHAM Report. (2022, October 31). Brain Health - The WHAM Report.

"The Influence of Information Overload and Problematic Internet Use on Adults Wellbeing -ORCA." n.d

The Nutrition Source. "Protein," November 12, 2021.

Thorpe, Matthew, MD PhD. "10 Natural Ways to Lower Your Cholesterol Levels." Healthline, July 13, 2023.

"Thyroid Patient Information | American Thyroid Association." American Thyroid Association, January 23, 2023.

Tilgner, Sharol. Tilgner, Sharol. *Herbal Medicine: From the Heart of the Earth*. Wise Acres, 2020.

Toups, Kat, Ann Hathaway, Deborah R. Gordon, Chung H, Cyrus A. Raji, Alan Boyd, Benjamin D. Hill, et al. 2022. "Precision Medicine Approach to Alzheimer's Disease: Successful Pilot Project." *Journal of Alzheimer's Disease* 88 (4): 1411–21.

U.S. Census Bureau. 2021. "Women Still Have to Work Three Months Longer to Equal What Men Earned in a Year." Census.Gov. October 8, 2021.

Van Der Kolk, Bessel A. *The Body Keeps the Score: Brain, Mind, and Body in the Healing of Trauma*. Penguin Books, 2015.

"Waking Just One Hour Earlier Cuts Depression Risk by Double Digits, Study Finds." 2021. *ScienceDaily*. May 21, 2021.

"What Is So Sacred About The Number 108?," n.d.

"What Is Shift Work?" (Definition, Types and Jobs) | Indeed.Com

"What's in a Handful of Soil?" *Farmer's Weekly*, June 27, 2018.

Wikipedia contributors. 2023. "Default Mode Network." Wikipedia.

Williamson, Laura. "How to Boost Your Mood through Food", American Heart Association News, March 30, 2022

Wohlleben, Peter. *Hidden Life of Trees: A Visual Celebration of a Magnificent World*. Greystone Books Ltd., 2018.

"Women in the Workplace 2022." n.d. LeanIn.Org and McKinsey & Company.

"Women Still Have to Work Three Months Longer to Equal What Men Earned in a Year." Census.Gov. October 8, 2021.

"Women's Experiences with Health Care During the COVID-19 Pandemic: Findings from the KFF Women's Health Survey." 2021. KFF Health News. April 15, 2021.

"Women Have More Active Brains than Men, According to Science." 2020. World Economic Forum. February 6, 2020.

"Women Now Drink as Much as Men — And Are Prone to Sickness Sooner." KFF Health News. June 10, 2021.

"Women and Heart Disease Facts," n.d. https://www.cdc.gov/heartdisease/women.htm

World Health Organization: WHO. 2022. "Mental Disorders."

World Wildlife Fund. "What Is the Sixth Mass Extinction and What Can We Do about It? | Stories | WWF," n.d. https://www.worldwildlife.org/stories/what-is-the-sixth-mass-extinction-and-what-can-we-do-about-it?ref=walkaboutsaga.com

Walker, Lauren. "4 Simple Ways To Stay Grounded | Yoga Digest," n.d.

"Your Complex Brain." n.d. https://www.brainfacts.org/core-concepts/your-complex-brain

"Your Digestive System & How it Works." (2023). National Institute of Diabetes and Digestive and Kidney Diseases.

Zaccaro, Andrea, Andrea Piarulli, Marco Laurino, Erika Garbella, Danilo Menicucci, Bruno Neri, and Angelo Gemignani. "How Breath-Control Can Change Your Life: A Systematic Review on Psycho-Physiological Correlates of Slow Breathing." *Frontiers in Human Neuroscience* 12 (September 7, 2018).

Index

Note: Page numbers in *italic* and **bold** refer to figures and tables, respectively.

About the Authors

Rimi Chakraborty and Samantha Anderson rejoice in inspiring women to redefine success. Beyond Resilience to Rootsilience shifts consciousness toward a new leadership paradigm that is rooted in well-being, balance, and health.

Rimi Chakraborty is a keynote speaker, author, yoga teacher and leadership consulting coach for groups, teams, and individuals, dedicated to developing conscious leaders.

Rimi holds a B.S.E. from the University of Pennsylvania and an M.B.A. from MIT Sloan School of Management as well as various certifications in Forrest Yoga, Yin Yoga, Energy Healing, Energy Medicine, and Yoga for Trauma. She is the co-founder of MINUVIDA AZORES, an immersive travel and learning experiences business in São Miguel, Azores. You can learn more about her at www.rimichakra.com

Samantha is a National Board Certified Health and Wellness Coach (NBC-HWC) and certified as a Functional Medicine Health Coach. She has decades of experience as a nonprofit and philanthropy consultant, and is the co-editor of *Generating and Sustaining Nonprofit Earned Income: A Guide to Successful Enterprises Strategies* (Jossey-Bass, 2004). She speaks widely to a variety of audiences offering practical tools to help women leaders cultivate purpose and vision while connecting to their whole selves and to that which restores balance.

Samantha received a B.A. from Tufts University and earned a M.A. in US Women's History from the University of Wisconsin-Madison. She is a Qoya Inspired movement teacher, Usui Ryoho Reiki Master, certified in Functional Nutrition from the Integrative Women's Health Institute, and a SHE RECOVERS coach working with women on all forms of addiction. You can learn more about her at www.essential-wholeness.com

The "Chakra" in Rimi's last name is more than just a coincidence; it's a testament to Rimi's Indian heritage and her passion to translate ancient teachings from her roots into practical wisdom for the modern world.

Samantha's family name, Langbaum, translates to "Tall Tree" in German. Samantha's ancestral lineage imparts this valuable lesson: a towering tree with shallow roots can falter at the faintest wind, yet a tree firmly anchored in deep roots can weather any storm.

Rimi and Samantha share a love for nature, a belief in the strength of embodied conscious leadership, and a commitment to a life of sustainability, health and wellness. They have come together in search of their authentic selves, connected by their love for the earth they respect and revere.

Printed in the USA
CPSIA information can be obtained
at www.ICGtesting.com
LVHW020539080224
771185LV00057B/1569